EVERYONE HAS THE POTENTIAL TO DO BETTER AT EVERYTHING!

You *don't*   inner.

You *don't*   maximize it—   re.

You *can* learn how to control anxiety—to turn it on and shut it off.

You *can* teach yourself to make the most of all your inner capabilities, from athletic achievement, if that's your goal, to achievement in every area of your life!

"In this up-beat, eminently sensible guidebook, the authors provide a step-by-step program for toning minds and bodies into a state of dynamic relaxation as a prelude to achieving one's ultimate potential. . . . surprisingly readable and very, very persuasive."

—PUBLISHERS WEEKLY

Books by Laurence E. Morehouse, Ph.D., and Leonard Gross

Maximum Performance
Total Fitness in 30 Minutes a Week

Published by POCKET BOOKS

LAURENCE E. MOREHOUSE, Ph.D. AND LEONARD GROSS

MAXIMUM PERFORMANCE

ILLUSTRATIONS BY
PETER GREEN

PUBLISHED BY POCKET BOOKS NEW YORK

POCKET BOOKS, a Simon & Schuster division of
GULF & WESTERN CORPORATION
1230 Avenue of the Americas, New York, N.Y. 10020

TO OUR CHILDREN

Acknowledgments

We would like to thank the following people:

Peter Schwed, Nan Talese and Dan Green of Simon and Schuster for their creative support and enthusiasm.

Herman Roth, Debbie Cooper and Ron Zernicke for their research assistance and critical reviews.

Gayle Godwin, head coach of the UCLA women's tennis team and coach of the United States Junior Wightman Cup team, for helping Leonard Gross turn theories into realities.

Our families for their patience, tolerance and perceptive criticisms.

And finally all those colleagues of Laurence E. Morehouse in exercise physiology, sports medicine and athletic training whose work has amplified and assisted his own.

Laurence E. Morehouse
Leonard Gross

Contents

1

Unlock Your Better Self

WE ALL HAVE fantasies about achievement. We would all like to be better performers at everything we do— better producers, leaders, organizers, homemakers, athletes, dancers, lovers. We would all like to read faster and write more coherently, think more clearly and sleep more soundly. What few of us realize is how close fantasy is to reality.

There is in every one of us a better performer than we are. A modest adjustment in our habits can enable us to move with greater agility, function with greater economy, maximize power, minimize injuries, learn faster, score higher and win more often.

That better performer lies dormant in us for three basic reasons. The first is that various cultural and social forces have conspired to keep it hidden. The second is that it doesn't believe in itself. The third is that it literally doesn't know how to make use of its own potential.

But the potential is there. In 1960, a 123-pound woman, Mrs. Maxwell Rodgers of Tampa, Florida, lifted a 3600-pound station wagon off of her son, who was trapped underneath it. In 1975, Ricky Grill, a 12-year-old Santee, California, boy, rescued his father in the same manner. The unbelievable strength summoned by such life-and-death emergencies is not

1

normally available to us, but episodes like these show that we use a small percentage of our capacity when we think we are making a near maximum effort.

The study of the brain is still in its infancy, and the range of our intellect is unexplored, but everything we've learned so far suggests that we're using only a fraction of the brain's capacity. Once in a great while, we put ourselves to a mental test that demonstrates the brain's ability to function at a far higher level than normal. A solution to a problem that has eluded us for days suddenly materializes. An urgent need for a decision produces crystalline logic. When we compare such efforts with how we normally use our brains, we are astounded by the differences.

The same discrepancy is true of the body. Our neuromuscular system is a marvel without parallel in the physical world, yet unlike the inventions of man, it is rarely employed at anywhere near capacity. For most of our lives, in effect, we are driving a high-powered engine at twenty miles an hour.

Anytime we use our minds and bodies to a degree we haven't before, we develop heretofore unexplored areas of use into integrated, functioning parts of the whole. Use makes the organ—the brain, the heart, the muscles, even the sexual organ.

Maximum performance is the level that would be reached if all our capacities were developed to their fullest, perfectly applied and operating in harmony. But we never achieve that level. Even when we're working at maximum effort we are far short of our potential for maximum performance. So we all have a better performer to uncover, no matter how skillful or powerful we become.

The principles of maximum performance apply equally to work and play. They are based on more than forty years of my own multidisciplinary research, together with that of colleagues around the world, in the science of human performance. The study of human performance focuses on the whole man, his personal development and productivity. It considers the physiological, biochemical and psychological aspects of a problem, as well as the role of nutrition, drugs and exercise in performance. In studying the effects of exercise on the heart, for example, we don't just hook a subject up to an electrocardiograph; we study the various environments in which the exercise occurs. If he's watching a film while he's exercising, for example, does this change the effect of the exercise? In the course of my studies, I've worked with world-class athletes, astronauts, aquanauts, corporate executives and industrial designers. I've been consulted by federal agencies, the military services, manufacturers, labor unions and foreign governments, all with the same objective in mind—to make better use of human endowments. I've learned many lessons from all that work, but the central one is this:

Better performance is not a mysterious gift handed to a precious few; it's achieved in a step-by-step procedure that, properly followed, produces not only concrete improvement but psychological reinforcement, as well. You feel more confident, more adventurous, more capable of doing what you were formerly afraid to do. The success with which you perform each day —in business, sports, and sex—carries over into the other areas of your life.

THE EXPRESS ROUTE TO EXCELLENCE

WE'RE ALL FAMILIAR with the psychological tonic that being well-groomed produces. A woman enters a beauty salon to be "done over"; she leaves with the impression that she's a better person. A man eyeing a better job buys a new suit that dresses him in the image of the better self he envisions. The same phenomenon is at work when you enhance your physique by physical exercise. An accompanying new muscle awareness provides a heightened feeling of well-being. Seeing how much more work your muscles can do tells you you're stronger and more capable. Anxiety decreases; you become more confident, self-reliant, and gain greater self-respect. You become wary of habits that will diminish your newfound gains. So you smoke less, you're more careful about what you eat, you exercise more regularly and get the rest you need.

Once you see that you can improve, you no longer accept your old image of yourself. You know how well you can do when you invest the time and effort.

World-class performers constantly practice in an atmosphere of success. You're going to practice that way, too. You'll learn to organize your development in such a way that, at each session, you'll be successful at what you set out to do.

You'll learn how to break your activity into periods of effort and recovery that will enable you to achieve more, and with less fatigue, than you would have by constant effort.

You'll learn how to put yourself into the best mental condition before starting a game of tennis, approaching the first tee—or making a presentation to your boss. You'll learn how to arrange your office so that you remain alert throughout the day; how to break your tasks into more readily soluble components.

You'll learn that there are distinct body parts and systems that are overprotecting you—shielding you from nonexistent dangers. You'll also learn how to convince these systems that it's all right for you to go forward. This process, known as "deinhibition," is an express route to maximum performance.

You'll learn how to "undress" your motions, stripping them of nonessentials, so that you end up with a bare motion that gives you the greatest accuracy and effect with the least effort.

You'll learn about fifteen "Super Ks"—kinesiological secrets that are part of every champion's movements—and how to incorporate those secrets into your own performance.

If you're a parent, you are your child's first and most influential coach. There are good and bad ways to coach. We'll concentrate on the good ways, so that you not only create the right environment for your child but give him an image of himself as a performer that he can carry through life.

You'll learn how to use spare hours—such as driving to and from work, or walking, or performing some task that doesn't occupy your mind—to practice your gold swing, tennis stroke or bowling delivery, or even your competitive strategy. It's called "mental practice," and it literally trains your muscles to perform. If you're a poor sleeper, you can learn to use mental practice not only to make use of the time when you're lying awake but to lull yourself to sleep.

THE MYRIAD POSSIBILITIES FOR IMPROVEMENT

THERE IS NO reason to be discouraged because you consider yourself a poor performer. In fact, the less developed you are at this moment, the more readily and rapidly you'll improve. Increments of improvement are invariably larger at the beginning and become smaller and smaller as performance improves.

Nor is age a barrier to improvement. Recently, I've been training a UCLA pathologist who'd been a runner in high school and at the age of sixty decided he wanted to run competitively again. His goal was to become the fastest two-miler over sixty in the world. Within three years, he was in the record books.

If you are capable of motion, you can improve that motion. Take walking, for example. Everyone knows how to walk, but how many of us walk as well as we can? If you're the average walker, you may be raising your body as much as an inch more than you need to with each step. Suppose you weigh 150 pounds. Every time you lift that weight an extra inch, you're doing 150-inch-pounds of work. With a dozen steps, you've done almost enough work to lift a ton one inch. Smooth your walking motion by getting rid of that unnecessary inch and you've saved the energy required to do several hundred extra inch-tons of lifting work each day.

Or suppose you want to become a better runner. One way is to increase your endurance, which takes systematic training. Another, more immediate result can be achieved with a little practice simply by focusing your attention on one area of your body.

Years ago, Roy Cochran, a world-class 440-yard hurdler, was a doctoral candidate at the University of Southern California, doing research in aviation medicine. I was a member of his doctoral committee. Roy had been out of training for four years, but he suddenly decided that he wanted to enter the then upcoming 1948 Olympics. Because of his academic objectives, he determined that he could give only one hour a day to training. So we worked out a minute-by-minute schedule to maximize the yield of the hour, and we studied his techniques. One of the first things we learned was that Roy was always a bit short coming to a hurdle. As a consequence, he had developed the habit of taking hurdles on alternate feet. That would have been acceptable if he had been as agile and strong on both feet, but he wasn't. One foot was a better takeoff foot than the other. The only way to overcome this problem was to increase his stride length between hurdles. If he could lengthen each stride a little, he would, over a series of strides, make up the difference and be able to use the same takeoff foot at each hurdle. So I suggested to Roy that he increase the rotation of his hips by deliberately relaxing the muscles in the small of his back and around the hip area, allowing his pelvis to swing forward with each stride.

That simple adjustment gave Roy Cochran greater stride length with about the same amount of energy. He began running world-record times—and he won his Olympic gold medal.

The next time you're on a sidewalk, try a similar experiment. See how many normal strides it takes you to cover ten squares. Next, walk the same distance while consciously relaxing the muscles around your hip area and letting your hip swing forward, left hip preceding left foot, right hip preceding right foot. You should find that your walk is more fluid, as well as more efficient; you'll be covering a lot more ground with the same amount of effort. Then, try the same technique running. You'll run as you never have before.

Walking, breathing, driving, reading, writing, working, playing, keeping house—we perform such functions all but unconsciously each day. Were we to examine them critically, we would find that we perform them with far less skill than we might. Were we to apply the principles of maximum performance, we would be increasing our effectiveness and conserving time and energy in all fields.

Learning to be a maximum performer in one activity tends to habituate you to certain approaches and procedures in attacking other activities. Specific skills can't be transferred; you can't shoot baskets any better because you've learned to be a better bowler. What can be transferred from one activity to another—sports to business, for example—is the art of improvement.

There are numerous overlaps between sports and work. Both require endurance and strength. Both require a methodical approach. Both require a sense of pace and rhythm and timing. Both require, above all, an ability to focus—energy, attention and body parts.

The price of improvement has always come high. This book aims to lower that price. It will offer "take-home" techniques that can be applied to everything you do—because the art and science of maximum performance are applicable to anyone who's trying to do anything.

One word of advice as you proceed: Try to regard your performance record as a personal rating. People in their middle years, particularly, often judge themselves by comparison with others. This is a cardinal fault and the narrowest measure. Inevitably it leads to frustration, because unless you're the world champion, a Nobel laureate or the world's highest paid executive, there's always someone "better."

The only valid comparisons are between your present, past and future performance. What you've accomplished to this point is all to your credit and something to build on. Your only objective now is to unlock your better self.

2

Stop Trying So Hard

AT STAKE IN learning to be a better performer are some cherished notions of how excellence is achieved. Foremost among them is the idea that the harder we struggle the better we'll do. That's almost always wrong.

To strive to your utmost means to give everything you've got with all your muscles. The problem is that physiologically, when you're putting all you've got into an action, some of that force is holding you back. Muscles are grouped around joints in such a way as to oppose each other. While one group act as accelerators, another act as brakes. The muscles acting as brakes stabilize the limbs while the accelerating muscles move them.

Ideally both braking and accelerating muscles act in harmony to make the movement smooth and accurate. In order to move at your best, one system must be releasing while the other is hauling. You must feel that you're functioning with only a modest amount of power and effort. In rapid movement it's not the strength of the muscles that's important so much as the ability to relax antagonistic muscles.

Muscles contract swiftly. They relax less swiftly. Every time you contract a muscle to make a move-ment, you must then relax it so that it can recover its

9

original position before moving once again. You can speed up contractions by a determined effort. But the resulting tension spreads to the muscles that should be lengthening, or relaxing, and ties them up. Look what happens:

When you're running, your hamstrings (the tendons that bind the thigh) pull the lower leg back. The quadriceps (the large muscles at the front of the thigh) pull it forward. During the pullback phase, the hamstrings, which are relaxed at the outset, contract to create the desired driving movement. So far, no problem. Now the quadriceps take over to extend the knee and bring the foot forward. These muscles have relaxed while the hamstrings contracted, so they begin their contraction from a relaxed state. But they are pulling against their antagonists—the hamstrings—that are still partially contracted and thus not relaxed enough. In returning the leg to its extended position, this hamstring resistance must be overcome. To the extent that the resistance is applied, the speed of the return is retarded. The same problem exists the next time the hamstring contracts to repeat the cycle; this time, it's operating against a partially contracted quadriceps.

THE SECRET OF SPEED

SPEED RESULTS not so much from the swiftness with which you can contract your muscles, but the swiftness with which you can relax them so that they don't act as brakes on your acceleration. If they don't relax fast enough, not only is the speed of the leg impeded, the momentum of that leg swinging forward pulls against a partially contracted hamstring muscle and tears it. A pulled hamstring, so common in sports, is an indication of a poorly relaxed athlete. It occurs most frequently during the latter part of a foot race, when the muscles are partially fatigued and the runner attempts to use extra force to maintain his flagging speed. The hamstring resists, and the rip occurs, proof that the runner has done exactly the wrong thing. If he wants to move faster, his concentration should not be on applying more power, but on increasing his relaxation.

The concept of relaxation applies to any motion. The more relaxed your antagonistic muscles, the faster —and paradoxically more powerful—that motion. It is the ability to relax that enables small men to hit a golf ball great distances. Most golfers would be elated to hit a ball 240–250 yards with a fairway wood. I was perplexed one day, therefore, to see a slight young man on the par-five, 577-yard fourteenth hole at the Bel Air Country Club waiting for the players ahead of him to clear the green. He was nearly 300 yards from the hole, and the wind was in his face. Nothing in his spare physique suggested the power he would need to hit the ball that far; if you saw him in the showers at the clubhouse—as I did later—you would judge him to be among the weakest men present. When he swung, it seemed that he would never make it, because his swing was so easy and relaxed. His ball landed on the green, fifteen feet past the cup. It was the greatest golf shot I have ever seen.

The source of such strength is simply explained. A relaxed muscle can be stretched to greater length than a tense muscle. Up to a point, the more stretched it is, the more forceful its contraction.

The benefits of relaxed muscles to performance are apparent in everything we do.

Try a little experiment. Grip a pen or pencil very tightly and write a line across a page of writing paper. Then relax your fingers and copy what you've written. Compare the two specimens. The second will almost surely be much more accurate and readable than the first. At first, the speed at which you write may be slower, but as you become accustomed to it, your speed will gradually increase until eventually you'll be writing legibly at a faster rate, and with far less fatigue.

YOU DON'T HAVE TO KILL YOURSELF
TO BE A WINNER

DESPITE EVIDENCE indicating its inefficiency, all-out struggle remains a national fixation.

Our tradition holds that the battle is won by the man who gives to the limit. We deify sacrifice. Death is the ultimate performance. "He killed himself" is a colloquial form of flattery with antecedents in the legend of the warrior Pheidippides, who ran from the Plains of Marathon to Athens to announce, "Rejoice, we conquer!" and fell dead. *There* was a sacrifice consistent with our own concept of achievement—which is that if you have anything left in you at the end of a contest, you haven't given your all.

In working life, we often rate others' performances in terms of the cost to them. If I give you a job to do that I think is pretty difficult, and you return an hour later with the job well done but with no apparent cost to you in terms of emotional drain and physical energy, I tend not to appreciate that effort. If, on the other hand, you don't show up until the next morning and you've obviously been up all night, I value not only your effort but the work itself. *Rationally,* I should have more respect for the person who can get the job done in an hour than for the one who had to work through the night.

Not long ago, a film producer gave a famous writer a great deal of money to write a script. The writer turned in a finished manuscript within two weeks. The producer decided the script was done too hurriedly; he demanded a rewrite. The writer did the revision in four days—at which point the incredulous producer got another writer. Impartial readers of the script said it was superb. But the producer was incapable of truly critical judgment; he felt that he had been abused, because no one could make that kind of money so fast and easily.

In education, the idea that learning can be fun is still novel. Play is the mode in which children discover their world, but the moment they get into class, the joy of discovery is quashed. "We're through playing now," is the message. "We've got to get down to work." The assumption is that anything that's good ought to cost the learner something. He must "give it every last ounce," "keep his nose to the grindstone"—or "kill" himself.

Sad to say, such sacrifice diminishes rather than enhances performance. The child who can't play is deprived of a learning experience and an essential educational process. The child who can't laugh is deprived of an important physiological releaser of tensions, as well as philosophical perspective. Such children grow up bewildered as to why their serious efforts have not gained them maximum rewards.

Underlying the idea that deprivation is necessary to success is the religious notion that sins are purged through denial and suffering. Prisoners break rocks on the premise that they must exhaust themselves physically in order to purify themselves morally. Our religious and secular heroes are those who suffered in dying.

The notion that excellence can come easily is antithetical to our tradition. Look at the family hero, out there killing himself for his wife and children. He accepts this as his burden, bringing home work at night, taking on extra jobs, courting a heart attack. He feels terribly righteous, and he expects admiration and sympathy from those in whose behalf he strives. The posture touches something deep in us—the old fundamentalist notion that if it doesn't hurt, it can't be effective.

The same attitude carries into physical and athletic performance: we should always make the supreme effort. Physiologically, however, the idea makes little sense.

THAT "EXTRA EFFORT" CAN
HOLD YOU BACK

WHETHER YOU WANT to run fast or think fast, over-effort diminishes your prospects. The way to perform at your best is to learn to ease off all extra tensions by switching off all untimely reactions.

Take, for example, thinking and doing. We try to think while we're doing, which impairs the doing, and we try to do while we're thinking, which prevents us from thinking clearly.

In our ambition to succeed, we're driven to do everything at once. This isn't the way the body/mind functions. You can't abruptly "stop and think," as is so often counseled. Stopping is an active process. What you can do is stop, pause and then think. There needs to be an interval between doing and thinking and thinking and doing.

While you perform, you mustn't think about the technique of your performance. While you think through the details involved in performing, you mustn't perform. You can do both at once, of course, but you won't do either well. To think or perform at your best, you must keep the functions separate.

When you try too hard at anything, you produce extraneous effort; you quiver and become tense; your motions are inefficient. When you play too hard, you make a business of recreation, which deprives you of its expressive, restorative benefits. Working too hard and playing too hard are roads to self-destruction. Consider the word: re-creation. That's its function.

To work hard and play hard should mean working productively and playing ecstatically. Peak experiences result when all elements fit harmoniously together and you become as one with your game or task. That state arrives spontaneously. It's almost never achieved through extreme effort—because such striving sets up bodily forces that disorganize and burden the essentials needed for the event.

In neuromuscular terms, a gentle forcefulness is produced by just the right number of muscle fibers coming into play at just the right time in just the right organization to move the levers and joints of the body through the precise motion needed to accomplish the objective. Extra effort upsets this balance. Result: A poor performance.

The basic purpose of neuromuscular training is to refine movement to such an extent that only those motions directed toward the final action are in play. Extraneous efforts by muscle fibers that drain the organism of its energy and cause general confusion within the neuromuscular system are eliminated.

Suppose you're playing darts. If you were to throw the dart as you might throw a stone in anger—clenching, winding up and heaving with all your might—your chances of hitting the bull's-eye with any consistency would be worlds less than if you were to take the dart gently in your thumb and forefinger and send it on its way with a relaxed and gentle motion. By refining the muscle systems in control of the dart and eliminating the extraneous ones, you have minimized your effort but maximized your prospects.

There was a period some years back when I took every opportunity I could to interview athletes who had either just broken a world's record or bettered their own record in an event to a remarkable degree. "What happened?" I asked each of them. "Tell me about that performance from beginning to end." By the time I had interviewed a dozen athletes, I could predict almost exactly what each of them would say. The scenario went like this:

> I didn't feel well that day. I was nauseated and felt weak. As a matter of fact, it crossed my mind to ask the coach to scratch me from the event. But before I knew it, my event was called. I hardly remember starting. All I knew for sure was that I was in motion. I don't remember any particular moment during the event. It all seemed

so easy. At the finish, the way the crowd was cheering told me I'd done well, but I had the feeling that if I'd only tried a little harder I could have done much better.

It was almost spooky. Here were different athletes in different events in different parts of the country, none of them communicating with any of the others, yet all of them giving me the same basic story. They were all astonished that they had broken their records on that particular day; not one of them felt that he had been really putting out his best.

In the years since then, every time I've been near an athlete who had vastly improved his performance, I've asked him to comment on these stories I'd been told by other performers under similar circumstances. The inevitable reply: "I wouldn't change a word."

These athletes are telling us something about maximum performance that every one of us can apply in our daily lives. If you're exhausting yourself trying to achieve, that's about all you'll do. The lesson is as valid in the office as on the field; the executive who strains at his work is no more effective than the baseball player who tries to hit a home run with every swing of his bat. Nile Kinnick knew this. He was a legendary football player and scholar at Iowa in the late 1930s, a Heisman trophy winner and a Phi Beta Kappa. When he died in a Navy training exercise at the start of World War II, a diary was found among his effects. "It is a sad mistake to try to be head man in everything you attempt," he had written. "The axiom, 'If it is worth doing at all, it is worth doing well,' has its limitations. Stay on the ball most of the time, but learn to coast between moments of all-out effort."

Kinnick was years ahead of his time in his understanding of maximum performance. Most athletes of his day associated great performances with pain, struggle and exhaustion. Today's enlightened athletes aren't like that. They don't spend their energy on

needless histrionics. When their race is called, they
shake out their hands and feet to get loose, kick their
knees up and down, run a few easy spurts and try a
few starts. John Smith, the world's record holder in
the quarter mile as of this writing, often sits in the
stands with his girl friend until his race is called.
Then he wanders down, stretches a few times, runs
loose as a goose and finishes as if he's just starting.

The record books tell us which is the sounder approach. The times and distances of today's supercool
athletes are far better than those of athletes in an
earlier day who gave everything to win. Certainly, the
excitement of a winning basket or touchdown or a
record-breaking time is just as intense today as it has
ever been. But the execution is done with much more
grace and ease.

Exhaustion is no longer the mark of top-class performance. It shouldn't be the mark of yours.

FORGET PICTURE-BOOK PERFECTION

YET ANOTHER enormous misconception under which
we labor is the conviction that there is a perfect way
of doing things.

We're a conforming society, and we've been taught
all our lives to perform in certain ways. Prompt and
uniform obedience is sometimes necessary to the pres-
ervation of life: abandoning ship, leaving a burning
building, fighting a battle. But conformity in matters
of human performance is a crime against yourself.

What has kept us back from our maximum as performers is not so much our lack of potential as our
belief that there is only one way to do something. If
we can't do it that way, we do nothing. It's our idea
that's deficient, not our capacity.

The reality is that there is no single perfect way to
execute a movement or perform a task. Every body is
different—which means that the movements of the

muscles and joints ought to be different and, in fact, will be different, no matter how hard you might try to be a sedulous ape, mimicking someone else's movement.

I remember once being at a physiology meeting in Atlantic City. From my hotel room on the boardwalk, I could see for miles down the beach. In the distance, about the size of an ant, was a figure walking on the beach. "There's Charlie," I said to my wife. Charlie didn't move strangely. He simply had a style of movement that expressed Charlie. He happened to be an extrovert, so he walked with an upright body, swinging arms and a long stride. Had he been an introvert, he might have walked "small," hunching his shoulders, lowering his head, keeping his arms tight to his body and his feet close together. Each person has his own style of movement, and any changes made in the execution of a movement must be undertaken within the individual's style.

In all probability you have a style of movement that is better for you than any style you might be taught. We call this style *idiosyncratic movement*. The attempt by well-meaning teachers throughout our lives to get us to conform to idealized models in motion has kept most of us from achieving maximum performance. *Your* ideal is the motion that conforms to your structure. Since the structure of every one of us is different—even if only minutely—it follows that each one of us will perform a motion in a different manner. The difference may be so minuscule as to be all but undetectable by the eye. Or the motion may be totally unorthodox in terms of conventional movement.

You need the professional's eye and a measure of advice. That advice must be given in a certain way if it's to do you any good—a point we'll be elaborating further on. What you don't need is the feeling that you must develop someone else's style.

You'll be your best if you learn to be yourself. This involves a whole new teacher-pupil relationship. You're going to learn to say to your coach, "Help me find my own way in terms of my idiosyncratic body organization."

That we're all different is a fact so inarguable it would not bear repeating if its meaning were truly accepted and its consequences understood. It is the most obvious and yet the most ignored lesson of human existence, and its consequences transcend the playing field.

Physical training is a joy when it's done in a way that's right for you. Improvement is swift. But the biggest payoff is when the logic and method of conditioning for maximum performance are applied to daily life.

You may figure that you can't apply the principles of body conditioning to life-style improvements because life is so complex. But if you consider all the adjustments the body makes to improve the movement of the intricate system of levers in the body, adjustment of life outside the body by comparison becomes a fairly simple affair.

3

Optimal Anxiety

PERFORMANCE REQUIRES TENSION; without it, your muscles would become disorganized, you'd stumble and fall. You'd be hard pressed to keep your head sitting correctly on your shoulders. The trick is to perform with exactly the right degree of tension—just enough to key you up, not so much as to tie you up.

Anxiety, which accompanies all performance, is not only inevitable, it's desirable provided it's completely under control.

It's that delicate balance, the ability to relax under pressure, that eludes most of us. That ability is often the critical difference between winners and runners-up, and perhaps *the* vital factor in competition at the world-class level, where skills and physical attributes are all but indistinguishable.

Knute Rockne of Notre Dame was a great football coach, but he was the embodiment of one unfortunate myth—that highly charged players play better. The myth has been perpetuated by sportswriters and Hollywood to a point where every high school and Little League coach thinks he can lift his players to unparalleled heights by the power of extreme emotion.

There is one potential benefit to such "psyching up" sessions. A player who is fearful of imminent body contact in his approaching contest might be helped over this hurdle by an emotional charge. But the fact is that, most of the time, excessive emotion ruins performance. Coaches who work their players up in the dressing room and then lead them in a charge onto the field are doing players and themselves a disservice. Not long ago, the soccer coach at a West Coast college led his squad in a pregame tantrum that ended with imprecations to kill the other side. His team, the state champion, was held to a scoreless tie in the first half. Only in the second half, after a subdued rest period, did the team regain its form and win the match.

It's true that when you go beserk, you can become fantastically strong. But rage is unpredictable. You may do something super-human, or you may fall on your face. It's well known among prizefighters that if you can get your opponent angry to the point of fury, you've got him licked. His punches will be wild and easy to counter. He'll lose his coordination and sense of strategy. This is what is meant by "psyching" your opponent. It is bringing out his rampant—and self-defeating—emotion.

There's a difference, however, between uncontrolled emotion and emotion that's carefully used. A person performing in a state of controlled anger is truly someone to deal with. He has super strength, super alertness and super endurance.

Because emotions are energizing, they increase the body's alertness through the activation of the wakefulness centers of the brain; they increase strength by the flow of adrenaline; and they increase endurance by motivating the performer to continue beyond ordinary points of discomfort. So we welcome emotional responses. When emotion is allowed to play out freely into muscular activity, performance is enhanced.

Too often, however, emotion is accompanied by tension. The muscles of the body actually form an armor, providing a rigid defense against attackers. In this posture your body is in no condition to make a move.

Excess tension produces mental confusion: you

don't think straight or organize properly; you jump at the wrong conclusions; you dwell on negative, unproductive factors.

Everything that's happening within you is in involuntary response to environmental stress. You haven't willed your muscles to be tense. You haven't willed your mental processes to be in a similar state of confusion. It has all happened automatically.

World-class performers aren't exempt from tension. Because the stakes are so much higher for them, they actually experience tension to a degree few of us ever feel. But the difference between them and you is that they know how to deal with tension. They expect it, they're prepared for it, and they know how to utilize it to their advantage. When they perform, they're supercool.

Fortunately, tension is highly manipulatable. If you're in a state of emotional fright or feeling overwhelmed, you can do something about it by calming down the tension. If you're flat, dead on your feet, disinterested, you can turn up your tension to increase excitement.

For every performance, there is an optimal anxiety level. It can be described as a state of relaxed alertness. You feel somewhat excited, "up," light and strong, but not overeager. You may even feel a slight tingling sensation coursing through your body, a certain self-awareness and readiness. If you've never moved with the freedom or grace you'd have liked, you may have blamed it on poor coordination. Excess tension is the more probable villain.

Muscle tension levels are controlled by the intensity of the activity of the central nervous system, particularly the cortical centers, the layer of gray matter that covers the brain. This center receives impulses from the sensory nervous system and discharges motor impulses that control skeletal muscles. This discharge causes a general increase in tension.

When you're sad or depressed, your level of tension diminishes to a point where you may slouch and move halfheartedly. When you're happy and confident, your level of tension elevates, producing more erect posture, greater alertness and more direct movements.

HOW ANXIOUS SHOULD YOU BE?

SOME PEOPLE FUNCTION well in states of high anxiety. Others are paralyzed. There's no need to test yourself to determine which category you're in. We all know how we respond to stressful situations. We function either better or worse. The more sensitive you are to a high anxiety or arousal state—the more adversely it affects your performance—the more important it is for you to control this state. If, conversely, you're assisted by a high arousal state, then you may even want to induce it.

Your state of arousal is governed by what we call the "Reticular Activating Mechanism," known as the RAM. The mechanism, when active, produces showers of impulses that enhance muscular action. You can, if you wish, deliberately excite your RAM simply by talking to yourself prior to a performance. During an event if no one is cheering you, you can cheer yourself. Just before the peak of a performance, you may even want to let out a shout. Many weight lifters grunt as they lift, exciting the RAM. The same technique is used by shot putters, hammer throwers, and discus throwers, and sometimes even by tennis players. Listen carefully the next time you watch a professional tennis match on television. You'll hear some of the top players in the world grunting with each serve.

Generally speaking, high arousal states are undesirable in activities requring fine muscle coordination, but helpful in activities that don't require such precision. Thus, the quarterback looking for a receiver needs to remain as calm as he can, but the lineman protecting him can use arousal to good effect.

If you're going to perform a task that's well known to you and at which you have a high degree of expertise, you'll probably perform it best in a high arousal state.

I play golf with a number of distinguished actors. At one time or another I've asked all of them, "Can you tell before you go on whether or not you're going to give a good performance?" The answer is all but uniform: "If I feel frightened, my palms are wet and my heart is pounding, I know my performance will be good."

The key here is that they know what they're going to do. They've performed hundreds of times before and they can forecast the audience response. The only variable is how well they're going to do this time. If they're *not* anxious, their performance suffers. One actor flew two thousand miles to give a single performance. The promotion had been badly handled and he found only a handful of people in the audience. He shrugged, and went onstage, but he felt absolutely nothing—no anxiety, no arousal. The next day, his agent receved an outraged call from the chairman of the event, denouncing the star's lackluster performance.

It's very seldom, however, that most of us have a chance to use highly polished techniques before predictable audiences. When we're unsure of our material or unpracticed in our event, a high state of arousal can be devastating.

As a rule, the more difficult a task, the less value arousal contributes.

If you're doing something you've done a thousand times and you're the kind of person who works well under stress, then on an arousal scale of ten, you'll perform best at about eight. But if stress bothers you and you're unfamiliar with your task, you'll be better off at a lower arousal level.

Before you can perform better, then, you must learn how to control your arousal state so that it is neither too low nor too high when you start the job.

TURNING IT ON, SHUTTING IT OFF

IF YOU'RE IN an extreme state of anxiety, and would perform better in a lower state, you have two options. The first is to put off the task until time has diminished your arousal state. The second is to take steps to diminish that state.

If you're in a low state of anxiety, and would perform better in a higher state, once again you have two options—either to postpone action until you reach that state, or to take steps to increase the state at once.

Physiologically, when you increase or decrease your arousal state, you are controlling the flow of adrenaline through your body. Adrenaline is a hormone secreted into the bloodstream by the adrenal medulla, the soft, marrowlike center of the adrenal gland. This secretion occurs during stress. It produces an immediate increase in metabolism and an accompanying "jump" in blood pressure, cardiac output, oxygen consumption, blood glucose, blood lactate and central nervous system action. It constricts the smooth muscles of your gut and blood vessels in your belly, but dilates the vessels of the skeletal muscles, letting more blood into them to help them with their work.

The effect is to strengthen your muscular contractions, including those of the heart muscle. Because your heart rate increases and your blood pressure rises even though for the moment there is no demand for either, the body responds to this interruption in your normal rhythm as it would to a threat, and shunts the blood away from the digestive areas of the body into the muscular areas. What the body's doing is as old as man, preparing you to defend yourself.

From all this adrenaline comes a temporary increase in strength, alertness, coordination and reflex action. You require less exertion to accomplish your objective. In a way, adrenaline is like a high octane in fuel. You get more power. The hills seem easier.

Just as a heavy foot on the accelerator can mean danger, so too much adrenaline sweeping through your body can ruin your performance. You become exceptionally powerful—and tend to apply this extra power where it isn't needed. At high speeds there's a premium on driving skill. A concentrated boost of adrenaline requires a controlled use of the super power.

Obviously, a resource like this can be either an asset or liability. The first step toward controlling it is to appreciate that the nervousness you feel before a performance is vital to that performance. Without it, you're going to be flat; with it, you have the opportunity to excel.

It's not necessary to feel well in order to perform well. Sometimes it seems that the opposite is true: the worse you feel, the better you're going to perform. Don't worry that you don't feel like playing or giving your report. Your interior processes are working in your behalf. Be glad that you feel like throwing up as you unpack your bowling ball. If your mouth is dry, your palms are wet, your heart is pounding and you feel your neck hairs standing on end, under normal circumstances you could interpret these as signs of illness. In terms of performance, you're super well.

Test pilots welcome the "butterflies in the stomach" feeling they get just before they put a new type of high-performance airplane into its first dive. They call such surges of arousal "adrenal-burgers." They know they're going to perform to their maximum, with their system alert, in a circumstance where alertness and competence are matters of life and death.

Athletes recognize the feeling as "prestart phenomenon," a phrase invented by the Russians. Recall the champions I interviewed after their record-breaking performances. They all said that they had felt so bad just before their event that they had considered dropping out.

Once you accept that anxiety can be your ally, the next step is learning how to control it.

4

Dynamic Relaxation

THAT WE WESTERNERS are, as a rule, too committed, too zealous and too anxious has gained increasing acceptance in recent years. Americans by the hundreds of thousands have gravitated toward Eastern thought in an effort to achieve personal tranquility in a charged-up, aggressive, achievement-oriented world. This laudable quest for spiritual insight, however, has a significant deficiency: it concentrates on the static realm, and all but neglects the dynamic one.

I've seen many people go through Yoga, Zen Buddhism, Transcendental Meditation. The lines come out of their faces. They become serene. They achieve a state of bliss. If you consider the achievement of a blissful state as performance—and it is so considered in Eastern philosophies—then you must say that they are performing maximally.

But for most Westerners, who choose to live in the world of accomplishment, this is not enough. How, they ask, can a state of bliss be of benefit to one's work and home life and recreation? What does bliss have to do with getting ahead—or even making ends meet?

There is no positive relationship I know of between serenity and performance. Many serene people I know are content to be pretty sedentary. They become philosophical about getting things done. Achievement to them is no big deal. Since they won't perform, they won't be tested. They're satisfied with their position in the social order. They don't need to compete for status.

Several years ago, I had a student in my class on conditioning for maximum performance who had the potential, as well as the desire, to become the fastest sprinter of our time. No one in the world could match the swiftness with which Ron Welch got out of the starting blocks. At ten yards, he was always out in front. But by the end of the race, one or more runners would have passed him. Getting out of the blocks, for him, had become an almost unconscious reflex mechanism, but once he was running, we discovered, he was slowing down because he was trying to push his feet too fast—using force instead of relaxing. After we talked with him about that, Ron took up Yoga and meditation; he learned to relax and his performance improved. For a while, it appeared that he was going to reach his goal. Then he began to change. Instead of being uptight and tense in his dedication to competition, he became more whole and open. He lost his drive. Becoming the fastest runner in the world no longer seemed to matter to him. He had found a state of bliss, and there he stayed.

Relaxation can be an end in itself. There is nothing sweeter than some moments of calm in a turbulent day, when you steal away to a quiet place and undress your mind of its problems. But we can also use this blissful state for other than its own intrinsic merit. We can move from a static state of relaxation—a feeling of just-right and oneness with the universe—into a dynamic state. We can have these same sensations of just-rightness when we're doing something. We can relax in motion, feel the unity of self and the environment—a dynamic environment interacting with the dynamic self. We can combine both worlds, the feeling world of the East and the doing world of the West.

One way to achieve that unity is through the method I call Dynamic Relaxation.

This system is one I devised for world-class athletes and later adapted to everyday use. At its heart is the same method used in Eastern disciplines to release the state of tension in the neuro-muscular system. That method *focuses* the mind in such a way as to exclude antagonistic concerns.

FOCUSING

IF YOU ARE unfocused in your attitudes, objectives and conduct, time and nature act upon you in a manner that almost invariably produces a constant state of unproductive, enervating tension. By focusing on your inner state, and deliberately taking actions to control that state, you can reorder your mental and muscular activity.

In Hatha-Yoga, you focus on breathing and posture. By focusing your attention on the flow of air in and out of your body, you produce a soporific, almost hypnotic effect that induces general relaxation, ease and calm. It is this relaxed sense that enables you to ease into positions that extend the body's joints to their extreme range of motion. Were you not in that state, your muscles would quickly cramp and the position would become a strain.

In Transcendental Meditation, you focus on the reception of a word—your "mantra." Many hours of training and ritual precede the bestowal of his mantra on the initiate, but the objective remains a simple one: to eliminate that which is bothersome and intrusive by emphasizing a solitary act.

The principles of maximum performance are in exactly the same spirit as the Eastern disciplines. Here too, focus is the key.

The maximal performer does one thing at a time.

When he practices, he focuses on a tiny segment of the larger thing he's trying to do.

When he moves, he attempts to do so with such simplicity that his effort is focused on one phase.

The difference is in the objective: You are carrying this harmonious state into the workaday world. You're one with the universe—but you're still getting some work done.

Maximum performance occurs when you have eliminated all thought about how well you're doing something and are focusing on your objective.

Thinking, once again, is a mental process in which you let the mind work on all the elements of a problem in a free and unrestricted way, leading hopefully to a decision. Concentration comes after the decision has been taken. Focusing is the essence of concentration, in which you are using your senses to make small adjustments in timing and rhythm to match the work and eliminate extraneous movement and mental activity. In a performance, you can think too much but never focus too sharply.

THE MECHANICS OF RELAXATION

WHILE MENTAL and muscular tension are interrelated, it's in the muscles that the tension state is manifested. That's extremely fortunate, because it's infinitely easier —for most of us, at least—to relax our muscles than our minds. In the process, the mind becomes more quiet, since relief of muscular agitation removes some pressure from it.

There are four simple things to do that will give you instant relief:

Pause.
Breathe.
Move.
Take a break.

Pausing changes the state you're in. It assists you to erase where you were and get ready to start over again. It alters the relationship between you and what's bothering you. Preoccupation with a problem locks you into a process that reinforces your tension. Pausing unlocks the process.

Breathing induces concentration. You shift your focus to your breathing and away from bothersome things. Breathing a little more deeply and a little more slowly produces several beneficial physiological changes. First, a deep breath increases the negative pressure in your chest. This, in turn, helps to draw blood toward the heart through the large veins. An increased supply of blood in the heart helps to maintain the pressure of blood to your brain at the very moment when other parts of the body are competing for the blood. When your body prepares to go into action, the blood vessels supplying the muscles that will move you to fight or run away shift more blood into the action area. The body does this by squeezing the blood out of your belly—digestion isn't important now—and driving it to the muscle area where the vessels are opened to receive it. A sigh or two will help move the blood from your belly to your muscles and your brain.

When you breathe, focus on its four phases.

Feel yourself inhale.
Feel yourself pause.
Feel yourself exhale.
Feel yourself pause again.

Next, practice *belly breathing*. Sitting in a chair, put your hands on your belly. As you inhale, note whether your belly is rising or falling. It should be rising, but it often isn't because when we're tense we harden the stomach muscle as though in anticipation of a blow. If your belly isn't rising as you inhale, make a conscious effort to change the pattern. Continue monitoring your breathing for at least a minute by feeling the rise and fall of your belly.

Movement of any kind further reduces tension. Tapping the foot unconsciously; yawning and stretching; going through the motions of swinging a club, bat or racket; taking a walk; pacing the floor—all these motorize tension and help erase it.

Anything specific helps to calm emotions. If you're nervous about writing a paper, laying out your supplies will help to calm your nerves. If you're in a match, the way to combat the emotional backwash of a bad shot is to immediately rehearse a good shot by taking a well-executed practice swing.

The very best thing you can do when suddenly seized by tension is to take a break. Mentally, and physically, if possible, remove yourself from the arena that is causing your tension, so that you avoid further impulses that have locked you into a feedback situation. Ideally, you would go to a quiet, comfortable room where you could shut out the noises and smells that remind you of the arena. But whether an oasis exists or not, the break is the crucial thing.

Let's assume you're in your office, feeling unusually hassled. Six different people are lined up at your door, ready to ask you for a decision. Your phone is ringing. Your secretary is ill, and her substitute is driving you crazy. Everything that's happening to you right now is adverse to good performance. Your blood pressure is up, your heart is pounding, you're tense and mentally confused. For your sake and the sake of your firm, you should close your door, tell the secretary to hold your calls, remove your shoes, loosen your clothing, pause for a moment, take a deep breath and relax your belly, yawn, stretch and stay on your break until your composure is restored.

TAKING A TENSION INVENTORY

WHILE YOU'RE ON your break, you should make a tension inventory.

TENSION CHECKLIST

Eyebrows arched?
Squinting?
Staring?
Teeth clenched?
Pushing your tongue against your teeth?
Biting the inside of your mouth?
Scratching your face?
Biting your fingernails?
Neck tight?
Clearing your throat?
Swallowing unduly?
Shoulders hunched?
Hands clenched?
Tapping your finger?
Tapping your foot?
Belly tight?
Buttocks squeezed?
Are you sitting tensely on your chair, instead of
    letting your weight sink into the chair?
Thighs tensed?
Are your toes clenched?

Using the same principle you used in focused breathing, go down the checklist, focusing on each body part.

If your eyebrows are arched, relax and lower them. Then tense them again, and relax them once more. They'll relax more on the second try.

If your teeth are clenched, try letting the muscles of the jaw relax. If they won't relax, deliberately clench your teeth, and then focus on letting the tension diminish. Clench and unclench your teeth until your jaw muscles relax to the point that your mouth falls open.

Focus on the tension in your shoulders. Next, let your shoulders relax. Then let them hang, as though they might fall off on each side. Now tense and raise them again. Finally, let them relax and fall out to sides once more.

Now to deepen your relaxation even more, rehearse your belly breathing—breathe in, belly out; breathe out, belly in—pausing at the end of each phase.

THE DYNAMIC RELAXATION SYSTEM

THE SPECIFIC SYSTEM of Dynamic Relaxation is based on the "Jacobson technique," named after Edmund Jacobson, a physician, physiologist and pioneer in the field of relaxation methods. Doctor Jacobson's system has been used most widely in assisting people to get to sleep. You lie on your back, and focus on each part of the body, beginning with the feet and ending with the head. Increase the tension to a count of ten, then, counting backward, slowly relax each body part.

Dynamic Relaxation goes much further. It is a means by which you gain voluntary control over involuntary functions during any kind of performance. It is used during motion, rather than in a static state. I developed the technique when I was working with Mel Patton in the late 1940s at the University of Southern California. At the time, Mel was the world's fastest human, running the 100-yard dash in 9.3 seconds. I asked myself why he couldn't run the dash in 8.9 seconds. We studied his leg as we would a pendulum, figuring the mechanics of movement. Mel was tremendously powerful, as we had suspected; his strength measurements were far superior to everyone else's. If he was to run faster, it wasn't strength he needed. It was the ability to relax his muscles between their contractions at a faster rate. But Mel was a high-strung athlete, and he had used his great power against only partially relaxing muscles for so long that the muscles were torn and replaced with noncontracting scar tissues. Our discovery was not made in time to help him, but the system has worked subsequently for almost everyone who's tried it.

Dynamic Relaxation is accomplished in four steps:

1. You become aware of your present tension level.
2. You deliberately increase that level.
3. You then diminish that level, until you feel yourself slipping well below your initial tension level. You're getting so loose that your motions begin to wobble a little.
4. You bring your tension level back up to a degree that allows you to perform at your best; you have firm control and are free to move rapidly.

You learn Dynamic Relaxation as in the Jacobson method. While you are in motion, keeping a steady pace, slowly count to ten as you increase tension. Gradually tense your body all over, constricting the muscles, clenching the hands and feet, gritting the teeth. When you feel you're as tight as you can possibly be and still be able to move you should be at the count of ten. Then, counting backward to one, slowly let loose of your muscles, hands and feet, and let your jaw go slack. Let your body go limp. From this lowest tension point, increase your tension a notch or two, until you feel just right.

At the finish of the exercise, you'll be at an optimal level for performance, not so loose that you can't function, but not so tight that movement is restricted. If you were tense at the start, this level will be a good two notches lower than the level at which you began. You can never locate this proper level unless you dip below it and feel yourself coming "untied." Only then can you bring your tension back up to a level required to maintain proper function. In this optimal tension zone, your body is freewheeling, and you can move at top speed because there's nothing holding you back.

In the subtension level, you're so relaxed and loose

that you don't hold your body together, which means that you can't hold your technique or style together. If you swing a golf club without a certain degree of firmness, your swing all but collapses, and you don't hit the ball far or accurately. A certain degree of tightness is necessary to stabilize the joints and move them with accuracy and force. Golfers recognize this and go to extremes to achieve it, such as making sure that their shoelaces and belt are tight. This gives them a certain feeling of compactness. They feel that all their joints are properly bound together. Imagine swinging a golf club with no shoelaces in your shoes. You need this tightness in order to hold your feet firmly in the shoe and the shoe firmly to the ground. Your muscles are acting the same way. You can't move well with your muscles untied.

Conversely, too much tightness constricts you. Imagine trying to pivot if your shoes are too tight. In that case you don't get the proper footwork.

So the trick is to find just the right level. The trick is accomplished by exploring the *wobble*.

Measure out a distance—an estimate is good enough —the length of a basketball court. You are going to go three lengths to discover your own best level of tension. First, walk swiftly or run the length of the court. As you do, gradually tighten your body all over. Now, turn around and make the return trip. As you do, gradually let your structure "come apart." Deliberately let your coordination go. You'll feel it first in the knees and hips, where quite a bit of tension is normally needed to take controlled strides forward. This will slow your speed, and you will almost appear to be stumbling. A little further and you'd be staggering. Just before you get to the finish line, when you feel that you're as limp as a rag doll, begin to recover your tension—just enough to restore coordinated motion.

On the final lap, maintain that tension which gives you perfect function. What you've lost is the tension you didn't need. Repeat this three-trip circuit until you are able to achieve complete control of your tension.

The principle of Dynamic Relaxation can be applied in any sport. If you're swinging a golf club, for example, swing too stiff, then too loose, and finally just right a few times while you're warming up before you tee off on the first hole. After you've got it right, take one or two more practice swings to establish the feel of relaxed but firm control.

The Dynamic Relaxation system is good for any activity, athletic or otherwise. Whatever you're proposing to do that involves the movement of any part of your body, adjusting your arousal and tension will get the body's neuromuscular system into the right level of readiness—just enough to keep you up, not so much as to tie you up.

THE DYNAMIC RELAXATION RUN

LATER ON, when you're conditioned for intensive activity, you'll want to practice this advanced form of relaxation.

The difference between Dynamic Relaxation and the Dynamic Relaxation Run is that the first engages the entire body while the second isolates body parts and enables you to run with all brakes off.

Warm up for the Dynamic Relaxation Run by one bout of Dynamic Relaxation. When you feel that your body is at an optimum level of tension, try the procedure over again—but this time engaging only your lower legs, ankles and feet. As you run, increase the tension, then let it fade gradually until you find that there is a looseness or flipping action in your ankles that, if any more severe, would interfere with your running style. This is exactly what John Smith, the world-class quarter miler, looks for to give him top speed. Keep searching back and forth, alternating tensing with relaxing, until you feel that you've got the ideal degree. Then move up to the knees, thighs and hips, and repeat the process. Try to keep your lower leg area relaxed as you increase the tension in your thighs and buttocks, making yourself feel that you're running stiff. Then gradually release this tension until you feel that you're slowing down, even wobbling. At that point, bring the tension back to the point at which you control the running stride once more.

While you're practicing Dynamic Relaxation during running, try releasing the tension in your lower back in order to allow more than usual hip rotation. Such hip rotation should enable you to increase your stride length without altering your stride frequency. This little change could cause a remarkable increase in your speed.

Thus far we've approached the optimal state of tension for a maximum performance via the body. Now let's look to the mind.

5

Quieting the Mind

JUST AS CONCENTRATION is often impaired by self-induced distractions, so a great deal of tension is self-inflicted. Dynamic Relaxation works most effectively when you're aware not only of everything that contributes to tension but of what you can do to reduce it. It comes under the category of what world-class athletes would call "getting it together."

Much of what follows, once again, goes against the grain of accepted norms of how excellence is achieved. But it's the norms themselves, and commitment to them, that help produce the performance-spoiling tension.

PROTECTING YOURSELF FROM OVEREFFORT

WHEN BENNY BROWN, a world-class quarter-miler, was a student in my class on maximum performance at UCLA, he was absent a number of times and missed some important lectures. So I called him in for a conference. "Benny," I said, "you're not doing well in the course. Let's figure out how you're going to make up your work."

"We better not lay on me any more than I've got right now," Benny replied.

I immediately understood what he was saying. Between the pressures of competition, other schoolwork and social relationships, he had all he could handle. He could have gotten his A, but he had decided to settle for a lower mark in order to maintain his equilibrium. In terms of his priorities, it was a sensible decision, and very much in keeping with Nile Kinnick's dictum that it's a mistake to try to give 100 percent to everything 100 percent of the time.

Most maximum performers I know have this same solid sense of proportion. They know how much they can take on in addition to their highly focused training. In their resistance to the demands and pressures put on them by society, they show a mature wisdom. But the wisdom, itself, is childlike in its origins.

When you ask a child to run 100 yards, he knows innately whether he can or can't do it. He may try it —or he may sit down. In either case, he's made a fairly accurate appraisal of his capacity. If he does try to make the run and sees that he can't, he'll simply pull off to the side.

As we mature, we tend to lose this natural capacity to protect ourselves from the catastrophe of overeffort. Our innate clarity is compromised by rationalizations inspired by social pressures. In the name of success, we work ourselves to a frazzle, get ulcers, court heart attacks or have nervous breakdowns.

To perform maximally, you need to let your innate understanding of your own capacities govern your activities, just as you did as a child. But it is the nature of adult behavior to perform in terms of consequences. There are social rewards for certain behavior. The great irony is that the very behavior that's supposed to lead to better performance actually retards it.

When you see a sign in an office that says THINK, you know you're being urged to "be an adult," take responsibility, recognize the impact of what you're doing. The trouble with such injunctions, whether implied or expressed, is that they keep you from doing what's best for you—as well as your organization.

Suppose you're an actuary, and you've been asked by your insurance company to deliver, by a certain date, a figure on which policy rates will be based—a maximum mental performance. If, during this performance, you permit yourself to think about the consequences of being late or making a mistake, your work will suffer. Your most accurate and fastest performance will come about if you approach the assignment with childlike openness.

I attack day-to-day problems most effectively when I act on impulse, much as a child would. It's when I'm trying to assess all the ramifications and their possible consequences that things become a mess.

That may sound like a formula for impulsiveness. The fact is that your first impulse seems to be the best informed. It comes about by reflex, and reflex is conditioned by all past experience and knowledge. If there is such a thing as wisdom of the ages, it reposes in impulse.

When you try to construct a response on the basis of logic, several things happen that make a solution more difficult. First, by switching into a cerebration mode—trying to think it all through—you block out your experiental reflexes. Second, you see all the complexities. Third, you function with less conviction; having considered the alternatives, you've given them the legitimacy to act as censors on your actions. And fourth, by reverting to a harsh, rigid mode, you've lost your own naturalness and personality.

Whether you're thinking or doing, overeffort only spoils the act. You'll achieve less than if you develop a solid sense of proportion about how much you can do. Don't overload your system with projects and concerns and goals that you can't handle. You won't do them any good, and you'll only be hurting yourself. If you have a good sense of proportion, those things to which you do commit yourself will be done at your best, because you'll approach them in a state of productive equilibrium, devoid of useless tension.

Self-protection from overcommitment includes learning what you can and can't effectively influence—and limiting your concern accordingly.

I feel that the world affects me and I affect the world, but I don't feel a deep responsibility for everything that's going on in the world, and I don't think the world expects me to be personally responsible. I wasn't always like that. Over the years, I've dissipated a lot of energy because of my overresponse to what confronts me in the media. With the onset of worldwide communications, we've become spectators at an unending series of disasters. If we permit ourselves to become "burden bearers," reacting personally to every human tragedy even though there's practically nothing we can do about most of them, we drain our personal resources.

You can't live harmoniously in the world if you always try to tailor it to your own constructs. Sometimes, you have to let the world exist as it is and try to understand it. That, of course, is easier said than done; we may acknowledge validity in the proposition, but that doesn't prevent us from trying to make over the world in our image.

Years ago, the government of Egypt asked me to investigate the problem of low productivity among its industrial workers. The problem was readily located: an extraordinarily high degree of absenteeism. To my American mind, the solution was obvious: Identify those workers who didn't want to work, and replace them with workers who were more willing to stay at their jobs. But in the course of my investigation, I came to appreciate that Egypt was a culture formed by the rhythm of the Nile; all work and social life had for centuries been cycled to the flooding and ebbing of the river. There were brief periods for the planting and harvest, and long periods of inactivity in between. Egyptians, consequently, developed working rhythms all their own, and spent long periods among their families, to whom they developed close ties.

Even now, in an industrial age, the historical rhythms continued; the country's most dominant social feature remained the celebration by all members of a family of a special event in the life of any one of them. A marriage, a birth, an anniversary or funeral obliged every relative, no matter how distant, to attend the ritual ceremonies. And there were frequent festivities, as well, for which business shut down. In the spring, for example, there was an exodus to the Sahara to "smell the breezes" fragrantly scented by the brief bloom of desert flowers. Absence from work for such reasons was a cultural norm, readily accepted as more fulfilling than a few days' work on an assembly line. Nothing in my armament of human factors science could change that. I departed Egypt wondering if there wasn't a little something we Americans could learn from the Egyptians.

CREATING A RELAXED ENVIRONMENT

THE WRONG KIND of tension can be as contagious as the flu, and just about as debilitating. It's pretty difficult for you to relax if the people around you are tense. If, by chance, you're the one who is making them tense, your problems are compounded.

Leonard Gross worked for many years for a brilliant editor who was terribly uneasy with most people. The editor felt the best way to handle this was to be aggressive. If a freelance writer would come into his office with a story idea, he would say, "State the case," or something equally rattling. He so unnerved his visitors that they could rarely express themselves well. The unsatisfying episodes only served to further deepen the editor's unease with people and compound his tension.

If you're the kind of "businesslike" person who

doesn't believe in social amenities, who likes to get right down to cases, you're doing exactly the reverse of what should be done in the interest of maximum performance. The moments of amenities at the beginning of a conversation are more than worth the time they take. They set the stage for a maximum performance by both of you. When you say, "Hello Fred, how's your golf game?" both you and Fred know that you're not really that interested in his game. But you're opening up with some sort of relaxed casualness from which you can approach the business at hand with a clearer mind and a better use of the intellect.

If your own performance profits from reduction of tension, it follows that others' performances will, too. If you have a vested interest in seeing that others perform well—employees, teammates, your family—then you have to help them relax.

Suppose you're upset about a decision taken by one of your subordinates, and you say, "I want to see you in my office at once." When he gets there, he'll be unnerved. But suppose you say, "Can you drop by in a few minutes?" The chances are he'll be far more orderly in his thinking when he arrives and so will you. Both statements mean the same thing, but only the one allowing the pause is encouraging maximum performance.

If you're a parent with growing children, you don't need me to tell you how much tension the home environment can produce. It simply breaks my heart to watch how well-meaning, loving parents constantly put down their children. To say to a child, "You're a bad boy!" or "I'm ashamed of you!" is to ruin him for that day. Enough of that kind of put-down can ruin him for life.

The way to help your child perform to his potential is to make him feel good about himself. Encourage him to tell you how he feels. Show him that you respect his feelings, whatever they are. This gives the child a sense of worth. In the process of helping your child, you'll be helping yourself. Because he feels better and more relaxed about himself, he won't be upsetting you.

Remember that the less tension you create to begin with, the less you'll have to reduce to put yourself into an optimal state for performance.

TAKE A REAL LUNCH-HOUR BREAK

THE LUNCH HOUR, a natural break period, is terribly abused.

The business lunch is probably the worst time and place to do serious business. The continuity of work hurts performance. You're sacrificing time you need for personal recuperation from the morning, as well as preparation for the afternoon. Worse yet, you're making crucial decisions in what ought to be a rest period.

If the lunch hour is the time when decisions are habitually made, you'd be well-advised to take some time off just before lunch. Allow yourself a comfortable fifteen minutes for grooming, shopping or walking to a restaurant.

The executives with whom my son works all bring their lunch to work. At noon, they go out to a park, find a picnic table and have lunch together. That's good procedure, deliberately removing themselves from their place of business, but it would be even better if they removed themselves from one another for a while.

The nonbusiness lunch hour is a marvelous time for exercise. If you can't devote the entire period, then even a brief workout is beneficial. Many women have begun to use this time well by enrolling in exercise classes. If you have a weight-control program, work out before lunch. Vigorous exercise tends to diminish the appetite.

I once knew a man in Washington, D.C., who solved the problem of the business lunch superbly. He had an important luncheon every working day of his life. Each morning he would come to work unshaven. At exactly 11:45 he would leave his desk, go to the washroom, remove his shirt and shave leisurely. At 12:15, he would appear for his lunch date, feeling fresh, smelling fresh and looking well groomed. His primary purpose was to make the best possible appearance at his luncheons. In the process, he was also freshening his mind.

I walk to and from work each day, a distance of a mile each way. I often teach in the morning at the university and work in my study at home in the afternoon. As I prepare lunch, I turn on my television set and watch a soap opera. It's like reading a detective novel. I get involved in the characters. They take me into another world. If I were to start work immediately on my return from the university, I would still be on a "high" from my lecture. As it is, watching that soap opera erases my present concerns and eases the transition to new concerns.

However you wish to make that transition, the important thing is to make a real break. It's the first step in maximum performance—whether you're playing a sport, doing needlepoint or closing a million-dollar deal.

6

How to Maximize
Everyday Performance

WE ALL PERFORM, all day long.

Brushing your teeth is a performance. You can do it well or poorly. If you do it poorly, you eventually pay for it with complex, costly and uncomfortable dental work. If you do it well, you may avoid this problem. Yet dentists are aware that many patients don't brush their teeth well. They haven't learned—or, if they've learned, they haven't been impressed by—the major purpose of brushing, which is to extract particles of food from between the teeth before they cause decay. A scrubbing or polishing motion back and forth will refresh your mouth, but it may not dislodge the food particles, and it may even drive them farther into the crevices. A better motion is to place the bristles against the gums, then stroke the bristles away from the gums out to the biting edge of the teeth.

The manner in which we perform even the most mundane acts is a statement of who we are. We resemble our performance, and our performance resembles us. Every repetition of a performance habituates us more permanently to the style of that performance. By improving our performance, we improve ourselves as persons.

During World War II, I commanded a patrol ship based in Brazil. When we weren't at sea and I didn't have much to do, I started reading about graphology, a system that assesses personality and behavior characteristics through the analysis of handwriting. I became conscious of what my own handwriting purported to reveal about me. Crowded words are interpreted in graphology as a sign of stinginess. My words, I saw, were crowded. So I deliberately increased the spacing to portray myself as a more generous person—and each time I did that I was reminded to be more generous.

Most of us perform dozens of routines every day without thinking about what we're doing. We've done them thousands of times before, and it never occurs to us that we may be doing them in an inefficient manner. Yet, if we were to examine these activities, we'd find that we could do them more swiftly, with less energy and greater style.

The first time you made a bed, you probably followed someone's instructions—your mother's or your sergeant's. Like a rat in a maze who finds a route to the food and then repeats that route over and over without searching for a better one, you continue making the bed in the manner you were taught.

The next time you make a bed, take a job foreman's view of the project. Observe how many times you go from one side to the other before you're finished. The first time I tried this experiment I was surprised to learn that I was making six trips around the bed. I decided to see whether I could make the bed in one trip. I could, but it was a pretty sloppy-looking bed. So I modified my objective, and found that in three trips I could often make a bed as neatly as I could in six.

Using the methods of maximum performance you might well double your effectiveness, doing a job as well or better in half the time and with half the effort. To accomplish this, you have to pay attention—perhaps for the first time in years—to what you're doing. At the outset, you'll work with less efficiency, not more, because you'll want to become aware of everything you're doing, evaluate your useless movements and figure out a more direct method. Next comes the actual experiment, in which you see whether your new method works. After that come refinements, until there's no further way of reducing waste motion consistent with achieving the result you want.

As you proceed, you'll be tempted to return to your habitual method. Old habits are comfortable; you may feel more comfortable spending twice the time and energy just because you don't have to think about what you're doing.

There's a lesson here central to all improvement, be it making a better bed, brushing your teeth better, earning a better living, or playing better tennis. It's this: There is a thinking phase in all learning that makes any new process seem more difficult. But this phase is quickly left behind once you habituate yourself anew. Then the new habit is as automatic as the old one—but considerably more effective.

No matter what your objective is, everyday habits are a good place to start. We want to accustom ourselves to keeping improvement in mind. We start with readily changeable patterns. Once we've successfully changed those, we know we can change habits, period.

What could be simpler than getting into a car? Nothing, really, yet most of us enter a car in a cumbersome manner: We grab the wheel, place our right foot inside, then sit, then lift our left foot inside. The entry is inefficient and ungainly, and could conceivably cause a muscle pull.

Just as an experiment, try a new technique, one well known to sports car owners. Open your door. Turn your back to the seat. Sit. Then lift and swivel your feet into the car.

If you were to continue to climb into your car in the old inefficient manner, it wouldn't make that much difference in your life. But if you could make this new, more efficient way a habit, you would be preparing yourself for change in activities that do matter.

Let's try that principle out now by learning to be

better performers at an activity common to us all. In the process we'll learn about the method of improvement and, also, how improvement of a rudimentary technique all but automatically improves other things we do.

BEFORE YOU RUN . . .

NEXT TO BREATHING and talking, walking is our most frequently performed physical activity. You would think that anything done so consistently would be done well. Yet, as we saw in the first chapter, there's not one of us who couldn't walk more smoothly and with greater conservation of energy.

Learning to walk better is an accomplishment you can achieve yourself, without the benefit of coaching. Both psychologically and physiologically, it's an excellent beginning for adaptation to change.

To improve your walk, you must first pay attention to the way you're walking now. Are you swinging from side to side? Bouncing up and down? Flailing your arms uselessly? All these movements are nonproductive, and yet they all take energy. If you're walking a great distance—and most homemakers walk about six miles a day—an inefficient manner of walking can amount to tons of work. We've already calculated the energy cost of lifting the body an extra inch when you walk; a 150-pound person would use 1800 inch-pounds of energy every dozen steps—almost enough work to lift a ton one inch. There's the additional problem of the descent, when the walker's momentum puts a force more than twice his weight on his foot and knee joints, a needless strain on vulnerable tissue. Just as a heel-pounding job may provide a good cardiovascular workout but cause an orthopedic disaster, so a bouncing walk is a risky form of exercise. Better to smooth your walk and get your workout in a less damaging way.

The manner in which you walk derives in good part from the manner in which you hold yourself. If your head is bent forward and your pelvis is tipped forward, both your leg and arm action are affected. A tilted pelvis tends to make you walk with your feet splayed; you waddle from side to side. Ballerinas develop a splayed-foot stance; that's a classic position in that form of dancing but bad for general movement.

One day my assistant asked me what she could do to solve a problem of "secretarial spread." "Come on," I said, "we're going to do a little fanny research." As we took a walk through Westwood, I pointed out to her examples of good and poor posture among young women. Those women who walked with their belt lines parallel to the ground—meaning that their pelvis was level, as well—had compact behinds. Those women whose belt lines dipped in front—meaning their pelvis was tilted forward—had saddlebags on their thighs and flabby behinds. Were they to run, they would do so in a weak and wobbly position, and they wouldn't generate much speed. The girls with the tight behinds would have an agile, forceful stride.

Secretarial spread is caused by sitting continuously. This shortens the tissues in the front of the hip and elongates them in the rear. You can do all kinds of exercises to correct this, but the simplest and most effective is to lift the pelvis and hold it level when you walk. Every time your leg swings backward, you stretch the anterior hip tissues. This makes it increasingly easier to hold the pelvis level. The level pelvis automatically tucks your behind under you and draws the tissue together. More important, it forms the basis for a strong walking and running stride.

And there's another dividend: a smaller waistline. When your pelvis is held level, its bowl is upright, and the viscera—your guts—are contained in it. When your pelvis tilts forward, as when you slouch while standing, your viscera spill forward, out of your pelvic bowl, and press against your abdominal wall—your belly—giving you a pot. The weaker your abdominal muscles, the larger your pot.

Because of this visceral pressure against your belly, the size of your waistline increases. If you will just lift the front of your pelvis the viscera will shift back into the bowl where they belong. With this slight shift in posture you can take an inch off your waistline in one second.

Unless you're really fat, you can have a trim waistline simply by keeping your guts in the pelvic bowl. Using your belly muscles to lift the front of the pelvis

also firms the abdominal wall. These benefits are yours just by putting yourself into a good walking posture.

There's a simple way to encourage this posture. Take a "posture walk." Select some place, about a block in length, that you pass every day, preferably an area where there are store windows so you can see your reflection. Each time you get to that block, put yourself in the right position and hold it while you walk. Ideally, it would be the first complete block that you walk when you set out from home in the morning. Just raise your breastbone a trifle—half an inch will do—and lift your belt buckle or belly button the same amount. Your pelvis will automatically level. Your shoulders will fall naturally to the sides. Your head will rest straight on your shoulders. You'll be walking, and looking, better.

WALKING—AND RUNNING—FASTER

IF YOU'D LIKE to run faster, the best possible approach is to learn to walk faster. That will happen automatically if you train yourself to relax when you walk. Here's your opportunity to utilize Dynamic Relaxation.

As you start to walk, become aware of your present tension level.

Next, gradually increase the tension in your body, constricting the muscles while you count to ten.

Then, gradually release the tension as you count backward to zero. At the end of the count, you should be "wobbling," almost staggering.

Now, increase your tension a notch or two, until you're walking smoothly.

At this lower level of tension you'll discover that you've been walking all these years with your brakes on. You'll begin to feel where the movement of walking comes from. The first thing you'll notice is that your stride is led by the anterior thigh muscle, the quadriceps, which draws your leg forward. The next thing you'll notice is an increased looseness of the hips —the key to efficient movement in walking and running. A slight exaggeration of this hip swiveling will produce a marked increase in your stride length. Your walk will be less jarring because, in addition to your ankles and knees, you're adding a third shock absorber to your stride—the rotation of your hips. This added cushion to your walk enables you to keep your center of gravity on a more even plane. You eliminate all nonfunctional up-and-down motion. The effect of all this is to increase your walking speed. In addition, and particularly in women, your walk becomes much more sensuous.

The exaggerated movement of competitive walkers includes a technique you can adapt to good effect. By raising their chest, they put their abdominal muscles on a slight stretch. The abdominal muscles, in turn, function more strongly to support the pelvis in its swiveling action. The pelvic action helps the anterior thigh muscles lead the leg. If you try the same technique, you'll find that you feel loose in the small of your back. What you've done is to release a kinesiological lock. When you walk with your pelvis fixed, your lower back muscles are rigid. When you permit the pelvis to swivel, the lower back muscles unlock and assist in rotating the hips. You've forced nothing; you've simply relaxed.

To really feel the effect, try walking with your chest raised on a very slight downhill slope. This enables gravity to work with you and gives you a longer stride. As you let your hips rotate freely, you'll feel that you're practically flying.

The same technique you used to unlock your walking is used to improve your running. Raise your chest, and keep it raised as you run.

With your chest slightly elevated, your shoulders fall naturally and comfortably to the sides, and your arms are free to assist the legs in running, by stabilizing the body. Don't deliberately try to hold your arms in any position. They'll find their own best position with your hands close to your chest and your elbows well bent and swinging close to your sides. If your arms are tense, use a sprinters' trick. Press your thumbs against your middle fingers. All the tension will flow to that point. Now release, and relax. Everything but the driving muscles should remain as relaxed as possible, without affecting your posture or carriage. Even your face should be so devoid of tension that your jowls flap in the breeze.

When you run, your head should be comfortably resting on your shoulders rather than craning forward. Your back should be straight, not arched, and your buttocks tucked under.

Breathing while running is best left to nature. There is a tendency to coordinate breathing with stride rhythm. The less you think about and try to control your breathing, the more economical it will be. Although the energy cost of breathing can be more than 5 percent of the total energy cost of the run, we rarely think of what it's costing us to breathe. Instead, we're concentrating on our flagging limbs. Expanding the rib cage and lifting the chest involve muscle work. The muscle of the diaphragm is working, too, but at less cost. Any energy that can be saved in this respiratory work can be applied to the run itself. Natural breathing costs less than trying to breathe with a contrived rhythm. Sprinters in the short distances, up to 100 yards or meters, usually suspend breathing during the race without realizing it. The body's need to stabilize the thorax for the violent arm action is greater than its need for oxygen during those few seconds of effort.

If you've followed the foregoing simple procedures, you've greatly enhanced your movement. But what you've learned in the process is even more valuable than that. What you've just walked and run along is the route to maximum performance.

THE METHODS OF MAXIMAL PERFORMERS

THE GOLDEN ROAD to maximum performance is bricked with common sense. Analysis, conditioning, skill training and performance strategy are all put in proper sequence. Each element receives the attention it needs before you progress to the next.

The maximal performer who takes up a new sport will first watch it executed by skilled performers. Then he'll search his repertoire of skills to see what he already knows that might be applied to the new activity. If he's a former baseball player who decides to play golf, he'll analyze what possible similarities there are between the swing of a bat and the swing of a golf club.

What is most novel and refreshing—and perhaps surprising to the average performer who has experienced more than his share of failure—is the atmosphere of success in which the maximum performer functions. He's immediately successful, and he almost never fails throughout his adaptation to the new activity. The method by which he manages his success is critical to your own improvement, and readily accessible.

The maximum performer knows what he's proposing to do before he tries.

The task he sets for himself is so simple that he's almost sure to be able to do it.

Once he's prepared himself, he gets going right off —even if what he's doing is the barest suggestion of the way he'll eventually perform. Even though he knows a great deal about his eventual goal, he's content to begin at a child's level, if necessary. A child with a new pair of skates quickly discovers that he's got a new environment. First he holds on to something. Then he takes short steps. Finally, he glides.

The maximal performer never tries the next step until he's mastered the previous one.

He interprets failure as his having done something the wrong way.

He quickly discards what doesn't work and concentrates on what does.

The performance idiot who at first doesn't succeed because he's doing something wrong tries and tries the very same thing again. Such practice makes the error perfect.

The maximal performer specifies his target and focuses on it. If, for example, he wanted to learn golf, he would not go out to a driving range or practice tee with a bucket of balls, take out his driver and try to hit the ball as far as he could. That is the traditional manner. The maximal performer takes a putter and goes to the practice green. Why? Because, first, he knows that putting comprises half of par. Second, he knows that putting is the simplest part of the game. Third, he knows that almost instantly he can have some success.

The maximal performer doesn't try fifteen-or twenty-foot putts at the outset. He puts the ball down next to the hole and taps it in a few times. Then he moves the ball back six inches, and tries that until he's successful. He continues to increase the distance in increments of six inches. As he finds his putting stroke, he knows he's getting a good idea of the mechanics involved in striking the ball with the clubhead; he's learning about the roll of the ball and the effect on it of grass textures and slopes. He's also developing the habit of a steady head which he will need on the tee and fairway. By the time he's at the practice tee, he has confidence in one part of the game and a feel for the rest of it. And he's already been rewarded with a continuum of success.

THE CRUCIAL HABIT

MOST OF US are impatient to get into competition as soon as we can. Understandably. We're after either results or enjoyment, and the process of learning is no substitute for the real thing.

But the secret of maximum performance is exactly here: you must train for an event until conscious movements become so habitual that they're performed automatically.

Training and conditioning should not be so dull and frustrating that they kill anticipation of the event itself. The key to avoiding such boredom is to make each session so simple that a reward is guaranteed. There is no satisfaction quite like being able to do something that you couldn't do before.

On or off the field, failure is the worst part of any performance. And too often failure is the result of plunging right into the middle of a complicated activity and competing against a superior opponent. This is a mistake. Only when you have a good understanding of the complexities should you seriously challenge a better opponent.

Here sport and work intersect. Every time I become deluged with responsibilities, I find myself trying to do everything at once. It's no good; it doesn't work; but it's a normal human response. Only when I see that I'm doing everything poorly do I remember what I've learned so many times: One thing at a time, the simplest things first.

I belong to an automobile club whose employees utilize the one-thing-at-a-time principle, whether they know it or not, in their office procedure. When you go to a representative's desk, the only thing on his desk is your file. Everything concerning your business is transacted while you're sitting at the desk. If a form needs filling out, it is filled out then and there. If a phone call in your behalf needs to be made, it is made on the spot.

If a higher authority must be consulted, he is sought out at once. You're still sitting there when the representative makes out his report: who you are, what was done, and so forth. When you're finished, he's finished. Then he pulls the next customer's file and calls him in.

You may have to wait awhile to get such service, because the representative won't see you until he's completed work with the customer ahead. But contrast this service with the service you'd get if shortening the customer's stay in the office was the representative's primary concern. Papers would be put aside to be filled out later when you're not waiting. Phone calls would be made after you'd left. Consultations and reports, the same. An enormous amount of unfinished work would accumulate. Eventually all that work would have to be reviewed to see what was done, what still needed doing and what special concerns you might have had. Invariably, the representative would run across questions that only you could answer; that would require a letter or phone call or another visit, which would generate more unfinished work, more time and more delay.

Whether you're training for a sport or working for a living, the vital principle is the same: Take things in order, simplest things first. Complete one project before you start the next. Not only is it more efficient and productive, it's also easier to confront.

GETTING STARTED

ALL THE METHOD in the world isn't going to help us if we can't bring ourselves to begin.

We're all familiar with the work-avoidance phenomenon. We need time to "crank up," we tell ourselves, and so we fritter away hours in the process. "Getting myself together" is a way of avoiding work. I convince myself that I don't have in mind exactly what I want to do. So I fuss around, finish the newspaper or watch the rest of a TV program. My rationale is that my unconscious is getting me organized, so that when I do get to work, I'll have a better concept of how I want to proceed. Before I know it, I've blown the time I've set aside for the work.

The work-avoidance phenomenon is a rational and understandable process. It usually surfaces when you're about to do something uncomfortable. Either you've never done it before, or you don't feel competent enough to succeed. So you concentrate on the dreading, not the doing.

The remedy is a simple one: Begin by doing something that's related to the task, but doesn't involve any risks.

Suppose it's a tough paper you've been putting off. Write down your present thoughts right away without worrying about how they sound. Such notes don't pose the same hangups as writing the paper, because you haven't yet committed an idea for examination by someone else.

To commit yourself to an idea, for most of us, is not an easy thing to do. As Leonard Gross tells students in his writing courses: "Writing is easy. It's thinking that's hard. It's not what you write but what you think that's tough to come to terms with." He advises the students to get their ideas and convictions down on paper first, no matter how crudely they're stated. They can be prettied up later.

By the time you've finished your notes, you may well find that you have the outline of your paper. All you then need to do is fill in the gaps.

The phenomenon of work-avoidance is equally present in physical workouts. Getting started is a problem for most of us every day that we train. The solution is similar to that employed for mental work: Do something that's preliminary to the work you're supposed to do.

A warmup exercise is more than physiological preparation. It's psycholoical, as well. You're about to undertake something that you don't particularly relish doing, so rather than hit it head on, you take tentative steps in that direction—for example, moving a light weight before a heavy workout.

Another common excuse for putting things off is the feeling that you're not ready to perform perfectly. Your sense of what you'd like to do and what you're ready to do are so far apart that you're discouraged from even trying. There's a lesson to be learned from industry here: Your initial effort is and ought to be a crude one.

The first step in the development of a new product is to take scraps of whatever's on hand, whether suited to the final product or not, put the whole thing together on a work bench, and see if and how it works. This first device is usually called the bench model.

The next step is the engineering model. It requires the fabrication of parts that are going to be its central feature. Once the engineering model is assembled, it's tested for reliability, durability, accuracy and efficiency. From the results of these tests comes the final design of an attractive, easy-to-use and hopefully salable product.

To get yourself organized, you follow the same basic procedure. Set down what you've got, no matter what it is—a rough set of figures, sketches, fragmentary ideas. Organization doesn't matter. Once you have these items set down, then you can see what else you need. When you have the new ingredients, assemble them with the initial ones in a logical order. Now you have an engineering model. Then perfect that model until it's what you want.

So many people shy away from projects, saying, "I could never do it." If they were to see the effort in its initial stages, they would recognize it as something they could, indeed, do.

The important thing is to get started, no matter how—even if what you do at first doesn't necessarily appear in the final product. Any preparation that's related to the anticipated task will help—even if all you do is write a word or two on the back of an envelope or clip an article from a newspaper.

WORKING UNDER DURESS

PRODUCING ORDER from chaos in daily life involves the exact same procedure as training for a championship. When we find ourselves working under duress, it's usually because we've let ourselves be talked into trying to do several things at once.

If you've got a horrendous work load, your blood pressure's up, your heart's pounding, you're tense and mentally confused, and you'd like to run away, it's time for a coaching strategy session with yourself.

First, stop everything and wait a moment. Next take a deep breath and practice relaxation techniques— belly breathing, Dynamic Relaxation. Then, determine your top priority task, turn to it and set the others aside. You're not going to be able to do them all, you tell yourself, but the main tasks are going to be done and done well—*one at a time.*

When we're confronted with a threatening situation, our tendency is to bring all our resources to bear. We feel we have to be as forceful as possible; we try to marshal every possible ally—legal, financial or moral —that can be mounted against the foe. But an excessive response is not efficient.

Whenever I'm angered enough to respond, I grab at every argument I've got. My notes show it. After a night's sleep, I see the better effect of one argument simply stated.

REMEMBER TO SEPARATE THINKING
FROM DOING

THERE IS SOMETHING sad to most of us in the spectacle of the supercoach sending plays into a game. The athlete becomes the instrument of the coach's intelligence, nothing more. The truth is that those coaches who send in plays are right; by eliminating the need to think, they are simplifying the players' task and improving their performance prospects.

When it comes to physical performance, the preliminary mental factors should be out of the way before an action begins. To be a maximal performer, you have to refine your focus.

I was the founding president of the Human Factors Society of America and a fellow of the Fatigue Laboratory at Harvard's Graduate School of Business Administration. The concerns in both groups were the same: to increase productivity in industry and make work easy and comfortable. The question that preoccupied me was why workers needed foremen and supervisors. Why couldn't they do their own thinking? I soon discovered the reason for middle management: You can't plan and work at the same time. Planning requires an analytical process. If you try to analyze what you're doing while you're doing it, your movements become disorganized and you make mistakes.

Think when you need to, and do when you need to, but make it a rule to keep your thinking and doing separate.

7

Maximizing Energy

THERE ARE ANY number of things you can do to get more mileage out of your present supply of energy. They range from learning how to intersperse work and rest, to how to better arrange your office, to how to choose the desk chair that keeps you most alert. Later, we'll be dealing with ways to increase your energy, but right now let's work on how to conserve it.

We usually don't think of mental work in terms of energy, but your mind works very much like your body. If you're uncoordinated in your muscular motions, moving in several directions at once, you don't get much work done, and you soon are exhausted. Mental activity appears to follow the same principles. If you permit your mental energies to spread out, you get little done and you tire quickly. If you focus on a primary objective, you get the most done with the least fatigue. If you can learn to husband your mental and emotional resources as you do your muscular resources, then you will function maximally.

Heavy muscular work tires the nervous system as well as it does the muscles. That's another reason why muscle work and mental work in combination are never a good idea. Do your planning first, while you're fresh. Then do the physical work according to your plan.

Try to organize your work into a number of circuits, each consisting of a variety of tasks. If you're cleaning a house, for example, clean one room at a time, rather than making all the beds in the house, then vacuuming all the floors, then cleaning the bathrooms. Circuit training is an important component of conditioning for maximum performance, because it permits you to work intermittently at much higher rates and with less fatigue than if you were to practice one motion continuously. Suppose you were scrubbing floors, and tried to do all the floors in succession. Your arms would quickly tire, your knees would hurt from kneeling, your back would hurt from bending. But if you did one floor, then made one bed and dusted in the bedroom, your arms, knees and back would have been given the respite they needed. Imagine how fatigued you would become if you had to do all the polishing or furniture moving during one unbroken period. By alternating these heavy chores with lighter work, you're able to accomplish more work during the day and not get tired.

Most of us tend to take the time available to do a task. In keeping house we could take all day to wash up the breakfast dishes, read the paper, feed the pets, make the beds and put the house in order. The sensible alternative is to set a time goal. If everyone's out of the house by eight-thirty in the morning, we should try to finish the daily maintenance and be free for our own activities before ten.

Working efficiently retards fatigue in two ways. Psychologically, your accomplishment is motivating. Physiologically, you distribute your energy.

Recognize signs of anxiety or tension that are going to impair your performance, and take steps to deal with them. If you approach a backlog of work saying to yourself, "My God, I'm not going fast enough, I've got to get moving," the work will be done carelessly, and you'll quickly lose the energy you need to perform the task.

Industry has learned that the working day has to be

broken up by rest periods, but it has yet to learn what it should about individual pacing. When you attempt to speed up the work beyond the worker's natural pace, he becomes tense, careless and easily fatigued.

The same problems and solutions apply to the homemaker. When you have a house to clean, children to care for and a dinner party to prepare, you tense up exactly as a busy person does in an office. You strive to move faster and do more. Result: you do less, and do it poorly. Your remedy: Dynamic Relaxation, followed by a strategy session to identify priorities.

When you tire, you are tempted to strive harder to make up for your fatigue. This induces the very tension that holds you back. It's as though little bears are grabbing at your ankles, bigger bears are clutching your shoulders and the biggest bear of all is jumping on your back. At the moment you feel the little bears tugging at your ankles, you should recognize that you're striving too hard, take a breath, and try to go only as fast as you can.

WORK AND REST

PROPER REST PERIODS can anticipate and head off tension and fatigue. And inasmuch as a certain amount of tension accompanies all performance, it's helpful to remember that the best way to reduce tension is through the reduction of excess effort—reducing extra motions and easing feelings of tightness.

Work periods should vary with the intensity of the work. Low intensity, long work periods. High intensity, brief work periods.

Work of high intensity should be preceded by a warming-up period. The muscles that are going to be used in your effort need time to receive an extra supply of blood. By contracting those muscles you set in motion a reflex phenomenon called "shunting." The vessels in the parts of the body at the site of the mus-

the contraction open up so that more blood can flow in, and the less vital vessels narrow. At the same time, the nerves that are going to be involved go on the alert. The body, in short, is finding the proper state it wants to be in when the performance occurs and it can only do that by a rehearsal of the movements that will take place. The secret of strength is to get the most impulses to the working muscles. This does not usually occur in the first attempt. But after a few trials, you've usually found the maximum coordination that gets the most impulses to the working muscles.

An interval of thirty to sixty seconds should come between your warmup and your work. During that interval walk around and shake your arms. This short period of active rest is needed to let the body recover from the fatigue of the warmup activity. But don't prolong the interval; a wait of even five minutes between warmup and work will cancel many of the benefits of the warmup, and may produce a kind of stiffness in muscles and joints.

You should work while the extra blood is in the muscles. But you should interrupt that work with short rest breaks, so as not to persist into a stage of fatigue. That's when you ruin your style and pacing, begin to make mistakes, and often incur injuries. When you are tired, your standards of acceptance lower and you don't recognize that the quality of work is deteriorating. You think you are doing a good job, but you aren't.

You'll get more and better work done by working steadily for short periods and then resting than you will be working straight through.

Rest periods shouldn't be too long. Suppose you're working on math computations. It's exacting work, yet if you simply stand and stretch, you can get back to work in thirty seconds and have the relief you need to continue, without losing your concentration, as you might if you rested longer. Even with fairly heavy work, a minute's rest at frequent intervals is usually all you need to recover sufficiently in order to

nroductivity. If you
e, you begin to lose the

should try to rest in a
legs up on a chair. It
vise that promotes blood
I've been using is better
or seated position. What
g the tendency for you
extremities, which can
can conceivably be dan

s, a workplace that al-
lows you to alternate between standing and sitting
keeps fatigue to a minimum. Having a second desk or
bench so that you can do some of your work standing
up allays fatigue.

If you're in charge of a group of workers, remember that they'll benefit more from rest periods if those
periods are authorized, because then they can relax
without tension. Industry has learned to its sorrow
that when authorized rest periods are not provided,
"unauthorized" rest is usually longer than a scheduled
rest period would be, and the worker doesn't feel as
comfortable.

Any bout of strenuous work should be followed by
ample rest—at least one full day after exhaustive
work. Failure to rest could result in chronic fatigue or
injury.

PACE

WHEN YOU'VE GOT a lot of work to do, a long race to
run or a strenuous match that could last a long time,
it's tempting to blast off—to get as far ahead as you
can while you're still fresh so that you can slack off
when you tire. That seems to make sense logically,
but it is physiologically unsound. Acceleration at any

point costs an inordinate amount of energy; it takes six times more energy to sprint at 18 miles an hour than to run at 9 miles an hour.

You'll finish stronger and quicker if you set a steady pace that will carry you through to the finish. Seasoned runners have learned not to hurry up in passing an opponent. They run every lap in about the same time; the first lap takes a little more time because of the start, and the last lap a little less time because of the finishing sprint.

END SPURT

WHEN THE END of a work period is near, there is a tendency to perform a little more intensively. Long terms of work can be broken into brief, well-defined periods to get as many "end spurts" as feasible into the workday. I saw a good example of this a while back when the water company was installing a new main pipe in the hillside next to my home. The truck that contained the compressors for the digging tools and the generator for welding the pipe was equipped with an air horn. After each hour and a half of work, the horn would blow and the machines would shut down. The men would open up snacks and sit, occasionally bringing out a deck of cards, and relax for fifteen minutes. When the whistle would blow again, the men would return promptly to their work. The process would be repeated throughout the day; at day's end, despite the confining work, the men always appeared as fresh as they did at the outset. Work on the pipeline progressed at an astonishingly rapid rate—due, in part, I'm sure, to end-spurt productivity.

SNACKS

NOURISHMENT IS another important component of energy. Any demanding activity should be preceded a few hours earlier by a nourishing meal. This doesn't mean that you should have a heavy lunch before an important 2:30 P.M. conference. It means that you shouldn't skip lunch before that kind of a session.

You should eat enough to maintain normal body weight, and drink enough to continuously replace the water you lose.

Snacks during periods of hard work increase work output. A good snack would be a glass of milk or a piece of fruit. Marathon runners find diluted fruit juice most sustaining.

THE ENVIRONMENT OF MAXIMUM PERFORMANCE

THE QUALITY OF everyday life is determined by the level at which we perform common functions. Some of those functions can be improved mechanically. But much of what we do depends on the vigor and alertness we bring to the task. That, in turn, depends to a large part on the environment in which we spend the greater part of our day.

When we think of the ideal environment for getting a job done, we ordinarily imagine some place that's private, quiet and protected from interruptions. We picture the writer in his mountaintop retreat; day in and day out, there is only his work, and the view of the great outdoors to inspire him. The truth is that few people can function in such an environment. James Joseph, a prolific writer, once told me how he had left home and gone to a small, quiet hotel to finish work on an important project. He was home again within days, having been unable to work any better without the usual interruptions of his wife and children.

Industry has discovered that if you arrange a person's work so that everything is immediately accessible in a perfect environment with no noise, good lighting and comfortable ventilation, he won't be nearly as productive as he would be if his work was occasionally interrupted, he had to leave his chair from time to time, and his environment was occasionally changed. These interruptions in a constant, perfect environment provide the stimulation that keeps you alert.

The average person is much more sensitive to the presence of other persons in his environment than he is to minor alterations in light, temperature, humidity and air movement. Years ago, Western Electric decided to perform a series of studies to see how changes in the environment might affect work production at their Hawthorne plant near Chicago. The workers there were assembling a fairly complex device; the rate of production could be counted and the quality of production could be examined, so that at the end of the day each worker's performance could be scored. To conduct the experiment, the investigators put observers into the plant, armed with clipboards, stopwatches and scoring sheets. They were to test the effect of lighting changes and other alterations in the physical environment. The investigators were surprised to find that work efficiency improved whether the physical environment was made better or worse. The result confused them greatly, until it dawned on them that the workers were performing better because of the special attention showered on them.

This change in attitude of the workers due to the mere presence of the investigators became known as the "Hawthorne effect."

I observed a somewhat similar phenomenon in my own laboratory while doing studies using a device called the ergograph. A seated subject would raise and lower a weight with his hand. The weight was connected to a machine that recorded how much work he was doing. Then we varied the conditions at random to cancel out any possibility of improvement through training. First we left the subject alone in the room. Next someone was in the room but paid no attention to him. Then a researcher visited him to see how he was getting along. Finally we put a researcher next to him to monitor his every act and encourage him when his output flagged. The results showed improvement from the first condition to the last on every subject tested. Some subjects did two and one half times more work when interest was shown and encouragement given than when they were left alone.

WHY THE MOST "EFFICIENT" OFFICE MAY BE THE LEAST PRODUCTIVE

OVER THE YEARS, my work has taken me into the offices of some of the most successful men in America. They are, for the most part, officers of large corporations. I'm there because I've been asked to solve a problem relating to performance—anything from the manner in which men and women are working to the environment in which they work. Out of all this contact, I've discerned one quality in these executives that is invariably present.

The successful executives are the restless ones. They're usually relaxed and composed, but they're prone to move a lot. When you enter their office, they bound from their chair and meet you halfway. Within moments after you're seated, they'll change their position, and keep changing throughout your visit. They'll move about at the slightest excuse—to answer a phone or find a piece of paper.

This pattern of movement is consistent with everything I've learned about mental efficiency. The students who fidget the most during examinations seem to be the ones who score the best. Those who sit quietly generally do better on the first part of their exams than on the second. Movement keeps you sharp.

The most efficient office setting, therefore, is not the most productive setting in a great majority of cases. The ideally efficient office would seem to be the one in which all work is brought to you and/or placed easily within your reach. But that kind of setup leaves you in your seat, a factor that will almost invariably affect your performance adversely. Because your body isn't mobile, your mind isn't alert.

The brain circulation depends on the pressure of the blood flow. If one sits quietly for half an hour or more, or stands for ten minutes or more without moving, venous return—the flow of blood back to the heart—is diminished to a point that the heart doesn't have enough blood to pump in order to keep up the pressure to the brain. When this happens, your thinking gets sluggish.

Pacing the floor to think out your problems makes good physiological sense. I have my materials pretty well in hand on the days when I'm to lecture, but I always organize my presentation during my fifteen-minute walk to campus.

Your working environment should be structured not for comfort but for activity. Rather than having everything within reach, you should set yourself up so that you must move several feet to make a phone call. Ideally, the telephone should be on a shelf, with a note pad alongside, so that you're compelled to take all your calls standing up.

Reference books and supplies should also be a few steps away, so that when you need them you have to get out of your chair.

When we look at a functioning office, we can almost predict its level of performance in terms of the muscular activity we see. If people are locked into their seats and working away for hours at a time, we don't expect either creativity or productivity. Where people are bounding and twisting around, reaching out for supplies, standing and pacing, we find not only creativity and productivity but happier workers at the end of the day.

Union contracts sometimes provide that a worker may leave his place of work for a stated number of minutes during every hour. This is often interpreted to mean that a worker has to stay in one place during the remaining minutes of the hour. Time studies by large organizations like the Bank of America have established that where the stay-in-place mandate is either explicit or implicit, the worker actually takes nearly twice as many minutes out of the hour for his personal needs. If he's imprisoned, he's going to react by quitting if the restriction is enforced.

If you remain hunched over a task too long, you not only have blood circulation problems, but also get muscular contracture and contracture of the connective tissue—ligaments, tendons and fascia. This causes a pressure irritation of the sensory nerves, which results in discomfort, pain and, inevitably, distraction.

Even if you've organized your workplace so that you do a lot of standing, twisting and stretching during the day, there are four exercises you can do in your chair, in addition, to keep you feeling limber and keen. The exercises needn't be done all together. Do one whenever you get the chance. They're aimed specifically at the parts of the body that are most affected by seated work.

Reach: Standing, extend one arm above your head, stretching your waist as far as you can. Yawn or sigh. Lower your arm, then raise the other arm. Yawn or sigh again.

Twist: Bring your left arm across your chest and grab hold of the chair back. Reach your right arm behind the chair and grab hold of the other side. Tug, turning your shoulders gently at first, gradually increasing the pressure to stretch your shoulders and back muscles. Release. Tug again, this time a little harder, until you feel a thorough stretch. Then turn in the opposite direction.

Bend: Grab the front of the chair seat and pull your chest toward your knees. Straighten one leg, sliding the heel forward until the knee is only slightly bent. Put your hands under your knees and try to work your chest to your thighs. As you do, try to straighten the one knee a little more, feeling the stretch in your hamstring muscles. This exercise is done one leg at a time to prevent stress on the lower back ligaments.

Turn: Rotate your head to the right. Place your right hand on your chin, your left hand behind your head, and assist the head to turn as far as it can. Next, turn your head to the left and repeat the process, reversing the hands.

The best piece of equipment you can have in your office is an adjustable chinning bar. Just hang suspended for a few seconds, letting everything stretch out.

THE STANDUP CONFERENCE

THE TIME YOU TAKE to perform a task is related to the posture in which you perform it.

If you provide plush furniture in your office, your visitors are going to sit down and get comfortable. That kind of setting makes them think of a conference that could last an hour. A meeting at a conference table in comfortable straight-back chairs is only slightly less inviting to the subconscious.

There are times, of course, when such settings are propitious. But a great deal of office discourse can be accomplished in far less time without affecting its quality. The trick is to change the posture of the discourse. Some executives saw an inch off the front legs of their visitors' chairs so that the visitors are pitched forward and don't get so comfortable that they stay too long.

There are other, more straightforward approaches.

The next time someone comes into your office for a discussion, try standing near the front edge of your desk. In all likelihood, the discussion will be over in five minutes, with as much accomplished as would have been had you sunk into chairs for a twenty-minute conference.

Perhaps you and a colleague have a lunch date several blocks from your office. Save your discussion for that outing, and plan together to get the serious business out of the way while walking to the restaurant.

Corridors, elevators, drinking fountains, even washrooms are all possible sites for standup conferences. Decisions that might otherwise take an hour to reach sitting down can often be made in minutes.

It may be important to an executive's ego to have a plush office, with an executive chair, a sofa and coffee tables. If his job is to make the initial contact with important visitors, and that contact requires a certain amount of sociability and the presentation of an image of largesse, a loungelike office has a useful function. But in reality most business interchanges need no more than ten minutes. A few moments of amenities are important to make people feel at ease before a discussion, but if your office resembles a private club, those moments can stretch into half hours.

THE PERFECT CHAIR

COMFORT IS NO PROOF of a piece of furniture's worth. Bed manufacturers have learned that lesson the hard way. For years, they featured supersoft mattresses— only to discover that such mattresses produce backaches. Chairs that seem comfortable at the outset may become uncomfortable before long. Among older people, or those with heart conditions, a fixed position in a deep chair can actually lead to death. English doctors learned this during World War II, when persons who entered bomb shelters in apparently good condition suffered thrombosis of the heart, lungs or brain after sitting in sling-type reclining chairs for eight hours or longer. The crossbar under the thigh cut off blood flow. After World War II, when television viewing became universal, the same phenomenon produced by the pooling of blood when the leg is slung over the arm of a chair and the viewer falls asleep led to what doctors call "television deaths."

After your bed, the chair you work in is the most important piece of furniture in your life. You spend more time in it than in any other chair, and the manner in which it supports you affects your physical condition, your mood and your intelligence.

Over the years, I've studied the human factors in the designs of seats and chairs. I've worked on aircraft seats, race-car and tractor seats, dental chairs and office chairs. These studies of comfort, fatigue and work capacity during long-term sitting in various models have convinced me that contoured chairs are not suitable for prolonged human use.

Contours deny you one of the fundamental principles of kinesiology—the need for frequent changes of position. Designers of contoured chairs assume that you're going to stay in that one position as long as you're in the chair. In automotive parlance, this is called the "showroom" seat. The potential car buyer gets in and sits in the contoured car seat for a few moments. The seat around him gives him a nice, cozy feeling. Once he's bought the car, it's a different matter. After a few hours in the seat, he finds himself trapped.

The ideal chair puts the body in good mechanical condition in a variety of postures. You can sit with both feet on the floor or with your legs crossed. You can slouch, or lean from side to side. This, in fact, is what the body wants to do. In our studies of the effect of seating on driving performance, we made a "stop-motion" picture, in which one frame registers every five seconds. When this film is played back at normal viewing speed, the drivers appear to be more active than monkeys in a zoo.

We have the impression that people sit quietly in chairs. They don't. They twist and squirm and lean and stretch and crouch. The ideal chair permits you all these movements. Otherwise, it's a trap.

The key to prolonged sitting is motion. Anything that prevents a change of posture or motion while sitting is going to be fatiguing.

When you select a chair, you should look for these features:

The seat should have a "falloff," meaning that it neither goes straight nor bulges up at the front, but curves downward. This eliminates pressure from the front edge of the chair against the backs of your thighs. Such pressure cuts off your circulation, mainly the venous return of the blood to the heart, which eventually can affect brain function. The pressure also causes your feet to swell.

The seat should be fairly flat, without identations, and fairly wide, so that you can shift in any position on the chair without feeling a lump or ridge. It should also be somewhat shallow, so that it doesn't hit you behind the knees when you turn from side to side.

The padding shouldn't be so thick that you sink into it. Most of the weight when we sit is borne on the ischial tuberosities, two bones that you can feel under your buttocks. In most people, these bony protuberances are cushioned by the gluteus muscles. So the chair's surface doesn't need to be thickly upholstered to be comfortable. If you can feel the pressure of your bones on that chair, then you need some kind of thin padding. An inch is plenty. A chair seat that's too soft is uncomfortable for the same reason a contoured chair is uncomfortable; it traps you in one position.

The cushion should be covered with a fairly solid

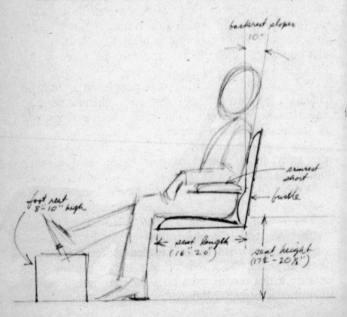

material, such as heavy leather or vinyl. This will give you an action surface to slide around on while cushioning the bone pressure. The part of the seat that's under your sitting bones should be tilted back about three degrees; if the seat were perfectly horizontal, you'd have the feeling that you were sliding off of it. At the point where the slope approaches your knees, it should reverse angle and start down.

The muscles of the hips and knees are two-joint muscles. When seated with the hip flexed to ninety degrees as in upright sitting, it's uncomfortable to have the feet elevated and the legs straight. For comfort, the hips and the knees should be at the same angle. With the feet propped up, it's more comfortable to slouch. If that's the way you like to sit, your chair should provide for this widening of the hip angle by having a reclining feature.

Arms on the chair are a good idea; they enable you to take your weight off your back once in a while. But it's best if the arm rests are short, about twelve inches, just long enough to catch the elbows. An armrest that comes out to the wrists is just in the way most of the time.

The backrest should have a ten-degree tilt in the upright position. The height of the backrest should be about up to the middle of your shoulder blades. Your lower back should be supported by a "bustle," a small pad made of firm foam rubber and covered in leather or vinyl, five inches high, as wide as your chair seat and two inches thick. This bustle is located just above the seat and provides a cushion for the pelvis, helping to hold it comfortably erect and taking the strain off your lower back.

Ideally, you would have one foot higher than the other, as well, which also takes the strain off your lower back. A kick stool or old-fashioned hassock next to your chair would be an excellent addition to your office. If you sit back to read, put a foot on the footrest, on a drawer, or even on your desk. Judges who sit in a courtroom all day would probably make better decisions if they kept their feet up on their desks. The least they should have is a footrest that they can move around to different positions during the course of a trial.

A chair with an adjustable seat and back is more desirable than a rigid chair. Anything that gives you more variety in seating postures is a benefit. Many automobile seats have this adjustment, but few drivers recognize the antifatigue value of using it.

PREPERFORMANCE NAPS

PROLONGED BED REST is not the proper way to prepare the body for action. Every person has his optimal sleep time, but in general if you stay in bed past nine hours a day, you are deconditioning. There is a possibility that midday sleep before an afternoon athletic competition may diminish your performance. Your body becomes sluggish.

But a period of calm prior to a stressful *mental* performance is another matter. It helps to reduce overanxiety.

Some years ago, I flew to Warsaw to lecture at the invitation of the Polish Government. My hosts met me at the airport and took me to the lecture hall, at which point they led me to a little room with a cot at the side of the stage and indicated that I was to rest. I did. Later, I learned that this period of repose is expected of all speakers, on the theory that it will rest an overloaded brain.

Among great achievers, the habit is widespread. In the middle of planning his strategy for the survival of Britain, Winston Churchill always went to bed. Billy Graham prepares to address a crowd of 100,000 by taking a nap.

If you're in too high a state of anxiety prior to a performance, you should try to bring it down. Otherwise you'll have little energy left for the performance itself. You know unmistakably when your body is feeding itself an "adrenalburger." You feel uncomfortable. Your pulse is racing. The hair on the back of your neck is standing up. Your skeletal muscles may be relaxed, but you're making an effort nonetheless. All of those sensations will be welcome at the time of the performance; the trick is to hold them off.

First, identify the tension by deliberately increasing it. Tighten your body to a count of ten, until it simply couldn't be tighter. Then slowly, counting in reverse, relax your body until your tension slips well below its initial level. Shake your arms. Let your body sag. Now bring your level of tension up just a bit, until your body function is normal, but you're still below the initial tension level. If you feel better, the tension may have been muscular. If the tension and discomfort haven't diminished sufficiently, it's time to break the vicious cycle in your reticular activating mechanism (RAM), those sensory inputs into your control center that are exciting the organs, muscles and glands into action.

The way to manipulate your RAM is to shut off all sensory input, just as you do when you retire for the night. If you're in your office, go to a quiet room, if there is one. If not, close your door and draw the blinds. If there are background noises, use earplugs. Lie down. If you have no couch, slouch in your chair, lean back and put your feet on a drawer or on top of the desk.

If the respite is insufficient, you must then take the final step, which is to rehearse the ritual of going to bed. What you're doing is making use of a conditioned response to induce sleep during the day. President Lyndon Johnson, a highly charged man, always undressed for his brief afternoon naps during the years of his presidency. Johnson lived and worked in the same house, which made it easy for him to go to bed. If you can't do that, you can condition your response to some extent, in any case. Take off your shoes, and turn out the lights. Just as the sight and smell of food get your digestive juices going at mealtime, so a focused, ritualized pattern of behavior prior to naps will induce the desired response.

MAXIMUM REST IN BED

IN ONE SENSE, preparing for sleep is no different from preparation for any other activity. You *focus* on that objective.

If you're the kind of person who falls asleep the moment your head touches the pillow, you obviously don't need assistance. Most of us aren't like that. We carry our waking battles to bed and fight them over again. Our apprehension about tomorrow ruins the end of today. Physiologically, our reticular activating mechanism is still sending showers of impulses through our muscles. Before we can sleep, we must quiet our RAM.

This process should be the same each night. It should begin at the same hour, leading to repose at the same hour. If your bedtime is eleven each night, your preparation should begin at ten, or ten-thirty at the latest.

If you've brought work home from the office, are working on your income tax return, balancing the checkbook or studying for an examination, you should break off at least half an hour before your fixed retirement time.

The next half hour should be given to some activity that changes your mind set. Television, recreational reading, a tub bath, conversation and sex are all good transitional activities leading to sleep.

During this transitional period, you should avoid stimulants such as coffee, tea, soft drinks or tobacco. A glass of milk, preferably warm, is an excellent tranquilizer.

Next, your sleeping environment: It should be quiet

and dark. There is no ideal room temperature for sleep. Some people like to sleep warm, others cool. A room cold enough to make you shiver will set off muscular activity and hinder rest. A hot room can produce enervating sweat. Anything between those extremes that feels good to you will assist sleep.

Even mild sweating can make you uncomfortable. A damp skin sticks to bedclothing; you feel sticky and can't turn over easily. It's amazing how much easy movement in bed helps sleeping, a prime reason for sleeping in the raw. We normally move quite a bit during a night; if it's hard to move and change position, we don't sleep as well.

For some persons, the movement of air seems as important as temperature and humidity. You don't want wind blowing directly on you because that would activate your sensory impulses, whereas you want to quiet them down. But a room with little or no air movement seems to make some people uncomfortable. The reason for this is unclear, since there's no problem with the supply of oxygen or elimination of carbon dioxide if the room is adequately sized. One possible explanation can be demonstrated with a simple experiment in a room with no air movement: Close your mouth and breathe through your nose for a while, paying particular attention to the resistance of the air that flows in and out of your nostrils. Now pick up a sheet of paper or a folded newspaper and wave it like a fan in front of your nostrils. You'll note immediately that it seems easier to breathe. The movement of air somehow seems to make inhalation easier.

When you want to sleep, be sure to shut out all other stimuli: light, noise, the touch of another person. Lie on your back so that your arms don't touch the side of your body and your legs are separated, knees and feet falling outward. Now that you've shut off your vision, hearing and tactile sense, the remaining task is to shut off your mind. This is the position in which to do it, but it is not the best position for sleep because it puts a strain on your back. The best sleeping position is on your side. You move to this position after you've quieted your mind.

To do that many people successfully use imagery. They think of the blackest velvet they can imagine, or butter melting in a pan, or grain spilling from a sack. But what works for some has an exciting or worrisome effect on others.

The best method, by far, would be to learn to think of nothing. Mental inactivity seems all but impossible when you first try it. You may cause your mind to go blank for a moment, but almost immediately you realize that you're thinking again. Don't panic or give up. Simply let your mind go blank once more, even if only for a second. Eventually, the periods will grow longer and the lapses will be less frequent, and you will achieve a state like that you experience on awakening after a night of restful sleep. Your mind is absolutely quiet, and you can close your eyes and go back to sleep again. This is the state you want to fall into in the process of quieting your arousal mechanisms.

Everyone's objective is an uninterrupted night of sleep. Whether you get that or not depends a good deal on what you had for dinner and afterward. I know that I can't eat garlic without punishment. Other people can't eat melons or bananas, because they're gas forming. Others can't drink liquids with impunity in the evening, particularly beer, wine, coffee or tea. If they do, they'll be up for sure at some point during the night.

But getting up during the night to urinate has one advantage. It restores normal circulation. We often hear others boast that they didn't move all night. If you sleep like a log, you wake up in the morning feeling like a log.

We've all had the vexing experience of being unable to get back to sleep once we've awakened during the night. The phenomenon is particularly prevalent when we have a problem we cannot solve. The best thing to do if you find yourself worrying about your problems in the middle of the night is to focus on one problem, and a specific piece of that problem. Rather than let the process control you, control the process. Begin to rehearse what you're going to do. If you're to make a presentation the following morning, make it in your mind as you lie in bed. Be as specific as you can be. Get a mental image of where you will stand, whom you will look at and how you'll begin. Think of the very words you propose to use, the points you intend to make, the charts you'll employ.

This is "mental practice." You're dreaming through the motion, without conflict or interference. You feel the rhythm and the sense of execution. In the process, you perfect it in your mind. Then you can relax and drift back to sleep.

Naturally, we'd be best off if we hadn't taken our problems with us to bed in the first place. Since most problems relate to fears of failure, let's focus on that problem now.

8

Extending Your Maximum

Two TOOLS ARE needed to break through the wall that keeps your performance in check. The first is an appreciation of what maximum means in terms of your own reality. The second is an understanding of how you can persuade yourself to overcome your inhibitions about venturing into the unknown. Between the two, you can sizably diminish the prospect of failure, both psychologically and physiologically.

DEFINING YOUR MAXIMUM

FIRST, WHAT DO we mean by "maximum"?

What follows applies to all activities, including work, but since sports are more measurable, let's express it in that language.

There is a maximum expressed by a world's record. That record keeps improving. We once wondered if man would ever break four minutes in the mile. So many men have done that since Roger Bannister achieved it a quarter century ago that we now wonder when—not whether—man will break 3:40.

Remembering the little lady who lifted a car from

her son, and the boy who similarly saved his father, it would be foolish to assign any limits to man's potential.

Even though the amount of time and energy—not to mention the natural endowments—required to achieve record performance is available to very few, the art and science of maximum performance are available to everyone. You can develop to any degree you choose, consistent with your own reality. If you are starting at a low point, your maximum, too, is theoretically without limits.

Your maximum capability is directly proportionate to the time and effort you're willing to give it. You're at your maximum today considering the investment of effort you've made up to now. If you want to increase your maximum, it's mostly a matter of doing more. *Anyone* will improve who works at it in the appropriate manner.

There are, to be sure, genetic qualities that enable some people to achieve more than others.

The governing hereditary factor in performance is the quality of your nervous system. It determines how fast you react, and it is a given that usually can't be modified. Disease, injury and malnutrition can also permanently affect the system. The normal nervous system can be affected by early child care. Margaret Mead discovered that children who are swaddled in infancy have a delayed motor development. Yet they also have a compensatory keenness in observation because all they had to work with at the outset were their eyes. It's the same principle at work that enables a blind person to develop hearing acuity: use makes the organ.

The quality of other body tissue—bone, muscle and blood—and their chemistry also determine your limits of strength, endurance and flexibility, but they are more modifiable than the makeup of your nervous system.

The different lengths of bones, as well as the slightly different attachments of tendons to bones, decide what activities each person is most suited for. One configuration will make you fit for weight lifting, another for sprinting and jumping. If you enter an activity for which you are anatomically unsuited, you're at a distinct disadvantage compared with others whose configurations are ideal for the event.

Basically, any sport is good for you that gives you pleasure, and you can improve at it by conditioning for maximum performance. If you're just starting out, however, or if you have a child who will profit from some direction, it's a good idea to have an understanding of what activities your organism or your child's is best suited for. If your young daughter is on the plump side, and has been since she was a baby, it would be cruel to lead her toward a career as a professional ballet dancer. She could, however, enjoy dancing as a hobby and fitness activity.

There are individual differences in your capacity to develop attributes such as speed and flexibility. For the most part, sprinters are born, not made. Either you have an innate ability to move rapidly, or you don't. It's difficult to improve this characteristic; about all you can do is modify the mechanics that enable you to start rapidly. The person who is last off the mark, and can't get his legs moving as rapidly as most people, should seek a sport that doesn't make these demands, if he wants to compete well. Between golf and tennis, he should choose golf.

Flexibility, the extent of the range of motion of one's joint, is also pretty much an inborn characteristic. Some people's joints are so lax that they risk injury; others' joints are so tight that they swim with difficulty. Flexibility can be increased to some extent by stretching exercises, but the extremely tight person should probably not aspire to be more than a recreational swimmer.

The heavier you are in relation to your musculature, the greater the limitation on your physical skill. Added weight in the form of fat increases the effort needed to perform a movement, and also obstructs the movement.

A tall person displaces his center of gravity through a greater distance than does a short person when the same movement is performed by each. He runs farther with the same number of strides. But the shorter person has many skill advantages. With his shorter body segments he is able to rotate faster and with less resistance with the same effort. His limbs have smaller moments of inertia. His errors in sports like diving and gymnastics are less noticeable. He appears to be better coordinated than his gangling peers.

Environmental conditioning has a marked effect on performance capacity and capability. A typical example is a young boy I once knew who literally seemed to have no delicacy, finesse, smoothness or rhythm. His concept of performance was to apply superstrength to everything he did—to smash, thrust and overpower. He liked to lift heavy things and throw them around. He was a formidable tussler—and one of the world's worst performers. He had great difficulty with sports like tennis and golf, and he was really lost on or in the water. In any water sport, be it swimming or scuba diving or even canoeing, you have to have a sensuous connection with the water, almost as though you're having a love affair with it. This boy punched the water. Paddling a canoe, he could not dip the paddle in the water and apply the continuous force that allows the canoe to glide forward in the smooth way that increases the momentum. The result was that the canoe didn't go very far or very fast or very often in the right direction. "Let's not fight the water," I'd say. But he was expressing an idiosyncratic movement behavior pattern developed in early childhood: struggle, fight and strive to overcome.

The kinds of childhood traumas that affect performance in adult life are usually not terribly subtle. Suppose you were overprotected as a child—prevented from climbing trees or playing rough. As an adult, you might be timid at the tennis net or shy away from hard body contact. That's a realistic, but modifiable aspect of your performance.

If some factors that affect performance—the speed of one's reaction or one's body height—are unchangeable, most factors can be positively affected. Inherent weaknesses or defects can't be eliminated, but they can be conditioned or adapted in such a way that much better performance is possible.

One summer while in college, I worked as a riding master at a resort in New York State. One of the horses was a beauty with a wonderful gait, but he had a problem that made him unpopular. After fairly heavy exertion, he would develop the heaves. This made him uncomfortable to ride, both physically and psychologically. Riders felt the horse was about to give out, and were understandably reluctant to run him. A veterinarian had examined the horse and found that his lungs were in good shape. So I determined to train the horse and get it into such good condition that it could run a long time before starting to heave. Then I would trade the horse. Each day I ran the horse on a long lead, a little at first, then more each day and at a faster pace. At the end of the month, the horse was in great shape. I took him for a tough ride in the hills; he didn't heave. Then I traded him. A week later, the horse was back. The man who accepted him had kept him in a stable without exercise; the horse had deconditioned and had heaved his first time out.

By exercising the horse every day thereafter, I was able to keep him so fit that he could easily survive the average ride without getting the heaves. He became the most popular horse in the stable.

That horse taught me an important lesson: Even when there is no remedy for a specific physical problem, the capacity for active living can be enormously increased.

In my work in fitness and performance, I would estimate that better than half the people who come to me for help play what I call the "organ recital." They have a shoulder problem or a back problem or a knee problem. My approach has been to encourage a general conditioning of the body that will increase the person's overall performance capacity.

A person with a shoulder problem has two choices. He can become an invalid due to inactivity, or he can condition himself to lead an active life that does not make heavy demands on his shoulder.

If you let a weak back or a touch of asthma or a painful arthritic condition immobilize you, a vicious cycle sets in. Your body deteriorates overall, and your increasing discomfort persuades you to do less and less. But if you reverse the cycle and gradually do more and more, you often find that you can live normally and perform recreational activities with a minimum of interference from your disabilities.

The time to really concentrate on increasing your performance capability is when you consider yourself partially disabled, either physically or psychologically.

YOUR OWN PERFORMANCE PROFILE

NOTHING IN OUR CULTURE has more retarded performance than the propensity to perform by comparison. It's tempting, it's encouraged and it's common; but it's almost always discouraging and deflating.

I run pretty well for a man my age. My running suits my requirements. It keeps me in shape, and it meets my responsibilities in sports and daily activities. In comparison with the world-class runners who take my classes at UCLA, I would be classified as a very poor runner. In comparison with sedentary men my age, I'm a streak of lightning. Almost everyone can find someone more awkward than he is, and someone more talented. Comparisons are meaningless. Each person should view his own performance in terms of his wants, needs, limitations and gifts.

Your performance is measured by how well you

achieve what you want or need in relation to the body equipment you have and the investment of time and effort you're willing to make.

The acceptance of yourself as a performer is based on two factors. The first is the quality of your work and how well it's organized. The second is your standard of acceptance: what you think you should be able to do in contrast with what you're doing. When those poles are far apart, it leads to frustration, discouragement and, often, failure.

The first factor is a remediable category: you simply determine how you can organize your work better, and what training you need to improve. The second factor is more difficult and dangerous. It's easy to set standards that are so unreasonably high that even an effective performance seems inadequate.

The adoption of standards lower than some idealized notion of your potential may seem demeaning, but it isn't. Once you meet the lower standard, you set yourself a slightly higher one. When you meet that, you raise the standard once more, until you reach a goal you are proud of and one that is within reason for your physical structure and your ambitions. This is true of groups as well as individuals. If the person in charge of a group sets an unreasonably high level of performance as a standard, he has constructed a formula for failure. The best performance comes from an objective analysis of the real working capacity of one's colleagues and/or employees, and an adjustment of expectations to reality.

Leonard Gross once played golf with a psychiatrist who shot an 84 and was elated with his round. "I'm four over," he announced gleefully at the end of the match.

"Four over what?" Leonard asked.

"Over par," the psychiatrist replied.

"Over par? Par is 72," Leonard objected.

"*My* par is 80," the psychiatrist replied.

My handicap—an unfortunate word, but there it is —is presently 22. For the amount of time I play and the attention I give to my game, my standards are in harmony with my performance. I can't expect better. If I were to decide that I wanted to improve, I wouldn't try to return to my old handicap of 14. A reasonable goal for me would be an 18. I know that I could achieve that goal without disrupting my life. But to try to be a 14 again would be inconsistent with what else I want to do.

In order to become world class in any single event, you just about have to give your whole life to that event. There's a lot of suffering in the process, but it's acceptable suffering because it provides continuous rewards along the way: recognition, admiration, power, money, the visible signs that you're improving. Improvement of this magnitude is selfish, in a sense. The energy you're giving to your improvement must be taken from other things, including personal relationships. Writing this book is a maximum performance for me. I have a belief, and the background and willingness to say what I believe. There are days when Leonard and I discuss the material that gives me a high unlike anything I've ever experienced; I don't know what else I could do that would give me a feeling like that. During certain times of the week, this book is more important to me than my wife. She knows it and feels it—and most of the time understands it.

To be realistic you have to separate performance from sociability and other behavior. To the maximum performer, the achievement of a goal comes first, whether it's training for a championship, the winning of a contract or the setting of a policy. He concentrates on his goal and lets friends, reading for enjoyment and other pleasures slip from his mind. If his goal is to get rich, he gets rich; if it's to write, he writes. There's an element of truth to the notion that winning is the only thing, as repugnant as some people find the idea, but to the maximum performer the satisfaction in achieving, competing and winning comes first. He cares that certain elements of his life were bruised in the process, but he figures it's been worth it.

Few of us can—or want to—narrow our effort and time down to a singular goal such as an Olympic gold medal, a Nobel prize, a high political office or a book that expresses our life work. But we can use the methods of those who do to improve our present standing.

Suppose you're a weekend golfer who shoots in the mid-nineties. By following the regimen prescribed for a dedicated athlete, you could drop your score to the low eighties. But part of the regimen is to postpone play in favor of practice for a period of many months, and you may be unwilling to do that. You may, however, be willing to postpone play for a few months— say one third to one half of the time—in order to score consistently below ninety. The goal you want to achieve and the duration of your training will be entirely up to you.

Suppose you're a tennis player. If you had the luxury of being able to stop everything in order to play tennis for a year, taking a lesson and practicing for several hours each day, you might double your present ability to play tennis, and be able to compete with players who are presently twice as good as you are. That might be a feasible goal for someone who is near-maniacal about tennis. But a more realistic person would say, "I want to be the best tennis player I can possibly be, consistent with the other demands on my life—including my desire to keep my game serviceable, to ski at winter holidays with my family and to break my training routine occasionally for other things."

"Maximum" now means a level markedly less than that achieved by the pure specialization of a professional or Olympic athlete. It means achievement of a satisfactorily high goal obtained by a serious and studied approach.

What you end up saying is, "I want to be as good as I can be in the time that I'm able to give." That is the human sense of maximum.

Once you achieve your realistic goal, it may well be that you'll have found the process so rewarding you'll want to improve further. That's the time to establish a new maximum goal and resume a new training cycle.

CONQUERING INHIBITIONS

IN TRAINING for maximum performance, we make gradual excursions into the realm of fatigue in order to discover where the limits of performance lie. When you reach a certain point of exhaustion, performance deteriorates, accuracy diminishes, you falter and slow down. As you condition for your event, you push back this threshold of fatigue. The more time you spend in the fatigue zone, the more familiar with it you become and the less distracting it is.

The end point of most activity, whether it's a brief maximum exertion of strength like punching, squeezing, leaping in the air or a prolonged run up an incline, involves a decision process in which the reward for continuing is balanced against the penalty of not continuing.

When you try to open a jar whose lid is stubborn, you're involved in a decision-making process about whether or not to keep trying, rather than a test of your real capacity to open it. Under life-threatening situations, that jar could surely be opened, whereas under ordinary conditions you might try with all your might and fail. The difference in your performance has to do not so much with your physical endowments as with your willingness to use them.

My dictionary defines inhibition, in the physiological sense, as "a restraining, arresting, or checking of the action of an organ or cell," and "the reduction of a reflex or other activity as the result of an antagonistic stimulant," and "a state created at synapses making them less excitable by other sources of stimulation."

What's important to understand about all three definitions is that they're describing an automatic process.

Inhibition is a convenient, life-preserving component of your makeup that can function like a safety fuse in an electrical system. When the system overloads, the fuse pops and the current is interrupted. Long before you might hurt yourself, your inhibitory fuse breaks the circuit, which stops you from putting further pressure on your system.

These fuses, or circuit breakers, exist at all levels of your system: in the brain, muscle spindles and other stretch receptors.

Any one of these fuses can break the circuit, but it's the fuse in your decision-making brain that's most influential. Consciously or subconsciously, you're weighing the possibility of pain or self-destruction against the importance of the performance.

When a runner drops out of a race, it's not that he's truly exhausted or has gone to his physiological limit, it's that his rational circuit breaker has told him the race has become too painful in terms of the potential rewards, or that his possibility of finishing well is so poor there's no use trying anymore.

The process of conditioning for maximum performance is one of "resetting" these circuit breakers to a higher level, so that they can accept greater loads. In effect, you're installing heavier fuses.

For our purposes, we can divide the circuit breakers into rational and sensorimotor nervous systems. Inhibitory reactions in the sensorimotor nervous system profoundly influence the reactions in the rational system.

The sensorimotor nervous system is "trained" at the Golgi tendon organs, we call GTOs, which are embedded in the muscle tissue and connective tissue. When you put tension on the GTO sensors by stretching them, they send out inhibitory signals, to wit, "You're straining me." Then they generate inhibitory impulses which knock down the motor impulses that are carrying your request for performance to the working muscle, and they cause the muscle contractions to let up.

Suppose you're doing some difficult pushups. The

first one you can complete without too much trouble. The next one you work for. Along about the third pushup, messages arrive from the sensorimotor and central nervous systems that your muscles are giving out and that this effort is getting pretty risky. At this point your rational process asks whether you really need a fourth. You decide that three is sufficient. How to affect that process?

You can argue with yourself, and say that you're going to do a fourth pushup no matter what. But the decision to quit is very strong in your subconscious, and that voice telling you you'd better not go on has a body, that GTO, that is sending inhibitory signals into the muscles themselves. It's not that the muscles aren't strong enough; it's that the nervous system has sent a message to those fibers that they're not to put any more units into contraction. You can feel the muscles trembling and recognize that your strength is on the wane.

Brute strength will never bull you past that system. It can't be coerced; it has to be coaxed. To go from three to four pushups is a magnum jump; it can't be made directly when your nervous system's on guard. Instead, you can educate your rational responses so that they are not so timid, and you can gradually condition your muscle sensors so they are not so sensitive to tension.

This process is known as *deinhibition*. It's a process of persuasion. It is central to all motor skill development, and a key to maximum performance.

Deinhibition, properly employed, can vault you into another class. It explains why just playing a sport alone can't get you where you want to go and are capable of going. When you play, you become habituated to giving up at a certain level. Or, if you please, your inner guardians have learned to cry, "Hold, enough!" at that point. Through the process of deinhibition you can train those circuit breakers in your nervous system to accept gradually heavier loads.

Deinhibition also explains why in training there is

no such thing as failure. You start out so far back in the process of determining what your body is willing to do that you never present it a problem it can't solve. You overcome the body's present level of inhibition by asking it to accept just a small extra load each day. We call this process *overload*.

All training is progressive. Your success each day is measured in tiny increments. You're continually being rewarded; for everything you do, you increase your capacity to do more. At a certain point, you ease past the old psychological and physiological barriers that made up your performance retaining wall, and find yourself in territory you've never occupied before.

9

Rapid Learning

YEARS AGO, WHEN I was a fledgling professor at the University of Iowa, I taught a beginning swimming class that was part of the physical education program. One of the skills I thought each swimmer should have was the ability to swim to the center of the pool, turn around and swim back to the starting point. There is a certain technique to turning in the water when no solid construction, such as the edge of a pool, is involved; you scull with your hands in a specific way in order to rotate your body. Each semester I would run my students through these movements on dry land. Then they would enter the pool and attempt the maneuver in the water. The failure rate was astonishing. We would devote two full class periods to this effort—far more time than seemed necessary. Finally I decided to take a radical approach. When the time for this lesson arrived the following semester, I said to my students, "I want you to swim to the center of the pool, turn around and swim back." To a man, they swam to the center of the pool, turned around and swam back.

That episode permeated my pedagogical approach. I recognized immediately that the less you tell a student at the onset about specific motions of a physical movement, the better he'll be able to execute it.

PARALYSIS BY ANALYSIS

NOVICE COACHES, recent graduates in kinesiology, know how to analyze the mechanics of a performance. They're eager to apply their learning. They shower their students with knowledge—and make motor idiots of them.

As a nation, we are almost invariably overcoached. We take lessons by the millions annually. Our teachers want us to feel that we've gotten our money's worth. So they explain more than we need to know, and thereby cripple our performance.

The next time you're on a stairway, try descending the stairs while thinking consciously of how one foot is coming down after the other. But be sure to hold on to the bannister. You may fall over if you don't.

That simple experiment illustrates one of the great impediments to maximum performance. As an anonymous poet once put it:

> The centipede was happy, quite
> Until the frog in fun
> Said, pray, which leg comes after which?
> This set his mind in such a pitch
> He lay distracted in a ditch
> Figuring how to run.

At one time or another, I've been given the following advice about my golf swing: Roll your ankles. Get your hips out of the way. Keep your heel down. Move your knees. Turn your back to the ball. Put your back into the ball. Keep your elbow straight. Hit with the back of your hand. Grip the club with the thumb and first two fingers. Keep your head down. Keep your eye on the ball. There is no way I can keep my mind on all those anatomical details. Any or all of them make me think about those body parts, rather than about my objective.

The body in motion doesn't think well in terms of anatomical parts. It thinks best in terms of movements and results.

It's generally assumed that the more you know about something, the better you'll be at it. When it comes to performance, however, knowledge is not always power.

I'm a so-so golfer. Considering that I've given my life to the study of human performance and have helped my share of world-class athletes, you'd think I'd be able to break 90. Actually, the opposite is true.

When you enter the field of maximum performance, you have to choose between being a performer with a pure mind uncluttered by analytical thought and being an analyst, investigating in depth every component of performance. It is unlikely that you can be both at the same time.

When I was in high school, I did a lot of wrestling. I was quite turned on by the discovery that I could apply the principles of mechanics I was learning in physics class to my wrestling with good effect. It occurred to me that if I would only analyze my performance and apply my learning to it, I could constantly improve. What I didn't know was that there comes a time in performance when too much knowledge is detrimental. Then you have to decide which you want to be—an analyst or a performer. It wasn't until I went to college and considered an athletic career that I realized I'd have to make the choice.

I liked to compete. I enjoyed being out there in uniform. But little voices were telling me that this wasn't me. I realized that I'd never become a champion, if only because I didn't accept the life-style that went with the time and effort required to train. What fascinated me was *why* I couldn't jump higher or run faster. I wanted to know what chemistry, biology and physics could tell me about performance, and how it could be enhanced. The choice I made was a good one. I traded a marginal possibility to be a country fair performer for a rich career of scholarly study of the elements of human performance.

I once had a student at the University of Southern California who was such a promising shot putter that thoughts of breaking the world's record were not at all unjustified. While he was taking a course from me involving an anatomical and physical analysis of motion, we determined to study the best posture, angle of trajectory and timing for putting the shot. We took high-speed pictures of him so that we could make a frame-by-frame analysis of his action. He was an excellent technician. He helped work out many of the photographic angles; he helped build a grid backdrop that enabled us to measure his motion; he studied the muscles involved. In the process of doing the film he saw where he could improve his mechanics and get better leverage, thereby applying more force to the shot. He worked on this analysis for three months, and did a magnificent job. The only trouble was that he lost his championship form.

From that time on, my student was never able to surpass his high school record. And I have held to a resolve I made at the time never to try to make an analyst out of a performing athlete.

Performance requires a certain innocence. When I perform, I can't keep analysis out of it. That's good for my profession, bad for my performance. I am typical of many coaches. Robert Kiphuth of Yale, Matt Mann of Michigan and David Armbruster of Iowa were three of the all-time great swimming coaches. Yet none of them were exceptional swimmers. Glen McCormick, once a student of mine, was a mediocre diver, at best. He went on to coach diving champions—including his wife, Pat McCormick, the greatest of them all. If performance is your objective, leave the analysis to the professional. If he's good, he'll have the skill to translate his analysis into cues or visual figures that tell you what to do.

Not long ago, I took up voice training. At sixty-three, I have no illusions about a new career. I am simply trying to strengthen my voice for the many demands that are made on it in lectures, public appearances and casual conversation. I had found in the last year that my voice had begun to give out after several hours of continuous demand each day.

To go into a strange room with a strange teacher is enough of an ordeal under normal circumstances. Under these circumstances, I felt more than a little foolish. But my teacher was a master coach. "I'm not going to speak in technical terms," she began. "We're just going to do it, do it, do it. I'm not going to tell you what is wrong. I'm just going to tell you what's right." She could have spent an hour on the theory of resonance. Instead, she moved my voice up from my throat into the voice box in my head—and I scarcely recognized the unstrained voice that emerged as mine.

Let me prove to you now why learning occurs most rapidly when you minimize your knowledge.

NEW MOVEMENTS, AND HOW
WE LEARN THEM

WE LEARN ON DEMAND. A new performance demands a modification of existing movement patterns to confront new situations and challenges. Such modification is not simply an addition or subtraction of motor skills; it requires some reorganization of your whole pattern of movement.

We know that the interactions of mind and body are almost instantaneous. The mind doesn't tell the hand to do something; they are, in effect, one and the same. If you move your hand, your mind receives sensory feedback from that movement in about a fiftieth of a second. You track it visually; you see its relation in space; you direct it in accordance with a preconceived plan as to where you want it to go. You thereby have an almost instant-by-instant mind-body interaction.

You have a mental image of where you want the hand to go; the image "corrects" the difference between where you intended the hand to go and where it actually went.

After you know where your hand is going, you don't have to track it anymore. You have a kinesthetic sense of where it is and where it's going but you don't have to think about it. You can put something in your mouth without having any memory of having done so. It has become automatic.

This is the ideal of motor learning.

The body is more conscious of movement than it is of muscle action. This is because the action of muscle spindles and GTOs terminates below the level of the conscious centers of the brain. The activity of the sensory receptors in the joints, however, is perceived by the conscious cortex. This explains why the mind thinks in terms of movement, not of muscles.

A shift in attention from the elements of a task to the whole action is the essence of motor learning. During the training process, the action becomes automatic, and the performer ultimately blocks out his attention to details. In this way he gains the quickness and positiveness of a nonhuman animal.

HOW SKILLS DEVELOP

THE DEVELOPMENT OF SKILL is essentially a reduction —or simplification—of neuromuscular activity. Films and electromyographic studies show beyond doubt that muscle contractions that don't contribute to efficiency are reduced and eliminated as skill improves.

You can't think through a complex movement rapidly enough to control that movement. To keep pace with the most rapid thought process, you would have to go through the movement in slow motion.

The mind thinks in terms of whole movements, not

in terms of the parts or the single muscle contractions needed to accomplish the movement. Any attention to the isolated parts interferes with the coordinative function of the brain.

The control function of the central nervous system integrates the various reflexes automatically, without depending on sequential decision-making in the process of the action. If, during the action, you decide you want to change it because one part of your body isn't performing correctly, you've interfered with the automatic reflex action—thereby breaking up the harmony of the control function and making your movement awkward.

When you have become highly skilled you can perform without thinking, moving efficiently, without extra motions, and at a rapid rate. When you start thinking about what you're doing, you try to reorganize and/or add extra motions. Your motions become uncoordinated, and because you're tracking, almost counting your movements, you inevitably slow them down.

When you're trying to learn something, the tendency is to try too hard to do all that you picture should be done. Rapid learning lies in the opposite direction. Your objective is to get rid of this excess motion and tension that are inhibiting you from a refined performance. The more your concentration can focus on the wholeness of the act rather than on the parts, the more skilled you will become.

FOCUSED ACTION

IN OUR CULTURE, the intellect is given higher rating than the physical side of human performance. This is a completely artificial value. The muscle is just as beautiful an instrument as the brain; without the muscle, the brain would be helpless.

When we write and read and even think effectively, we do so in "thought units." If we were to try to read or write or think word by word, the mind simply couldn't carry all those details. So the words have to be simplified into a single thought. We focus on a central theme.

So with action.

At the outset of any motor action, you may have to proceed step by step. The objective, however, is to train the motion until it becomes unconscious. You do that by grooving your response under circumstances that encourage you to stay in the new mode—i.e., without pressure. Once your response is grooved, you no longer have to think about it. It simply happens.

The object in a performance is to shut off your thinking, which you do by shifting your focus from the details of the action to the goal of the action.

This goal should be well within your capacity. Your time, energy and skill should be directed solely to its achievement—just that and no more. Stiffening or awkwardness during pursuit of your goal usually means that you're trying to do more than you're capable of doing.

Every time you move, you should do so with a clear target in mind. In tennis, you should never hit the ball just to get it over the net; you should hit it with a purpose. Even in that instant during a sharp exchange of volleys at the net, you've predetermined where you're going to hit the ball. Two things are accomplished in the process. First, you've established a strategy. Second, by committing your thought to your objective you've preempted the time; you're thinking only about getting there, not about *how* you're to get there. The first is important, but the second is crucial.

Focused action has an important corollary benefit. It prevents you from thinking you can do more than you can. That often happens on the tee in golf; standing up there, you're tempted to let one loose. The attempt usually ends in disaster because the muscles and tension are strained beyond comfortable bounds, and your warning systems go off. Eddie Merrins, the professional at the Bel-Air Country Club, tells his students to visualize where the ball is going to land every time they hit a shot. It makes you hit your shot so you'll be in good position for the next one; it keeps you within your capacity, and it sharpens your focus.

Focusing is the essence of performance. You're not thinking about your last shot but this shot. You're focsing not on *how* you're going to hit the shot, but on *where* the shot will land. It's the imagined result that focuses your body, literally organizing its fibers into carrying out your vision.

HOW YOU "BECOME THE ARENA"

THE SCENE OF ANY ACTION strongly affects you. As you perform, you and the arena in which you're performing become a feedback system. Letting this interaction occur, and using it well, is a vital component of learning—and subsequently of performing.

Suppose you're dribbling a ball. The relationship between you, the ball and the floor is constantly being reformulated. The resiliency of the floor determines the bounce of the ball, which then determines how much force you must apply in order to bring the ball to where you want it. The application of force affects the general tone of the muscles and the entire nervous system, recruiting muscle units and nervous system signals so that the next time the action occurs, you'll touch in a different way, and your eye will see the ball and the floor in a revised context. All of this is happening unconsciously and automatically. Your only responsibility—if you wish to profit from what's happening—is to be aware that this dynamic process is part of your experience.

The concept of becoming "one with the universe" —the goal of those attempting to achieve tranquil states—takes on a larger significance when it comes to performance. It's not sufficient to say that there is a structured universe you must recognize and adjust to until you become part of it. The reality is that in perceiving and interacting with the universe, you are more than becoming part of it; you are altering it, and it is altering you.

The achievement of harmony is a dynamic function, not a static one. When you enter an arena, your eyes adjust to the brightness or darkness. As you begin to move, the new demands insult your circulation; you aren't comfortable until your blood flow adjusts. Your strength adjusts to the need for it; your movements cease to exaggerate. Your sweat glands gradually adjust to the heat and the amount of wetness the skin needs in order to be comfortable. The sense of discomfort caused by the increased supply of chemicals in your blood decreases as you get used to their presence.

These kinds of experiences must be gained actively, not passively. It's not enough to attend a basketball game to know how it feels on the court; you have to be actively on the court. Your presence in the desert doesn't condition you to work in the desert unless you work. You don't acclimatize for skiing at a high altitude unless you ski. You become the arena by your performance in the arena, not by your mere presence in the arena.

During this acclimation even more subtle changes are occurring within you as a result of the recurrent stresses on your bone and muscle tissues. Consistent pressure on bone nudges its cells into better position to support its stress. The tiny fibers that make up muscles actually adjust their position within the muscles in a similar way. They literally shift into the best direction to support the stress that they must bear.

Suppose you're pulling on a rope. The muscle fibers adjust themselves to the force and arrange themselves to pull together. Every exertion prompts them to ask whether they are finally in the best arrangement for that effort, or whether they should adjust further.

A maximally performing muscle consists of a team of muscle fibers that have "gotten it together."

ZEN PERFORMANCE

YEARS AGO, Eugen Herrigel wrote a little book called *Zen in the Art of Archery*. When it appeared, it was viewed as a far-out philosophical tract that had nothing to do with performance. But subsequent readings gave the book the credit it deserved. The book mightily influenced me. Its central idea was that man, the bow, the arrow and the target could be made to interrelate until all were a harmonious whole. It offered the first glimpses of feedback phenomena: You are affected by your target, just as your target is affected by you. You're going to pierce the target with an arrow, but the target is organizing you by its presence.

Archery metaphorizes the interrelationship of all things in the universe. The slightest movement of a blade of grass can affect the course of the stars. The archer, through his archery, comprehends his relationship to other men, to objects, to his place in space and time.

Proficiency in archery through Zen—which really meant proficiency in living with full awareness of everything around you—was supposed to take something like eight years. My reaction at the time was that the whole was much too complex for the novice to comprehend at the outset. I could appreciate why it might take him eight years to gain proficiency. Today, I appreciate the concept in another light: It suggests that there is a wholeness to performance that gives you fulfillment and joy when you experience it.

Whenever I hit a golf ball really well it happens with such ease and rightness that I feel a certain harmony with the universe, as though I am part of the ball, and the flight of the ball is part of my existence. This may sound a little visionary at first reading, but you will find that your attitude toward the ball—and the arena, your opponents and everything else that goes into a play experience—profoundly affects your performance.

Let's revisit the maximum performer who's just taken up the game of golf. He began on the putting green, rather than the driving range, and now we can understand why. By starting with the driver, he would be trying to reach an understanding of the game with a complex stroke that is taken at a remote distance from the target. For him to achieve a "oneness" with the course, he would have to achieve a hole in one on a 240-yard, par-three hole; it's the only way his effort and the target would achieve a perfect relatedness, and until that happened, the wholeness of the game would elude him. The effort could easily take eight years—or a lifetime. But by starting with the ball a few inches from the cup on a putting green, the performer immediately puts himself in a position to comprehend the terrain, the ball, the club and his relationship to them. He studies the path of the ball, sees how it is affected by the grain of the green; he develops a sense that the ball should be dropped into the cup and not banged against the back rim. By starting with the first principles of golf, he is perfecting the most important single skill in golf. Because par presupposes as many putts as tee and fairway shots, the performer who masters putting has mastered half the game before he's swung another club.

Every game has interior components that can be peak experiences. To maximize your performance, your fail-safe route is to begin with these microexperiences. Later, as the microexperiences join together, you're able not only to express the whole idea, but to add an opponent to the arena. By dealing with the microexperiences first, you've made certain that you experience only success, never defeat, in your preparation for a new game or in retooling your present game.

Suppose you've decided to take up bowling. You would break the event into its components and practice each component until you feel a wholeness or oneness with the movement. Then you would put them together.

The approach in bowling is a simple walking step, but it has certain constraints. You must start in such a position that by your fourth step you're sliding to the foul line. After you've mastered the sequence of those steps, you assume a semicrouch position and work on your steps in that mode until the position and movement integrate. Next, you try your steps with the ball, learning when to lower the ball and let it swing backward and how to let it swing forward. By this point, you've gotten a sense of the smoothness of the terrain over which you're taking your steps, and you've related your body movement to the space in which you're moving. By the time you're ready to relate yourself to the alley, gutter and pins, you no longer have to think consciously about your stance, your steps or the backward and forward motion of the ball.

Zen in the Art of Archery suggested that you have to be content with failure until you achieve success. I'm suggesting that this is too much to ask of a non-ascetic person who doesn't feel that he needs to make a sacrificial ritual of his game. You can experience the joy of a peak performance earlier and more frequently by mastering the simplest components of a task first.

AN INTIMATE EXPERIENCE WITH
A BASKETBALL

SUPPOSE YOU'VE JUST hung a basketball hoop and backboard above your garage, and you've bought a new basketball and are going to work up your basketball skills. You may try a few shots, make half of them, and feel pretty good about it. But you haven't really developed much of a relationship between yourself and the ball and the basket. You're going through the motions, but it's not a complete experience. Nor are you performing as well as you could if you were to approach the experience as a whole.

Obviously, you may have no interest in basketball beyond this informal recreation. I'm simply using basketball to make a point that will be valid for any game you play. The point is that you have to discern the harmony in the event between yourself, the implements and the arena.

We tend to perceive all implements and elements to be used in a performance as hostile. Our unconscious thought is that we have to overcome this hostile environment in order to survive. The ball is our enemy because it can make us look foolish; the hoop is an unfriendly target, trying to keep the ball out. To succeed, we must somehow exert our will over the ball and hoop. We must achieve mastery over these objects, lest they master us.

Such perception is unfortunate. In any successful movement that makes use of your potential you are neither the master nor the slave. You, the implement and the arena are all one, interacting harmoniously.

To achieve that harmony, you would proceed in a series of logical, orderly steps.

First, you'd tune your senses to the size, shape and texture of the ball.

Next, you'd bounce the ball, to see how it rebounds and how much force you'd need to make it return to the right position. You'd develop the skill of making the ball continuously rebound while standing in one position.

Third, you'd move with the ball, "dribble" it, and learn what modification you have to make in your bouncing in order to keep the ball with you. You'd continue to work on that until you felt that the ball was a companion at your side. You're not chasing the ball, and the ball isn't eluding you. The ball is now your friend, not a foreign opponent you must deal with from an adversary position.

Fourth, you'd shoot the ball by standing at the side of the basket, up close to it, tossing the ball so that it bounces against the backboard and into the basket. What you're doing is getting the feel of the backboard and its relationship to the flight of the ball. Whereas before everything was down, toward the floor, now everything is up, toward the basket.

Fifth, you'd leap and shoot.

Sixth, you'd precede your leap with a few steps, shooting baskets in that manner until it becomes a shot that's almost impossible to miss. You'd also approach the basket from its other side.

Seventh, you'd go to the foul line and practice shooting from there.

Eighth, you'd finally take shots from conventional places on the floor.

By this time you'd be on intimate terms with the ball, as well as the environment in which it's used, and you would be ready to add an opponent to your arena in a one-to-one contest.

LOVE THE BALL

WHEN A DOG fetches a stick you've thrown and brings it back to you, you have a feeling of cooperation. When you bounce a ball and it rebounds into your hand, it should be with the same sense of friendliness. It's coming back to you because it likes you.

When the ball strikes your hand, your hand wants to accept the ball. Your fingers curl reflexively around it. If you throw the ball a little harder and don't close your hand fast enough, the ball will bounce away. So you learn to get your hand moving in rhythm with the ball in such a way that the ball gently overtakes your hand.

If you throw the ball to the floor in anger, it comes back with an angry force. Now your hand has to clutch the ball to trap it. There's a difference between accepting a ball and opposing it. If you accept it, you're more apt to catch it successfully. If you oppose it—throwing it bitterly—you tend to try to catch it the same bitter way and the ball seems to act angrily in opposition.

Your attitude toward the ball affects the flight of the ball when you hit it with an implement. If you're at bat in baseball and you think of the ball as an antagonistic object coming your way to make a fool of you, your tendency will be to conquer it by hitting it as hard as you can. With that attitude, you're more apt to miss the ball; you have no control over where it's going, and even if you hit it hard it's not a gratifying, harmonious experience. You'd be far more effective if you were to envision the entire experience: The ball is being pitched to you as part of a system in which you can place the ball where you want it to go. The ball is your partner, not your enemy. It wants to succeed as much as you do. It wants to fly as far and as straight as it was designed to.

You and the ball are one in the system of golf. It's an extension of you, just as the club is an extension of your arm. Help it take a long ride. Help it set down gently. Help it find the hole. Feel the hole welcoming the ball.

The next time you're on a driving range, experiment with the different reaction you get with "unfriendly" and "friendly" balls. Dump a bucket of balls into two piles, one "friendly," the other "unfriendly." Pick up an "unfriendly" ball, put it on a tee, tell it you hate it and that you're going to murder it. Then proceed to kill it. Now take a ball from the "friendly" pile, and address the ball as though you're going to give it a lovely ride. It's your messenger, in effect. It's working for you, and you're working for it. Pick a reasonable target, and send it off. After you've hit a dozen "unfriendlies," and another dozen "friendlies," notice what's happening. Hitting the unfriendlies, you're most likely clutching the club too hard and trying to push your muscles at the ball, in spite of the fact that muscles can only pull. Your swing is anxious, because you want to get the ball before the ball gets you. Your muscle action with the friendlies, by contrast, is graceful and rhythmic. Your timing is good. You're letting the forces summate naturally and harmoniously, so that the clubhead gradually develops maximum acceleration, the shaft bends as it gives in to the pressure of the ball, the ball compresses, recoils and flies out to your mutual target.

What is true for golf applies to all performance. Becoming one with the arena in which you play and the implements you use is what puts you into a condition of maximum receptivity for the acquisition of skills.

10

Maximizing Skill

To MAXIMIZE YOUR skill in any sport, you must set aside a separate period to learn, during which time you forego the pleasure of competing. The process of acquiring a new skill becomes your interim pleasure.

Suppose you're a golfer who plays twice a week. You're not satisfied with your game and you want to do something about it. If you take lessons during the week and continue to play on Saturday and Sunday, you'll find yourself incapable of playing in the new mode and probably unable to revert to the old one with any success. What you've done is to combine the foreman's and laborer's function—trying to think and do at the same time. It won't work.

The time to go to a professional is not when you want to prepare to play a match the next day, but when you want to reconstruct your skills and are willing to set aside a period of several weeks in which to do so. During this period, you'll take lessons, practice your new skills and not resume competitive play until they've been mastered.

Not long ago, a friend of mine returned from his first skiing trip of the season with a story and a question. His first day out, he related, he'd skied as well as he ever had. His success carried over into the morning of the second day. In the afternoon, his turns weren't quite so sharp. On the third day, his skiing fell apart. He was jerky in his turns, throwing his upper body—good skiers ski with their knees—and generally unable to make himself do what he knew he could do.

His experience should sound familiar to anyone who plays a sport. After an extensive layoff, it's not uncommon to play extremely well the first time you return to it. The phenomenon is known as *reminiscence*. Your body remembers motor acts that you once learned well. On that first day back, you don't have much anxiety because you don't expect much of yourself. You probably concentrate on your game more than usual because what you're doing seems more strange than it did when you were playing regularly. And you let things happen fairly naturally without trying all the little things you were trying when you were playing before. The result is a relaxed and focused performance that makes you think, "Hey, I've really got this game!" It's just then that you become conscious of some of the fine points of what you're doing and your game goes to pieces.

Reminiscence exists in the control mechanisms of the body. The moment you attempt either to visualize or to intellectualize your movements, you're lost. From his description of his skiing experience, that's exactly what had happened to my friend. His son, an excellent skier, had urged him to take some lessons, but my friend wasn't at all sure that that was the right moment to do so. What the teacher would see would not be the normal style in which he skied. Shouldn't he wait until his form returned?

His question begged the point. Lessons to correct a fault are not on the level at which the best instruction takes place. The time to take a lesson is when you recognize that your overall game isn't as good as you'd like it to be. This can occur at any level—at the outset, throughout your training or at the peak of your performance. A *good lesson doesn't deal with your er-*

*rors. It returns you to fundamentals and rebuilds on
the firm basis of the sound principles of the event.*

The secret of rapid training is to postpone the satisfaction that comes from a good score or a win. You
must put things in their proper sequence—and winning
or performing well comes last.

When you revert to analysis of body mechanics, you
almost invariably sacrifice performance. Such a rever-
sion should be avoided with someone whose performance is all important at the moment. If he does want
to improve, he must understand that his performance
will deteriorate for a while. This is one case where
things do have to get worse before they can get better.

When you take a poor bowler to a bowling alley,
you don't care how he scores when you teach him. It's
important to tell him so, because he'll really need
convincing that it's not the result that matters. What
matters is that he concentrate on the style of execution.
If he's bowling 140 and wants to get better but never
will with his present style, tell him that he can expect
the bowl 75 or 80 for a while, before he starts bowling
175. Otherwise, he'll more than likely revert to his
old style.

Old habits easily creep back into your performance.
I once had a golf game with a man who was suffering a slump and about to give up the game. His handicap was eight, but his score was in the nineties. It was
only after we'd finished our round that he understood
what he'd done. Several years before, he'd changed
the fundamentals of his game. Instead of pronating his
wrists on the backswing, he'd learned to keep them
square to the ball. The new technique had eliminated
a chronic fade and dropped his handicap by five
strokes. Now that he was having trouble, his body
memory had bypassed the newer technique in favor of
the older, more comfortable, less successful approach.

Because the temptation—both conscious and unconscious—to return to comfortable habits is so strong,
every effort must be made to resist it when you're
learning a new technique. There is no greater tempta-

tion than wanting to win; finding yourself in a pressure situation, you'll automatically and instantaneously revert to the more familiar mode in order to make your shot. You'll get by, but you'll never get better.

You must ingrain your new movement before you can return to competition without reverting to your old habits.

The process of reconstruction takes at least several weeks. The more time you give it, the better off you'll be in the long run. Your objective is to work on the new form until it becomes your natural style. By the time you resume play, the new style is so ingrained that you no longer have to think about it. The foreman or coach in you has retired to the sidelines; you're totally the performer, expressing your idea of the whole game, not bothered by thoughts of technique.

FOUR BASIC PRINCIPLES FOR LEARNING A NEW SKILL

EVEN THOUGH WE don't know a great deal about how learning takes place, experience has taught us some principles to follow when trying something new:

1. *Be sure that you have a clear image of what you are going to do.*

That image will have personal refinements, but it will be within a certain framework of efficient performance. If the image is faulty to begin with, you're obviously never going to achieve maximum performance. Suppose you want to deliver a bowling ball by bouncing it down the alley. You might keep practicing this until you become rather good at it, but even if the proprietor of the bowling alley were to continue to let you play, you would never be able to control the ball as well as you could if you were using a simple pendular delivery.

In learning a new skill you can't depend on visualization of the act too strongly because visualization involves a memory center, and your memory of movement experiences may be vague and not well related to the skill.

You can't get agreement as to what constitutes ideal form of play for everyone. To attempt in this book or any book to take every beginner through the same artificial set of motions, however mechanically efficient, would be meaningless because each person has his unique pattern of movement on which he superimposes the movement of the skill that he's trying to learn.

Each golfer puts his own signature on his swing. A chunky person who moves in a jerky fashion can have a jerky swing—and it can be very successful. A willowy woman will have a willowy swing. The chunky man should not try to imitate the willowy woman, or the willowy woman the chunky man.

What you're trying to do at the outset is not so much to execute a movement as to express an idea.

In learning a new skill you must let the body senses see and feel what it is you're going to do. This see/feel realm is actually the expression of the idea. It's not enough to separate thinking from doing. Something else has to take place: a rehearsal of a sensory experience so that you can understand how a movement is going to feel. Your muscles are actually previewing the experience.

Having watched a movement in its time/space dimension, all that's new for you is the force experience, i.e., doing it yourself to see how much effort it takes. Watching a skilled performer play tennis, for example, you get an idea of how much time you'll have to get set for the return of the ball; you get an idea of the space in which your return has to be hit. The only thing you haven't experienced is how much of his capacity has to be applied—but you even get an idea of that by watching the demonstration.

The point to remember is this: While you're standing and watching, you're learning in a way you don't

verbally comprehend. You physically *sense* what it is
that you're going to do. The greatest favor you can do
yourself as a performer is to realize that you have this
internal ability to conceptualize a new movement; trust
it and use it.

In biological terms we would call this your perceptual motor impression.

When you watch a performance that you're eventually proposing to emulate, electrical changes take place
in the muscles that, although very faint, are actually
rehearsing the movement. Suppose you were imagining that you were going to leap across a ditch. If an
electromyograph were attached to your hamstring muscles, it would register a faint contraction at the moment that you were imagining the leap.

Pia Gilbert, professor of dance and composer of
music for dance, once acknowledged that she used to
develop muscle strains while playing rehearsal piano
for her classes. "I would have all the same aches and
pains the dancers did at the end of the class because
my muscles were working in empathy."

I know what she means. When I was a collegiate
wrestler waiting on the bench for my event, I would
become exhausted just by watching my teammates perform. I was straining and groaning and resisting every
pin. I would catch myself pitting one set of muscles
against the other. Many have experienced this kind of
exhaustion at the end of a contest in which we've par-
ticipated only as spectators. We're wrung out because
we haven't made the movements that would have permitted our tension to be relieved; no extra supply of
blood has flowed as it would have through our contracting and relaxing muscles.

It's this empathy with a performance that gives you
your perceptual motor impression—if you let it. The
experience can be a skill workout provided you're
deliberately focusing on the movement in a manner
that gives you a feel for its proper execution. Watching
others play who are better than you, or watching a
smooth opponent, you only get a benefit if you delib-

erately transfer what you're seeing and feeling to yourself. You can watch in a detached way, in which you're registering what's going on without responding to it, or you can watch in an involved way, in which you attempt to sense what it is that the expert is expressing.

It's the sensation you receive that's important, whether you get it by watching or doing.

Suppose you're learning to swim. First, you would get comfortable with the sensation of having your face in the water, so that you know you're not going to suffocate. Then you would push off from the edge of the pool with your legs, and get the feeling of gliding and floating. Once you experience that delicious sensation of the body moving through the water, you're actually swimming. That is the expression of the idea—even though you have yet to learn how to stroke with your arms or kick with your feet.

Without this idea, you can do dry-land or shallow water drills forever without becoming comfortable with the idea of swimming. Once you have the idea, by contrast, kicking and stroking come easily. Each of these is a separate idea—but there is a natural and logical order to ideas in learning a complex movement, just as there is in putting together a written report.

What you need before anything else is an idea of how the movement is going to *feel*. You should have the attitude that you're ready to try it. It's a state of readiness in your whole being, not just a thought; you can't put it into words. The feeling is a mind-muscle image. Your body senses the action; you've actually had a miniexperience before you've ever tried it. When you finally try the movement, you're putting that miniexperience into a time/space/force magnitude. You've already rehearsed and felt what it is you're going to do. The act is a manifestation of what you've already previewed. You say to yourself, in effect, "Aha!" If you haven't said that, or something similar to it, you're not ready to perform because you haven't yet got the idea.

2. *Determine your starting point by seeing how far your present skills can take you.*

The basic rule of rapid training is that you build on an existing set of skills, no matter how crude or simple.

One summer, when I was in college, I took a job as a counselor at a girls' camp. I was the riding master, the waterfront director, the archery teacher, expected to be an expert at just about everything. I had my Red Cross Water Safety Instructor's certificate, so the water part was no problem. Before going to camp, I had taken six lessons in horsemanship and spent a week at a riding academy, learning how to care for the horses and to saddle and bridle them. In addition, along with my change in goals at the start of college—from being a performer to being an analyst—I had ceased training to be a champion and had determined to play every sport and make every team. In three years, I would play on nine teams and win my letter in every sport. So I already had a habit of adapting. But nothing I'd done had prepared me for archery. Nonetheless, I had to teach it. I'll never forget my first lesson.

The only bow and arrow I'd had as a child had been made of twigs. So I got a book on archery and learned the terminology. Then I studied, desperate to understand enough that I could talk about. I committed five or six points to memory, studied the photographs at length and, armed with equipment, walked with foreboding to the archery range. "I'm going to demonstrate the principles of archery to you," I told the class of assembled girls, "but you're not to pay any attention to where the arrow goes because I'm concentrating on what I'm telling you and not on the shot." With only a mental picture of what I was about to do, I took my stance, held the bow in front of me, notched the arrow, drew it back to the tip of my nose and, talking all the time about what I was doing and how to release the fingers, let the arrow fly. It flew into the center of the bull's-eye. The girls all oohed and aahed. Naturally, I didn't try it again that day.

The point is that even though I had never held a bow and arrow in my hand, my kinesthetic vault had enough of value in it to enable me to do what I needed to.

It's best to start out by trying. If you succeed, you're that much farther ahead; your mind is uncluttered by details of the technique.

3. *Divide the skill into its component parts—and start with those you can already do well.*

If a tennis ball was hanging from a string above your head, you could probably hit it with a racket the first time you tried to serve. But if you can't get the ball up in the air and hit it, too, then throwing the ball is a component that's going to have to be learned. Even that component, however, may be breakable into several components, only one of which needs work. You may need to throw the ball higher, or more to the left or right. Once you've perfected the toss, try the serve again.

There's no reason to work on all twelve parts of a movement if the reason you can't perform the whole movement is because of a single hitch.

As a general rule, unnatural, highly complex skills are learned more readily when the elements of the movements are taken one at a time, simple elements first, more complex elements later. Movements that are simple in their entirety can be taken up whole. Running is an example of an almost reflexive event. There's no need to separate the arm action and practice it by itself; you can work on your arm movement as you run, keeping the arms fairly close to the body, in an intermediate position, not too high or low.

4. *Move as soon as possible to the speed of the performance.*

Nothing should be done in slow or separate motions or with less than game strength for any longer than it takes to get you moving at game speed. If you hit softly in practice, you are teaching yourself to hit softly in a game. If you fragment your movements, you'll never move beyond the tension-inducing details to the purpose and meaning of the act.

In practicing a new stroke, you'll probably want to do it in slow motion in order to get the general idea. But learning comes best if you gradually increase the rate of movement to game speed within a few weeks, and practice at game speed thereafter.

Coordination, posture, muscle tone and balance are all related to game speed, and they will vary if your movements are either slower or faster. It's the practice at game speed that improves performance at game speed. The sooner your practice sessions get you to game speed, the more rapidly your performance will improve.

In bowling, it's almost impossible to practice at anything but game speed, and you should be near there at the end of your first lesson.

In tennis, you should hit your shots in practice as you hope to hit them in the game. Obviously, you don't strike every shot with equal force, or you will wind up with a game that is lacking in variety. But any sport in which speed is the dominant factor should be practiced at the rate you're going to play it. You'll get initial accuracy if you practice at a slow speed, but your accuracy will decrease only slightly as the speed of the event is increased. The idea is to accustom yourself first to the speed of the event, *then* to accuracy in the event at the speed of the event. If you work in this order you'll achieve early success at game speed —much like a racehorse that is ridden by a lightweight jockey in training so that it will retain the similar speed in a race even though carrying a heavier jockey.

The all but inevitable tendency of the tennis novice is to say to himself, "In order to get accuracy, I've got to hit the ball easily." This is not the route to maximum performance; rather, it leads to a game style usually referred to as pitty-pat tennis.

When you give priority to game speed you keep concentrating on accuracy within that pace from the very beginning. You don't just let your shot or throw go anywhere and hope to become accurate later. Every motion, regardless of its speed, is made with a precise target in mind.

MYTH: PRACTICE MAKES PERFECT

PRACTICE MAKES PERFECT only if you're doing it right. The endless repetition of a motion not only is unnecessary but can be damaging. Practice doesn't make perfect if you're just repeating a wrong motion.

The saying, "If at first you don't succeed, try, try again," ought to be changed as follows: "If at first you don't succeed, give up." Quickly discard what doesn't work and try something else. Hitting a golf ball the wrong way a thousand times may give you a fitness workout, but it won't do a thing for your skill; to the contrary, it will only groove more deeply a neuromuscular habit that will eventually have to be changed if you're to make any progress.

The only advantage of errors is that you learn the consequences of a bad move. But the pitfalls of repetitive practice exist even when your performance is basically correct.

When horse trainers are trying to refine a horse's movement, they will work the horse until he does it right, have the horse repeat the movement perhaps once more and then leave him alone. In their experience, forcing a horse to do the same movement over and over again kills the horse's enthusiasm.

I'm convinced that the endless repetition of an act once you've got it right probably does more harm than good. It changes your attitude toward an event as an expression of an idea—a satisfying, harmonious act—to a dull, mechanical movement. When you repeat an act over and over, furthermore, you're actually tiring some of the controlling muscles to the point where you must substitute other muscles that don't really belong in the performance but are needed now for support. The result is that you begin to perform in an indirect and awkward manner. Neither the fibers that are fatigued nor those that are substituting are getting the proper training.

What we call "practice" ought to be an exploration of the idea of what you're trying to express—until you feel, "That's it, that feels good, I've got it right." Once you have that feeling, you should execute the movement just once or twice more to reinforce your memory of it, and then put it together, with something else.

The purpose of any movement is to express yourself. When you reduce this performance to repetition of technique, you're removing it from the realm of esthetic experience. When, after prolonged use, certain of your muscle groups give up and you must use a different coordination, the whole objective of practice—to polish your expression—has been lost because you're not using the tools with which you're supposed to be working.

When you repeatedly drill a movement, moreover, it makes you conscious of the central action. That puts your attention in the wrong place. The attention should be on the goal, not the process of getting to it.

FRAMING AND SIGHTING

EVERY PROLONGED COMPLEX activity seems overwhelming at the outset from the perspective of the novice. He doesn't see how he's going to get from where he is to the other end—mastery of the event. In this circumstance, the way to attack the task is to break it into components.

Suppose you want to get from point A to point E.

You don't try to make it in one trip. Rather, you identify the "frames" of the activity—A to B, B to C, C to D, and D to E—and you see that you can easily make it from A to B, and so on.

Framing—as music professor Theodore Norman of UCLA calls it—is an excellent device for taking the dread out of a long recitation. Instead of worrying about your ability to remember an entire speech, you concentrate on moving from one central idea of the speech to the next one, and then the next one, and so forth, until you reach your conclusion. Framing works equally well when you're executing a long piece of choreography or playing a musical composition.

Within each frame, there's yet another technique to assist you. Whether you're drawing a violin bow across the strings of the instrument or shooting a basket, you perform best when you don't think about anything during the travel between start and finish. Your attention is best directed at the end of the movement, a process known as *sighting*.

If you're conscious of what the body is doing as you're moving between points A and B, the action won't be as smooth. If, instead of concentrating on the moving, you concentrate on the end of that movement, you diminish your attention to the process of movement, and have little or no awareness of the effort of getting there. As you learn to do this, you'll be enhancing your ability to express your idea of the act, rather than grinding your way through the act.

Theodore Norman wants the attention of the performer who is playing a phrase of music to be on the first and last notes and not on the notes in between. As Professor Norman tells the story, he learned this lesson, not from any of the European masters with whom he studied every summer, but from a cat in his Los Angeles backyard. The cat would sit in front of a fairly high fence, as though studying it. Then, in what appeared to be an unconscious act, he would crouch and fly up to the top of the fence. His movement was completely relaxed, as though he recognized that if he was straining and worrying about what was in between, he wouldn't reach his destination.

The day Professor Norman told this story to my class, he had with him a student of his who was a collegiate hurdler. The student explained how he had applied framing and sighting to his hurdling. Previously, he had been thinking in terms of so many steps between hurdles, then a stride over the hurdle. By eliminating all thought of his intermediate steps and concentrating instead on the final step before clearing each hurdle, he was able to improve his time substantially.

Mastery of a complex continuous event such as a hurdling race is facilitated by breaking the whole race into frames. In the preceding case, the final takeoff step would constitute the end of each frame. Now, instead of thinking about all of the steps between barriers, the hurdler can envision the race simply as a series of takeoff steps; after each takeoff step, he sights to the next one. This process brings him closer to experiencing the race in its harmonious whole.

Anything you do in the process of executing a movement that introduces extraneous tensions or motions destroys the quality of your performance, and fatigues you in the process. When you're trying to perfect an act, accordingly, you gradually let all thoughts of technique, the one-by-one process, fade as you simply "frame" the idea, and effortlessly leap from the end of each frame to the next.

Suppose you're retooling your tennis game. Your coach has determined that you have a tendency to hit shallow returns. She tells you that she wants you to get all your returns deep into the last three feet of the court. You know you're going to have to hit the ball in an entirely different manner to accomplish this objective. What you concentrate on, however, is not the technique, but the destination of the ball. Each time the ball strikes the target just within the base line, it "frames" the event. The positioning and stroking are relegated to mere process. You now give no conscious attention to what goes on between the frames. Without such concern you have no tension.

When your mind is on technique, you're driving your muscles through a prescribed framework, and directing them in the process. Technique simply gets in the way. When you reduce the whole motion to the practice of a technique, you're limiting the way the body is meant to function.

If you can't immediately express an idea in its totality, then frame it by expressing each of its components. Eventually, you'll be able to fit them together.

MENTAL PRACTICE

THE SAME PHENOMENON that assists you when you watch a performance is at work when you think about your own performance. If you simply go through the motions in your mind, you'll induce a training effect. An electromyograph placed on the involved muscles would show tiny signals of activiy in those muscles. Contractile changes take place that, although faint, are rehearsing the actual movement. The mechanism of mental practice is probably a modification of neuromuscular coordination. Even though no movement may be perceptible, you're actually learning by doing.

The best time to engage in mental practice is when you're in bed, with the lights out, waiting for sleep. It's quiet. You can practice without interruption. And you may well repeat the practice in your sleep. In the process, not only will you benefit your performance, you may also improve your rest.

Pat McCormick, who at one time or another during her career held every major springboard and platform diving championship, often had trouble sleeping because she worried about her dives. I suggested that instead of worrying about the dives, she visualize the motion of the dives. I advised her to start with her first dive and imagine going through her entire program, emphasizing in particular the parts that she'd been working on the hardest, so that she would get the feel more clearly in her mind.

Pat's program consisted of five required and three optional dives. She developed the mental practice technique to a point that if she didn't do one of her dives properly in her mind, she would go back and do it over. It wasn't just her imagination working; the reason it didn't feel right, in all probability, was that the little bit of contractile activity in her muscles wasn't well coordinated. She would sense that, and repeat the dive until she got it right. When she returned to actual practice, she noticed that movements that had been hard for her to do were now coming easily. And by converting worry to positive practice, Pat slept better.

When you engage in mental practice, you rehearse your entire performance. You play at game speed, creating a real environment. If golf is the game you're playing, you include your practice swing as well as your "waggle" as you address the ball. The waggle gets your signals started; if you were to leave it out, you wouldn't have the same muscle sense of the position of the club and postural preparation of your body.

Suppose you've been having trouble with your backswing, and you've learned what you want to do to regroove it. You'd pay particular attention to the moment when you take the club away from the ball. If it didn't "feel" right in your mind, you'd rehearse it again until it did. Once it was right, you'd complete your swing.

You play a perfect game in mental practice—perfect, that is, for you. If you're the kind of golfer who gets at least a couple of pars on every round, then in your mental practice you should par or birdie almost every hole. This isn't Walter Mitty fantasy. If you're not capable of hitting your best shot more than two hundred yards, you don't do so in mental practice. You drive to where your ball would be within your limits of the game. What will make the difference is that each shot is your best possible effort.

Not only are you helping your swing with mental practice; you're creating a game plan in your mind. Most novice golfers lose because they don't plan their shots with care. The same holds true of fledgling players in almost every sport.

VISUALIZE A PERFECT RESULT

THE DIFFERENCE BETWEEN the novice and the champion in the sandtrap is that the novice thinks, "I hope it gets on the green," whereas the champion visualizes the flight of the ball, how it will land on the green and run up into the cup.

You should always visualize a result as being perfect before you make your attempt. At the top of a ski slope, imagine yourself going down the slope taking the turns on the moguls. Feel the rhythm with which you're going to accomplish a perfect run. Visualizing in this manner will refine your coordination, giving it a directness and sureness.

The body follows the mind's suggestions because the whole motor nervous system is geared to the visual signal—"visual" meaning not just what you see but what you conceptualize as well.

If you visualize a negative result, you increase your chances of producing one. Worry that you'll shank the ball and you'll probably shank it. Visualize the result you want, and your body will do its best to comply.

Visualization is a whole-body phenomenon, a sense of awareness—of your position on a court or field, of the position of your opponent, of your movements and the movement of implements and ball. This envisioning concept is what organizes the nervous system to make the muscles respond in a coordinated way to accomplish your objective.

Returning a shot in tennis involves just two ideas. The first is to respond as quickly as possible to what the ball coming off the opponent's racket tells you—whether it's going to be deep or shallow, whether it's been hit with unusual spin, and what side it's coming to. The second is to visualize your return. Think of the result, not the execution; it's the thought of the result that organizes the execution.

If you don't have an image of what you want to do, your muscles won't be organized in the best manner available to you. Just as the artist or sculptor has an image of what he wants to put on his canvas or block of stone before he starts brushing or chipping away, so the performer needs to know what result he desires before he starts to move.

Our fantasies increase the likelihood that reality will match them. The ultimate in performance is when your body and the objects you're using in play actually take the course you had planned for them.

MAXIMUM SEXUAL PERFORMANCE

EXPRESSING THE IDEA of an action, rather than dwelling on ingredients of the action, applies to all performance, be it on the playing field, in the office or home. All of us may differ to at least a slight degree in our choice of events; let's try to illustrate this central fact of performance in terms of one event that we all perform sooner or later—and want, more than any other, to perform to our maximum.

What is a maximum sexual performance? A single kiss can be transporting, and a violent, athletic bout of coitus, complete with fifty variations, can be as boring as running in place. Sexual performance shouldn't be judged on the basis of variety, endurance, heart rate or sweat production. The real measure of sexual performance is the degree of satisfaction it produces.

The notion that there is some kind of ideal scenario or method to the sexual act is as fallacious as the idea of the "picture-book" golf swing. The surest way to diminish your performance is by trying to fulfill a predetermined scenario because it's expected of you.

Most sex manuals give you the elements and mechanics. It's assumed that you're going to put what you've learned into some kind of portfolio that you can experiment with and gradually work into your repertoire. This has an advantage and a disadvantage. The advantage is that it broadens the scope of the activity and introduces pleasures that wouldn't otherwise be enjoyed. The disadvantage is that the act becomes someone else's, not yours.

The best performance occurs when you follow your urges. Sex should be an expression of your feelings, not the practice of techniques. Your objective ought to be to enjoy what is functioning, rather than trying to control function.

The important thing, for the male in particular, is to allow oneself to function as a reflexive organism, and not try to hurry or program one's sexual response, imitate others' ideas or copy others' styles. Let things occur the way your reflexes guide.

The champion, we've said, always practices in an atmosphere of success. This is no less true in sexual performance. You try to do what you know you can achieve. If you have used one position for many years and now want to vary your technique, don't program a performance involving several new positions. Try one new one at a time. A new position with a habitual partner can be a fantastic experience.

Sex is both an individual and a dual sport. The duality has been explored and extolled. The individual aspect of the sport shouldn't be underrated.

If you let your own feelings grow, and respond to those feelings freely, all of the sexual reflexes from tumescence to lubrication to orgasm are intensified. If, however, you are preoccupied with your partner's response, trying to match the stages of intercourse to where you suppose your partner is at each moment, yours becomes an outer-directed performance, and your reflex action is impaired.

Intercourse as a dual sport is the apogee of the feed-back phenomenon, in which you are reacting to the stimulus of your partner's physiological emotional responses. You can feel and smell and taste and hear the changes taking place. These responses enhance your own reflex responses. But the closer you get to climax, the more nearly sex becomes an individual sport. It's then that a little selfishness is very much in order—for your partner's sake as well as yours.

Let your sexual actions follow your impulse; it's then, and only then, that the actions will reinforce the impulse—and you will find your experience becoming what you, and your partner, hoped it would be.

11

Super Ks:
The Champions' Secrets

WE'VE SAID THAT there's no ideal way to execute a movement, to which all of us must conform. There are, however, fifteen basic principles of throwing, striking, kicking, catching and moving into position that, once understood and employed, maximize performance. I call them "Super Ks," kinesiological secrets employed, for the most part, by champions. Any or all of them are immediately adaptable to your game —whatever that game may be.

1. *Use as much of your body in the motion as the play allows.*

Throwing, striking and kicking are the most common movements in play experiences. In all three, you're imparting velocity to an object, usually a ball, by using your foot or your hands, or your hands extended by an implement, such as a bat or club. If the objective is to impart maximum speed to the object, then you want to get your hands or foot moving at the maximum possible rate at the time the object is contacted or released. This result is best achieved by a whole-body action, rather than by the action of a single body part.

What most distinguishes the inferior from the su-

perior performer is the failure of the former to involve
one or more parts of his body in his movements.

To give you an idea of what kind of power is potentially available to you, let me tell you about my
experience with Ken Foreman, once the national
champion in the rope climb. This is such an arduous
event that performers have only one chance in a competition. Foreman would often travel several thousand
miles to a meet, compete for about seven seconds and
then return to his home. When I first began my study,
I noted that Foreman and others were performing the
event entirely with their arms. I sensed that this was a
mistake. The strongest pulling muscles aren't in the
arms, but in the shoulders and back. Overreliance on
the arms is a common error in golf, tennis, batting,
bowling, swimming—any sport that involves a stroke
or swing. I knew from my experience with swimmers
—I had been the freshman swimming coach at the
University of Iowa—that it's the shoulder and back
muscles, not the arm muscles, that should propel you
through the water. It occurred to me that Ken
should try to "swim" up the rope—but before I
suggested it to him, I went off to the zoo to watch the
monkeys. Sure enough, the monkeys scarcely used
their arms at all when they swung from branch to
branch. Their power came from their backs and shoulders.

I waited until Ken had won the national championship—I had learned that lesson from my student the
shot putter—and then I said, "Let's try something.
Let's use your arms for support, but let's climb with
your shoulders and back. Think in terms of flinging
one arm above the other, pulling with the back and
shoulders, in a sense like swimming up the rope."

At first, Ken couldn't do it. His times were terrible.
Then, suddenly, he caught the idea, "swam" up the
rope—and cut seconds off his best time.

Using all of your body—back, shoulders, hips and
legs, in addition to your arms and hands—can add

fantastic power to your movements, thereby permitting you to refine your motion, rather than straining to execute it.

2. *Move your center of gravity.*

You hear coaches urge their players: "Move your tail," "Get your butt in gear," and other expressions to that effect. Actually, the part of the body they're urging be put in motion is its center of gravity.

The center of gravity is located in the middle of the body, near the waistline in men, a little closer to the hips in women.

All striking movements are—or should be—initiated by the legs to move the center of gravity. Prizefighters know this; they watch the waistline for the signal of a knockout punch. Once they see that, there's just barely enough time to take defensive measures before the action is transmitted from the body to the fist.

Force is generated when you push off with one side of the body against the other. The action begins with the relaxation of the side toward the target—legs, hips, lower body. This is followed immediately by the contraction of the opposite leg, which starts the body's center of gravity moving toward the target. The force from this contraction in turn is translated from the hips through the back, shoulders, upper arms, forearm, wrist and fingers in throwing, and from the hips to the thigh to the foreleg to the foot in kicking.

3. *Give each force in a movement enough time to peak.*

One of the means by which we gain power in physical movement is called "summation of forces." It means that we wait for each component of a force to develop to its peak before applying the next one. We don't try to put everything together at once or do everything at once. We lose an enormous amount of force if we hurry.

To demonstrate the principle of summation of

forces, take a ball, go outdoors and perform a little exercise:

Holding the wrist of your throwing arm with your free hand, use your hand alone to throw the ball as far as you can. It won't go very far.

Next, hold the elbow of your throwing arm with your free hand, and use your forearm and hand to throw the ball. This time it will go a good bit farther.

The third throw is made with your free hand holding your throwing arm at the shoulder. The ball goes farther still when the movement of the upper arm is added.

The fourth throw is made with your free hand clutching your belt, to restrict rotation of your hips. An even better throw when you can use your upper torso.

Finally, throw the ball with no interference at all. Now, every body part participates in order: legs, hips, back, shoulders, upper arm, forearm and finally the wrist. The ball sails far down the field. If you wait for each part to develop its peak acceleration before adding the next, you'll make your maximal throw.

Most people hurry their motion too much, which tends to lock the body parts together and produce one combined action before each separate action has made its contribution.

Perfect timing occurs when each subsequent force is applied at the peak instant at which maximum acceleration is developed by the previous movement. To show how important this is, try to throw a ball while moving all the body parts at once, starting with the ball behind you and your shoulder stretched, as though you were going to throw a spear.

Next, break your throw into two motions. First, turn the whole body. Next, as you approach the peak of the body turn, throw the whole arm in one piece. The ball will go much farther than it could if you made the turn and the throw at the same time.

Now, move the hips, back, shoulder, upper arm, forearm, wrist and fingers as separate entities, one right at the peak of the other. Feel each part, but let them flow, each in its turn, and at its proper time. You'll probably throw the ball farther than ever before.

There are two major timing errors: too early and too late. Too early occurs when you hurry the forces involved in a movement and don't let each "summate" at its peak. Too late occurs when you delay the application of forces, so that the previous one is partially dissipated before the next one is applied.

Giving each force in a movement an opportunity to contribute to the overall movement can make the difference between good and excellent, or excellent and great. A subtle change of this nature helped Bill Sharman enormously in his playing career. It was the late 1940s, Bill was playing basketball for USC, and I was preparing my first book on kinesiology, a part of which was to be devoted to basketball. Studying films, Professor John Cooper and I noted that players who powered the ball into the basket with stiff arm and hand action were the least accurate. The final release of the ball, we reasoned, ought to be via the delicate action of the fingers, so that minute corrections could be made. After the season ended, we asked Sharman, who was a great all-court player but not that good a shot, if he'd like to test our theory. He agreed. We taught him to make his hand movement independent of his arm action, after the arm action had been completed. Bill's shooting improved so markedly that he became an outstanding professional.

4. *Take a windup that puts your muscles on a stretch.*

A stretched muscle is infinitely stronger than a relaxed one. Using a muscle that hasn't been stretched is like trying to shoot a rubberband that hasn't been stretched. Most average players fail to turn their back to the ball before swinging through. This turn stretches the back muscles. Then the arm and wrist are cocked in a slightly exaggerated backswing to put their action muscles on a stretch.

In throwing, you reach back, then throw.

In kicking, you stretch the hip, then kick.

Take a few minutes to watch a baseball game. Watch the pitcher as he throws and the batter as he swings. Each puts his back to the other, i.e., winds up prior to throwing or swinging.

The next time you take a swing, try putting your back into it. You'll add yards to your tee shots or put zing into your ground strokes.

5. *Stabilize supporting segments.*

The trunk of the body is like the handle of a bullwhip. The action is initiated there, and the trunk then becomes the supporting framework from which the following actions are linked. Without the trunk, you've lost your handle.

In order to achieve maximum speed of movement of the arms and legs as they are whipped from the trunk, the trunk must be held firm, even brought to a near stop and held rigidly, in order to provide stability. This firmness in the trunk is quite evident in skilled throwers, kickers and strikers.

6. *Let your head control your movements.*

Control in all skill motions of the body is centered in the head and neck. The head orients the body in space and provides a reference point from which accurate body movements can be made. If you focus on a ball with your eyes and keep your head steady so that the head and neck are reference points around which the body moves, then the movements will be made with the greatest accuracy and you'll have the greatest control over the throw or the strike. If the eyes are allowed to wander, a basic reference point is lost. If the head is turned, the body tends to follow the motion of the head, which may be contrary to the desired action of the body.

The body is so organized that its parts move in certain sequences; each part has an effect on the next part. If they don't start right, they won't finish right.

The body follows the head in any movement, so if the head starts abruptly—picking up before a ball is hit, for example—the body will jerk through a swing or stroke. If the body is not to be shifted, the head shouldn't shift. A coordinated movement by the head will lead the body in a reflexive body motion. If you were a springboard diver, you would know that the way to do a front flip is to bend your head forward; to do a back flip, to bend your head back; to do a twist, to twist your head. The body follows the head in follow-the-leader fashion.

For instance: when you start to fall, you reflexively pull your head back. This stimulates your neck muscles to organize the neck-righting reflex, which sets off a whole chain of reflexes that restore the body to an upright position by an action of the legs and trunk.

7. *Keep your body relaxed but together.*

Relaxation is commonly thought of as absence of all tension, a state of "letting go." But relaxation in action is a different phenomenon.

You want to be relaxed when you're moving. Otherwise, your brakes are on, and you're getting in your own way. But, as we learned, in order to have a fluid motion, you have to have an amount of stability that enables you to move in a smooth way, uninterrupted by excessive muscular contractions, yet retaining your coordination. You can feel that everything is firmly drawn together, and yet relaxed at the same time. When it comes to motion, being relaxed does not mean being sloppy.

Before training, when you tense one part of the body, the tension spreads through the entire body. But with practice, you learn to relax the tension where it isn't needed.

8. *Keep a tight grip.*

In all striking implements the shaft flexes and stores energy during impact with the ball. High-speed pictures of a tennis ball on impact with the racket show the head of the racket bending backward about an inch, springing forward, then fluttering to a stop after the ball departs. A viselike grip is crucial to power; a loosely held implement will not bend as much on impact; it will simply give in your hand, and you will have lost a lot of the energy that would have been stored in the implement, then transmitted to the ball.

To take advantage of the tight grip, it's necessary to have great strength in your wrists and arms. This is especially true in tennis because of the great force encountered when ball meets racket. So great is the force that a weak, unskilled tennis player would be better off using a lighter grip, sacrificing some power in order to save his arm. The reason: When the ball strikes the racket off-center—as commonly happens among inexperienced players—there is an additional recoil shock. The tighter the grip, the more readily this added shock is apt to pass to the arm.

9. *Finish the stroke.*

In swimming and rowing, it's the last third of the stroke that delivers much of the power—yet that's the phase during which the novice usually quits in anticipation of starting the next stroke.

10. *Move with, not against, a force.*

If a ball stings your hand when you catch it, you're catching it the wrong way. Catching is, or should be, a process of slowing an object in flight to a stop or, in the case of fielding a baseball, transferring the direction of the flight of the ball as it is being caught and thrown so that the ball never comes to a stop. In proper catching, the hand doesn't oppose the ball, or isn't being stretched out to meet it. Your hand is never going in the opposite direction of the ball; it's always going in the same direction. You have to reach out to prepare for a catch, but before the ball reaches the hand, you start drawing the hand in so that hand and ball are traveling in the same direction.

To demonstrate this direction of forces easily,

bounce a tennis ball on the ground with your hand, let your hand stay down until you're ready to catch the ball, and then raise your hand and let the ball float into it. If you wanted to catch the ball on its downward flight, you would let your hand stay up near the ball, as it descends.

If you put your finger in a baby's palm, the baby's fingers will reflexively curl around yours. In catching, a similar grasping reflex can operate unconsciously if you let it. If you're too anxious to catch you will probably close your fingers before the ball touches your palm and you'll either drop the ball or break your fingers.

11. *Use momentum.*

If you try to push a car from a position of complete rest, you won't be nearly as successful as if you first develop a rocking action of your body. Rocking is felt to be so important in weight lifting that it's not permitted in competitions. But there's no proscription on popular use. Whenever you've got something heavy to push or pull, get your momentum going first.

Momentum has a great deal to do with your effectiveness in any event involving response to a signal— a foot race, the snap of a football, a ball suddenly coming your way. We all have a movement characteristic called ataxia, which means that when we're standing, we're constantly swaying, not only back and forth but from side to side. If you were wearing a graduation cap with a piece of paper tacked to the flat surface, and above that surface was a pen or pencil whose tip lightly touched the surface, you would make a series of small scribbles by your swaying motion.

You start fastest when you make your move as your body is swaying in the direction you want to go. You start slowest when you make the start opposite the direction of the sway. You have to stop that sway before you start forward again.

If an experienced starter in a race detects any perceptible motion on the part of the contestants, he shouldn't fire his gun. An expert swimmer on his marks, waiting for the gun, is gradually relaxing the tension in his toes and allowing his body to sway forward ever so slightly so that the motion won't be detected by the starter. Runners in crouching-start events have the sensation of more and more weight going over their hands, being shifted to the knuckles or fingers. The shift in weight has to be gradual not only to deceive the starter but to be sure that the end of the sway isn't reached before the gun goes off. In that case, a runner would have to reverse the direction of his sway in order to retain his balance. Result: a miserable start.

If you know the direction in which you're going to move, you want to be sure that you're swaying in that direction at the time you get the signal to start.

Often, however, we don't know which direction we'll be moving in until the instant we get the signal. In this case, it's best to have the body as still as possible. It's not possible to still the body completely; but there are a few things you can do—as the next several principles will demonstrate.

12. *To improve your balance, focus.*

Any time you can focus on an object, or touch something, it will improve your balance and reduce the sway. In many sports, just watching the ball will do it.

Touching an object gives you a reference point, and thereby stills the body. Even a thread, which gives no support, would help your balance if you could touch it. Putting their toe to the service line helps some tennis players. A basketball player, guarding an opponent, touches the opponent's back lightly.

13. *Watch for signs that tip off your opponent's action.*

If you have a good working knowledge of body mechanics, there are other telltale movements on which you can focus. Watch your opponent's head; his body will follow his head. Or watch his waist for the tipoff to a power movement. In kicking sports, focus on the kicker's base foot; the ball will probably be kicked in the direction the base foot is pointing.

14. *Stay as low as you can, consistent with your sport.*

A stable position will greatly reduce swaying. The best position for tennis, basketball, baseball, soccer and other sports involving a ball whose flight is indeterminate is the one you would naturally assume if you were on a ship in a rough sea or riding a lurching subway. The feet are a shoulder's width apart, one foot half a step ahead of the other. Your weight is on dead center. Your knees are slightly bent.

By widening your base of support, lowering your center of gravity, and positioning it centrally in the support base, you can achieve greater stability, but at some sacrifice of your ability to move off in any direction.

15. *Use gravity to help you get started.*

To move most swiftly from an upright stance, you would first drop an inch or so before starting off. This is in accordance with a principle in physics that an immobile body requires a force to overcome inertia to start the motion. The natural and most rapid response is upward, but that puts your center of gravity so high you can't get your legs behind it. You want to assume a semicrouched position similar to a spring start. When you try it, just practice the feel of sinking and moving. You'll be redirecting the momentum from a downward path to the direction you want to go.

A batter running to first base after hitting the ball drops initially to get force behind his center of gravity. A wide receiver drops for an instant as the ball is snapped before starting downfield.

SPEEDING UP RESPONSE TIME

SEVERAL OF THE SUPER KS we've just discussed affect the speed of your body's response to action.

When you touch a hot object, an impulse goes up a nerve to the spinal cord and back again, and a reflex reaction takes place. Whether you react swiftly or slowly to the sensation depends on the type of nervous system you've inherited. Some people simply react faster than others, and nothing can be done to change your reflex time.

Response time is another matter. You have choices to make: in which direction you're going to move, how far and how fast you'll need to move, whether to move at all. Is a ball going to your left or to your right, high or low, fast or slow? Faced with these decisions, your response time may be five times slower than your reaction time. You can never eliminate that gap, but you can narrow it with training.

Obviously, experience is helpful. The same focusing techniques that reduce your sway can help you to anticipate movement: Watch your opponent's preparatory motions for cues as to force and direction. Observe his beltline and the position of his base foot. With experience, you will respond to these signals without resorting to an extensive decision-making process.

In sports involving an implement and a ball, the timing of the impact determines the flight of the ball. A right-handed batter swinging early sends the ball to left field. The same is true in tennis; if you hit early the ball will go cross-court; a ball hit late will go down the line.

But the best assist you can give yourself in cutting down your response time is learning to play relaxed. Dropping that inch or so from the ready position and moving toward the ball can be done a good deal faster with relaxed muscles than it can be with rigid ones.

Remember that it's not force of contractions that limits speed of movement; it's the swiftness with which muscles can lengthen following the contractions. If the muscles are tense, they'll lengthen slowly; if relaxed, swiftly.

You can do a great deal to diminish your tension, to begin with, by learning to focus on the things that matter in a game and dismissing those that don't. Tennis, for example, is perceived as a game between opponents. Actually, it's a game of you and the ball. Your primary concern is what's happening to that ball. The fact that there's another person on the court, manipulating the action of the ball, should not dominate your attention. Your concern is how the ball is being manipulated, not the personality of the person manipulating it. You watch the ball come to you, and you hit the ball the way you want to, and then you watch where it goes and see what happens to it once it gets there. The fact that your opponent fell down in the process can alter your strategic plans, but is irrelevant to your execution of the stroke. If you, by contrast, can get your opponent thinking about you rather than the ball, you'll be that much farther ahead.

12

Choosing a Coach/ Coaching Your Child

THERE IS A PERIOD in the development of a skill when you—or, if you're a parent, your child—would benefit greatly from some coaching. This is not to say that you can't perform without it. Millions of people learn how to swim, throw, catch, strike—all fairly complicated skills—without taking instruction. They watch good performers, read an instruction book, dip into their portfolio of existing skills. The notion that no one learns anything unless he takes a lesson from a professional is ridiculous. But what the professional can do is provide you with a useful skill sooner than you could achieve it by exploring on your own. He can also help you avoid poor mechanics that might become habitual and affect the quality of your game later on.

Once you've made the decision to take some lessons, choosing a good coach is about as vital as choosing a good broker after deciding to invest in the stock market. A coach who knows what he's doing can move you into a new class of performance; a bad one can cripple your game.

The criteria you should use in selecting a coach are identical with those you should set up for yourself when coaching your child. You are your child's first and most influential teacher. What you teach him and how you teach it shape him as a performer forever. Short of neglecting your child, there's no way around that responsibility. His first catch is with you. His first race is with you. His first questions and requests for help are directed at you. If you're like most parents, you wouldn't want it any other way. But when you give him help, you ought to know what you're doing.

In the process of learning how to choose a coach, you'll learn how to coach a child. The standards are interchangeable.

Before we examine the criteria of good coaching, however, let's consider the child as a performer. This understanding has two major benefits. First, obviously, it gives us an appreciation of the child's special idiosyncracies—vital knowledge whether we're parent or professional coach. Second, it gives us insight into our own performance profile.

What happened to you as a child by and large established your present performance level. To move to a new level of performance, you'll be greatly assisted by an understanding of what went into establishing the old one.

THE CHILD AS PERFORMER

CHILDREN ALMOST ALWAYS try too hard. They become overexcited and tend to overreact to their mistakes. They're rarely persistent; when a nine-year-old feels tired, he falls down and quits.

A child needs an image of himself as a performer. He needs to see himself as something, and he can't really do that without some support. Playing with my grandchildren on the beach one day, I noticed that one of them could run quite fast. So I put a label on him. "You're a runner!" I said. That's all I said, but I said it emphatically. Every time we've been together since, he's shown me how he can run. Not only does he enjoy it, but he sees himself as a runner, and puts himself into competitive situations where his running can be used to advantage.

The image a person has of himself and the injunctions given to him by the important people in his life pretty much dictate his life performance.

At every age, you continue to try to find out who you really are, and you depend to a great extent on the models others furnish you. It's left to few of us to break new ground.

It is a mistake to assign a role to a child that he clearly is not capable of playing; but if he picks up a bat and swings it well and hits a pretty good ball, it's important that he should be noticed. You can't make a silk purse out of a sow's ear just by saying, "You are a silk purse." But the silk purse might be going around thinking that he's a sow's ear unless he's told otherwise.

When a parent conveys his disappointment in a child's performance to the child, with either words or looks, he is not just creating added tension, he is molding the child's image of himself. Without the confidence conveyed by parents, the child can't accomplish very much.

I think I can say without immodesty that I've led a productive life. One reason—perhaps the most important reason—I have is that my parents and relatives functioned as a cheering squad for as long as I can remember. I lived in a big, three-generation home in Danbury, Connecticut. In addition to my grandparents and parents, our house included some aunts and even a few close family friends who just happened to end up living there. I was not an only child, but when my sister died at the age of four, I was at age seven the only child left. So I became the performer. I always had an audience, and I always got encouragement for what I did. Our backyard was half an acre in size. I was able to build just about anything I wanted. If my new bicycle racetrack interfered with my grandfather's garden, he would move his garden. Once I decided to build a miniature golf course on our lawn. Friends would view the construction and ask my parents, "Why are you letting Laurence mess up your lawn?" But my parents never disapproved. They, my grandparents, aunts and family friends were always ready to function as approving inspectors. Even when I played trumpet in the school band, some member of my cheering squad was present at every performance. As a result of all this reinforcement, I became a performing fool. Win or lose, I have managed to feel good about myself throughout my life. Even today, if I took you to see my eighty-five-year-old mother, you would be struck by the admiration she showers on me.

When you have an audience like that, you perform. Here I am, sixty-three years old, my colleagues are cleaning up odds and ends preparing to retire and I'm on projects that are going to last me another twenty years. I do them because they're fun. For me, work has always been play.

CHOOSING THE RIGHT EVENT

YOUR NOTION OF YOURSELF as an inept performer may have little or nothing to do with your original potential. Rather, it may be almost entirely due to an improper selection of your sport years ago by a parent or coach. If you weren't successful, you didn't have fun—and you lost confidence in your ability to perform.

Helping a child select an activity that's right for him at this moment in his development may be the most important coaching advice you or an instructor can give.

At each age level through adolescence, you find children who are physically elite. These are the young people for whom organized competition is designed.

Rather than playing with ordinary children their own age, they want highly organized team play, with coaches, referees and all the trappings of competition.

For the physically elite this is fine, but any kind of undue pressure that forces a child to compete who doesn't want to or isn't physically qualified to is tantamount to a life sentence. When a child strives because of parental or peer pressure to fit into the competitive mold before he's ready to, he sets up a crippling conflict between the external image of a Little League uniform and the internal reality of noncompetence. The groundwork has now been laid for poor performance through life relative to his real abilities.

A child doesn't have the maturity to put such things in their proper focus. He wants to receive the same attention as his physically gifted friends. He needs his parents desperately at this moment. It is they who must encourage him to recognize who he is and what he does best.

If your child's skill is such that he doesn't quickly adapt to the requirements of such high-skill sports as basketball, baseball or tennis, you can encourage him to go out for soccer or track or other sports that put a lower premium on skill. He can get all the thrills of competition and recognition in these sports. In the meanwhile, he's getting a good basic conditioning, so that when his skill attributes do develop a few years later, and he's ready to enter the skill sports, he'll have the advantage of superior condition.

High-skill sports are those whose movements are so specialized and complex that they require nearly full maturation as well as considerable practice. Not all Little Leaguers, for example, can pitch or play first base because of the advanced ball-handling requirements. In a few years, however, when the slower-maturing players have "caught up," some of them may play these difficult positions even better than their more precocious teammates.

Maturation is as important as experience in determining the child's ability to perform in organized sports requiring a high level of skill. Until the more slowly maturing child catches up, he can experience the joys of expression in movements requiring skills of intermediate complexity, in recreational games.

Intermediate skills are those that can be acquired with very little practice and can be performed by immature players. Such players may not yet be able to pitch a baseball into the strike zone with reliability, or throw a curve ball, but they can, after a few guided trials, successfully master the horizontal throw for distance, which gets them into the game in center field. At the intermediate level the child may be able to jump for distance but not yet be able to master the high jump; be able to tumble well but not be ready for formal gymnastics; be able to handle a street bicycle expertly but be a long way away from organized cycling competition; be able to skate like a dream but be all over his feet in ice hockey; and be as at home as a fish in the water but be incapable of executing the racing starts, speed strokes and fast turns required in competitive swimming.

Below the intermediate level are the elementary skills found in child's play. Elementary play skills are those that every baby seems to be able to perform without practice. Grasping an object and throwing it down are performed reflexively. Fortunately for the parent, throwing horizontally doesn't come naturally. Shortly after a child commences to walk, the hopping action appears as a further generalized movement. Hopping is so elementary that it doesn't have to be taught or even encouraged. The child is happy just to be hopping.

There is no profit to child or parent at this point in trying to teach him to jump. When he needs to do it, and is mature enough, he will quickly learn to jump— and do it just about as well as a child who was trained to perform such tricks as a baby.

Other forms of child's play are splashing, paddling and primitive swimming in warm water, pedaling a tricycle or other stable vehicle, climbing and sliding.

In this play, the spirited and well-coordinated child may be forecasting a talent for championship sports performance, but more importantly at the moment, he is a maximum performer at child's play.

The important lesson to give a child is that maximum performance is not just for the elite. It's *his* maximum, rather than some ideal or comparative maximum, that should concern him.

One further word about physically precocious children. Among a group of 20 eight-year-olds, there will probably be one who stands out as far superior to his peers. He or she may be better suited to play with twelve-year-olds, provided the play is serious fun and not serious work. Physically precocious children have no problem with skills; where they have trouble is in a game with high emotional impact—being booed when they make an error, or receiving body contact that communicates itself to them as an attack or form of rejection.

The way to help such a child—or any eight-year-old, for that matter—is to direct his attention away from his opponents and to the ball. The eight-year-old has little or no sense of the game. For him, the game is a man-to-man experience; he wants to wrestle, play the man, pile on. Directing his attention to the ball will do wonders for his game, not simply in terms of his ability to execute, but in his ability to handle the game's emotional components.

THE PLAY'S THE THING

SINCE CHILDHOOD, we've used play as a means of expression, development and communication. When you examine it, play is a serious thing; when you're playing a game to your utmost, it's no laughing matter. But it is fulfilling, and it does provide a harmony of spirit in action.

In this age of science and industrialization, however, there is a strong tendency to make the conditioning process for maximum performance a production-line experience. Every step of the way is rigidly prescribed and formally executed. This method contradicts and at times annuls the play element of sports, and thereby inhibits learning.

There are scientific principles that lead to improvement of the body and its performance. We'll be getting to them in the next chapters. But these principles don't have to be practiced in an industrialized way to be effective. If they are so practiced, they may prove to be self-defeating.

I always loved to run. The rhythm, the air rushing past my ears, the sense of progression as I rushed toward my goal gave me a joyous feeling that nothing else could duplicate. Both my high school and college coaches told me that I had an excellent running style and could be a champion if I worked on it. They prescribed rigid training programs—and running was suddenly a business. I no longer enjoyed it and soon gave it up. Looking back, I think that if my coaches had been like the people in my home, and had just let me run, finding my own rhythm and style in the process, I might have become a first-rate performer.

Conditioning and skill development should enhance the sport, not take the fun out of it. We have the phenomenon today of girl swimmers, champions at fifteen, retiring from the sport. They've been in the water since they were eight. Now they're at an age when social relationships are changing and important. They say, "Now I'm going to live a full life. No more life-consuming practices." The proper conditioning should help to shorten practice periods, make them more enjoyable and enable the competitor to live a full life in addition to her conditioning program.

Roy Cochran won his Olympic gold medal working out just an hour a day. You may not have to ruin your life to perform to your maximum or become a great performer.

Today's world-class performers resist the kind of coach's schedule that calls for repetitions of a given distance or execution of a performance at a prescribed pace monitored by computers. They are so wise. There is a scientific basis for believing that if you adjust your work to what's going on inside you, you're most apt to do the amount of work that's required for ideal training, whereas if you train by external measures, you do either too little or too much.

A child doesn't analyze or pay attention to his mechanics. All he knows is what he wants to accomplish. This innocence is the ideal frame of mind with which to approach performance. Somehow, we want to get back to that childlike innocence and wonder, trusting our bodies to do what we ask of them. For sheer performance, and even rapid learning, we need the wholeness, the positiveness and the zest for exploration of children.

As far as I'm concerned, it's an appreciation of these attitudes that most distinguishes the good coach, whether it's you or a professional. From this attitude flows the most constructive approach to teaching.

Now for its particulars.

THE GOOD COACH LETS HIS PUPILS
FIND THEIR OWN WAY

THE GOOD COACH knows there's no "picture-book" way to perform. He knows that no two people move exactly alike. He respects your idiosyncratic movement behavior and suggests movement habits that are already comfortable to you. He starts you where your movements indicate you should start. He might show you how to execute a movement, but he lets you develop your own style, helps you refine your excess motion, and allows your own motion characteristics to persist.

You have to have some image of what you're trying

to do to begin with. It's the manner in which that image is presented that's so important. If you're coaching a child, for example, and you say, "There is only one right way to do this, and I don't want to see you doing it any other way," then you're not allowing the child the right and freedom to perform in terms of his idiosyncratic movement. Far better to say, "Try doing it something like this." Then demonstrate your concept of what the movement is supposed to achieve. The child gets the feel of the movement and its result, with no requirement to mimic exactly the postures of the demonstrator.

As quickly as possible thereafter, the movement should be executed with the implement of the sport and at game speed.

It's possible that you can express the complete idea to a child right from the start, without breaking it down into component ideas. If you can, you're that much farther ahead. I would certainly advise you to take a crack at it. I've seen children not much older than toddlers so determined to swim that they just fall into the water and start swimming.

THE GOOD COACH FIRST SEES
WHAT YOU CAN DO

NO MATTER HOW INACTIVE you've been, you already have a repertoire of skills to apply to almost any event you undertake. A good coach finds out what it is you can already do, rather than asking you to try something strange. For example, the serve in tennis, as complicated a motion as it is because of simultaneous movements of both arms, is, at its base, almost exactly like the movement involved in throwing a ball. The good coach will ask you to throw a ball before he ever asks you to try to serve. Better yet, he will have an old racket with him and ask you to throw it just as you would a ball. In the actual serve, the difference is that you hang on to the racket.

THE GOOD COACH NEVER MENTIONS
BODY PARTS

HE HAS ANALYZED the sport, knows the rights and wrongs, sees the hundreds of things that are taking place, but transmits all this knowledge to his players in terms of a simple, workable cue. That cue is almost never expressed in terms of body parts. Instead of "Bend your knees more," the good coach says, "Stay low so that you can play from under the ball."

"Move into the ball," is a cue that says nothing about the mechanics of the body, the position of the legs or the rotation of your trunk.

Keeping your eye on the ball is vital in every sport because it keeps your body in position. The way that translates in golf is usually, "Keep your head down." A bad cue, because it calls attention to a body part. Far better to say, "Focus sharply on the back of the ball until after the ball has left." That keeps your body in position without focusing attention on your body. "Focus" in this context says nothing about the eyes.

Instructions should be conveyed in terms of a movement or a goal or a feeling.

"Move your clubhead through the ball" says nothing about the physics or the body parts involved, even though both are involved in the movement. "Take your racket back" doesn't make you think of your back and shoulders, even though the objective of taking the racket back is to cause the body to turn in a windup motion so that the powerful back and shoulder muscles can assist your stroke.

The body responds better to suggestion than it does to specific detail. Suppose you want to convey to someone that he should be lighter on his feet while dancing. You wouldn't want to tell him to rise on his toes or move with his knees flexed, chest elevated and elbows raised slightly from his sides, even though these are postures characteristic of persons who are light on their feet. You'd say, instead, "Behave as though you weigh less. Feel that you're all but flying." The changes you're seeking to induce would then come about naturally and automatically.

Movement comes from the suggestion of how it's going to feel and what the result is going to be. That integrates the whole organism, gets it synchronized and brings forth the proper coordination. It takes care of postural adjustments. Taking each one of these things separately in an anatomical and physical way destroys the sense of what you're trying to do. The only time you may need to do that is when a beginner is so confused that he needs to be led through the basic movements or positions. But it should be emphasized that mentioning body parts is an artificial means to get started and will be dismissed as soon as the student gets the feel of the action.

At the outset, teaching without mentioning body parts may seem impossible to coaches used to more traditional methods, but every sport can be taught better using imaginative analogies, and once a coach is convinced of that point, he can become quite creative. As we were preparing this book, for example, we asked Bob Schimke, a skiing instructor at Bear Valley, California, if he could invent an image that would assist a practiced but mediocre skier to move to a new level of performance. The skier's problem was perhaps the most vexing one in the sport—an unwillingness to commit her body in such a manner that her weight helped turn her skis. Like many beginning and intermediate recreational skiers, she unconsciously drew away from the snow, as though that would keep her from falling, whereas the closer one skis to the snow, the more security—and effectiveness—increases. To cure the problem, Bob proposed to his student that she think of herself as an engine, and her skis as tracks along which she was running. Instead of asking her to bend her knees—the most common plea in the sport— he exhorted her to use her "drive mechanism" to power around the turns. Once she got that feeling of power and sense of security, Bob changed the image. Now he asked her to imitate the lumbering up-and-down movement of a gorilla. Within four days, the student, who had been hung up for years in the stem christie, was making linked parallel turns. "I must have done a significant up-down," she noted later, "because I split the seat of my long johns."

THE GOOD COACH ACCENTUATES THE POSITIVE

A STUDENT SHOULD be told what he should do the next time, rather than what he did wrong the last time. The bad image doesn't provide a helpful feedback cue. If I say to you, "Don't do this," and imitate what you did wrong, it gives you nothing positive to work on.

Your history of learning has to be a history of success. You build the second block on top of the first, and you don't go on to block three until blocks one and two are cemented together. Showing a player what he's doing wrong can be an irresistible temptation, but the coach should realize that the improper movement results from a lesson that's been too difficult to grasp. The sequence of skills must always be kept at the level of success of the student.

ABOVE ALL, THE GOOD COACH KEEPS THE ANALYSIS TO HIMSELF

THE COACH KNOWS an enormous amount about why things happen—but he never communicates that knowledge to you. He knows that too much knowledge will turn his players into motor idiots. It's not necessary for you to know what you're doing wrong, or the mechanics of it, for you to change your stroke. When the teacher talks to a player in terms of body mechanics, bone levers and muscle function, he's not teaching performance, he's teaching kinesiology. That knowledge might be fascinating, but it does nothing for the person's play, and almost certainly hinders him.

It's a characteristic of a naive instructor to try to teach too much. Instead of taking one aspect that is basic, rehearsing and perfecting it, the novice instructor tries to take the sport from every aspect and teach and drill in too many elements. Now he's being an analyst rather than a coach.

He might discover from analysis of high-speed motion pictures and sessions with a kinesiologist that a pitched ball is released well before the arm is fully extended. This is important knowledge to him. Now he knows *not* to tell his pitcher to do anything with his wrist or hand when the arm is near full extension, whereas before he probably told his pitcher to flick his wrist and hand at the end of the delivery on the assumption that this is what made a baseball curve. He knows that a curve comes solely from finger placement. His cue to the athlete is only a fraction of the above—how to place his fingers on the ball. The athlete doesn't need to know why. To explain the why of performance to an athlete is overcoaching. You're messing up his neuromuscular coordination.

There is a great temptation for the novice or parent coach to violate this principle. They try to tell all they know to the person being taught.

THE ANALYST, THE COACH AND THE PLAYER: THREE APPROACHES TO THE SAME RESULT

THE ANALYST, the coach and the player all have the same goal in mind—to maximize performance. But they all approach that goal—or should approach it—from three different viewpoints, speaking three different languages.

Let's demonstrate that statement in terms of a single objective—hitting a ball hard with an implement.

The analyst knows from research data that the velocity of a ball, which gives distance in golf, home runs in baseball and the big serve in tennis, depends on two major factors. The first is the velocity of the implement as it strikes the ball. The second, as we mentioned in the chapter on Super Ks, is the firmness, almost the rigidity, with which the hand holds the striking implement.

To the analyst, this presents a problem, as well as an opportunity. He has isolated one secret of power, but he must now figure out how strength can be applied to the grip without destroying the rest of the swing.

It's obvious that you can't hold an implement with a steel grip through the three stages of a stroke—backswing, central action and follow-through—because this would produce the very muscular tension you're trying to eliminate. It's equally obvious that the shift in gears of your muscles can't be done in a jerky motion—which means that you can't suddenly clench the implement any more than you can abruptly remove your foot from a clutch. So the analyst reasons that the grip should be tightened smoothly throughout the central action, and that the grip should be firm throughout the stroke so that the transition needn't be so great. All of the tension should be in the hand; the rest of the body should remain fluid.

So much for the analyst. How does the coach make the transition from analysis to player action? Somehow he must convey what it feels like to accomplish the objective, but without making his pupils conscious of his body parts.

An innovative coach might have his pupil begin by hitting two nails into a board. He tells the pupil to hit the hammer "through" the nails—that is, to have the feeling that the hammer is actually following through. But one nail is to be hit with a light grip, the other with a tight grip. The pupil soon sees that a well-aimed stroke with a tight grip drives the nail farther into the board and with less vibration than does a well-aimed stroke with a loose grip.

All the player needs to know is that the ball must be struck with unyielding hands. He should never be concerned with the tightening process. His cue is a word or an experience that gives him a sense of tightness. "Pound the ball, just like you pounded the nail," the coach might say. Were you to pound a nail, you would see that the hand naturally grips the handle harder as the head approaches impact; after impact, the hand releases somewhat, but the grip remains firm throughout.

The player knows nothing about the change in pressure of the grip, nothing about the time at which that pressure change occurs, or the spatial relationship; all he knows is that when that ball is struck, it should be struck as though the implement and hand are welded together. He learns to do it just by doing it—hitting the ball from different positions, all with this feeling of power.

The coach may be an analyst, but when he talks to the performer, he talks in terms of the performance, not in terms of the analysis. He formulates a "do it" cue.

Suppose you're hurting your elbow throwing a fastball, and you go to a pitching specialist for advice. The specialist might take a high-speed motion picture, study the action and watch the position of the elbow joint throughout the pitch and the follow-through to see where the traumatic stresses are occurring. The analyst needs to know the detailed anatomy of the bone, muscles and ligaments in order to understand the mechanics of these stresses. But once he's figured out where in that pitching motion the trauma is taking place, he must—if he's to be successful—translate all that knowledge into what the pitcher should do, not what he'd been doing, or why what he'd been doing had been hurting his arm.

If you as a pupil are interested in why something happens, the good coach waits until you are away from the arena and then cautions that you are trading performance for analysis if you push him for details.

THE LESSON

A GOOD COACH never gives more than three new elements in any lesson. This is about all a person is able to learn. And he never gives a lesson on the day you are to perform. You should never ask for one, because the lesson will almost certainly ruin your performance.

Your first lesson with the coach is a trial lesson in every sense. You can't really rely on his reputation or the judgment of a friend. Each person has a different experience with the same coach. Basically, you select a coach who can give you the cue that makes sense to you, one that results in almost immediate improvement and doesn't devastate your game.

Never sign up for a series of lessons blindly, even if the price is advantageous. There are things you want to know about your professional before you make a commitment. Take one lesson to see what kind of coaching you get.

Remember that it's you who are learning. It's your task to improve your game. Evaluate your lesson in terms of what you've been given to work on. Is it simple, comfortable and workable for you? Has the task been assigned in terms of what you can accomplish? You can respect a coach for his knowledge of the game and his own playing ability, but he's not the coach for you if he hasn't led you into an easy system of change.

13

Conditioning for
Maximum Performance

REACHING MAXIMUM PERFORMANCE is a step-by-step
process that produces changes in your body and in the
work the body is able to do. The changes in the quality of your body have to do with fitness. The changes
in the work the body is able to do have to do with
skill.

Because both fitness and skill are measurable, the
steps leading to them are minute but definite. The effort required to take each step should be about the
same—so that the body never needs to be taxed beyond its physical capacity or ability to perform.

First, you condition your body to improve fitness.
Then you work on skills. If you try to learn when
you're weak, you'll invoke extraneous motions that
soon become habitual and have to be unlearned when
you begin to perfect your event.

The nervous system uses the path of least resistance.
If you try to execute a motion with weak muscles,
your nerves will tend to enlist stronger ones to take
over if possible. This can result, for example, in a limp-
ing gait. The more you walk in this manner, the weaker
the unused muscles and the stronger the substitute
muscles become. Ultimately the habit becomes so embedded that your hip flexors, the ideal muscles to move
your legs, are excluded from the movement altogether.

The result: muscle imbalance, less than ideal movement—and possible deformity.

Any complex use of the organism magnifies these possibilities. That's why it's imperative that you build your body *prior to performing*. This doesn't mean that you have to take off for six months from your favorite sport in order to undertake a body-building regimen. It means that you should proceed in a logical fashion as you learn a sport for the first time or renew an old sport, never taking the next step until you've prepared your body for it. A world-class hurdler, for example, breaks his training into three parts: body-building, running, and hurdling. Since running is part of body-building, he integrates these two phases *prior* to setting up his hurdles. By the time he approaches the hurdles, he's in top condition. If he were to start running hurdles at the outset of the season, less-than-ideal execution would be the least of his problems. Injury would almost surely result.

When you train, you're accomplishing two things. First, you're increasing your body's capacity to do more—the muscles to contract more strongly, the circulorespiratory system to endure a higher level of activity for a longer period of time. Second, you're increasing your ability to use a greater degree of your available capacity.

The second aspect—which may well be more important than the first—combines two factors. One is motivation. The other is training. Motivation is simply your desire to do something. The more you desire to do it, the more you're willing to extend yourself—a point that, obvious as it may seem, is critical to training. By performing within a limit beyond which you feel you shouldn't go, you experience a certain degree of comfort. You might stay there forever, were it not for motivation. Now additional motivation is needed to carry you to higher levels. Because the experience of getting to your present level was so redeeming and well within your capacity, you're willing to go a step farther. Success at each step is critical; you must avoid the experience of exhaustion, injury or failure, lest you lose your desire to improve. This is why you must be content to take your time if you want to use more and more of your capacity. Ideally, the progression is so gradual you scarcely realize that more of your capacity is being utilized.

THE MIRACLE OF TRAINING

MANY PEOPLE, probably most people, are turned off by the thought of training because they believe that it becomes progressively tougher. The truth is that as you train you perform better and better without any increased degree of exertion. If you're training properly, it may even seem that, day by day, you're getting the same workout. You can do more, you can do it faster, but your degree of exertion isn't any greater. Once you realize this, you've made a fantastic discovery.

The world-class champion doesn't train any harder than the novice. They're both exerting the same amount of effort. In fact, the novice may be knocking himself out more than the world-class champion, because the champion has come to recognize the degree of discomfort beyond which no further benefit will accrue. So he doesn't extend himself any farther.

When you start to train, you'll exert yourself, and four months later you'll exert yourself, but your perceived exertion at four months will be no greater than it was at the outset. You'll simply be getting more done.

Your greatest risk in this phase is overeffort. You won't get where you want to go any faster by hurting yourself through overeffort than you will by working up to the point gradually, so that your body at all times is able to tolerate the new limits of your performance. This is the key to exhaustion-free exercise training—that you are always exerting at an effort that relates to your ability to exert. You never do less or more exercise than you need to achieve and maintain your desired level of fitness to perform at your best. Your guide is not the amount of work you do, but what your body signals tell you about the effect the work is having on you.

Any increase in activity to which you're unaccustomed excites your systems. Your heart rate and blood pressure increase. You breathe harder. Your muscles become more active. All these things feed back into your senses and tell you how much effort you are expending, and how close you are to your limit of exertion.

Let's use some round figures to comprehend this relationship. Ordinary manual labor is usually conducted at less than 50 percent of your capacity to exert. Fifty percent is a moderate effort, something you can do all day long. Once you go to 60 percent, this greater effort produces a slight strain on your organism. An untrained person can't work comfortably at this rate throughout the day without taking some rest periods.

At 70 percent of maximum exertion, the work feels a little bit heavy. It's not something you want to keep up for very long, whether it's playing basketball or shoveling sand. Half an hour to an hour at a time will do for most of you.

Eighty percent exertion is very heavy work. The maximum time you'd want to spend on this work would vary between one minute and half an hour at a time. Chopping wood is a good example of an 80 percent effort for all but a lumberjack.

Ninety percent effort is extremely heavy. Thirty to sixty seconds at that rate is about all you can take, unless you are trained for it.

One hundred percent effort can't be endured for more than 30 seconds by the untrained person.

The magic in training is twofold: What required a 70 percent effort for a particular task at the outset needs only a 60 percent effort for the same task in short order, primarily due to an improvement in skill. And your ability to sustain a fairly heavy effort for a longer period of time increases, mostly due to an improvement in fitness.

We said at the outset that one objective of maximizing performance is to get twice as much done with half the effort. Just practicing the event itself will improve both skill and fitness somewhat, but won't give you that extra we're working for to make the difference between a mediocre and a maximal performance. The event itself probably does not stress the various systems of the body adequately to produce an optimal training effort. It is necessary to supplement the practice of the event with other activities.

OVERLOAD: THE KEY TO TRAINING

You MAY RECALL the story of Milo of Crotona, who lifted a calf each day until it became a bull. The story illustrates a primary principle of training. To become more proficient at whatever you attempt, you want to do just a fraction more each day. This principle is known as "overload."

If the load on your body is constant from one day to another, you'll gradually adapt to that load. Very soon, the load will produce less and less training effect. You'll still be better off than had you done nothing, but you won't be in nearly as good shape as you would have been had you gradually increased the load.

There are a number of ways to make certain that the benefit of training is continuous.

Recently a young man in my class on conditioning for maximum performance made a five-dollar bet with one of his fraternity brothers that within 60 days he could do 100 pushups. At the time he made the bet, he was capable of only 40 pushups. He presented the problem to the class: what was the ideal training program to help him reach his goal? Some of the students suggested that he follow a straight-line program—an extra pushup each day. But that was training by overload, back to the Milo principle. Other students reasoned correctly that he couldn't train by load alone, because he would exhaust before reaching his goal. You never train to exhaustion, because you're always pitting capacity against injury if you do. If he pulled a muscle or inflamed his tendinous tissue, his chance of reaching his goal was finished.

The next alternative suggested for the student was that he do an enormous number of pushups in an easier position. But the class concluded that the strength gained in a different position may not transfer to the standard pushup position.

Progressive overloading, it became apparent, has to be approached through a variety of means. You can't just keep adding a pound a day and you can't keep adding one more repetition each day. The day comes when you can't do more. The big mistake in any kind of training is to set a number and try to achieve that number and assume that, if you do, you've done your training. You may by chance be getting just the right training effect—but you are more probably getting either too much of a strain or too little training effect.

Finally, the class reached a consensus. The best approach would be to begin at a comfortable level of pushup exercise and intersperse repetitions of that exercise with periods of rest. This method is called *interval training*. To use it effectively, gauge the pushups in the work interval in terms of achieving a fairly heavy perceived effort rather than a number of pushups. Gauge the period of rest by the feeling of recovery rather than a number of minutes. Then experiment with these variables to see how the body responds. Change one variable, then another and another until the goal is reached.

There are three variables: intensity, duration and frequency.

Intensity is effectively varied when each bout of an

activity is performed with a shade more exertion than the previous one. To a person at a low level of fitness, this could mean something so simple as walking more briskly than he is accustomed to walking. Just that will give him the overload he needs to produce a conditioning effect. The athlete working at near capacity must employ variables in addition to intensity in order to achieve a training benefit.

The *duration* of an exercise is determined by the time required to produce a training effect or overload. In the case of a muscle contraction, the effect is almost immediate. Beyond ten seconds, you're getting little additional benefit. In the case of circulorespiratory training, the duration must be at least three minutes, the time it takes for the heart to respond to the body's need for oxygen, and for the chemical adjustments to be made in the working cells. Until these things happen there is little training benefit. Duration should be progressively increased until it's somewhat in excess of the duration of the event you're training for.

Frequency of training has to do with the time that elapses between successive bouts of exercise. After each bout, a training effect persists for about a day; then there is a gradual decline in your adaptation, and you de-adapt. If you cease training for more than three days, you're in effect losing a great deal of the benefit of the workout that you had three days before.

The training program his fellow students worked out for the young man whose goal was to do 100 pushups made use of all three variables.

First, he would cut the number of pushups he could do in half, and make that his "set" for training. Then he would double his target number. Every hour, he would do 20 pushups, until he had done 200 during the day. If he found that he couldn't do that many, he would cut the "set" until he found a number that he could do each hour until his total reached 200. Once he had succeeded at that level, he would then add one pushup a day to each set until he could do 10 sets of 20. Then he would start reducing the time between the pushups—say five minutes every hour—until he reached the point where his period of recovery was insufficient for him to maintain his sequence. Then he would increase that time slightly, and gradually add more pushups to his sets.

My student lost his bet because he caught the flu and couldn't train, but his task illustrates perfectly the application of overload: Ideal training involves changing just one of many variables, until that variable reaches a constant. Then you change another, and then another until you reach your goal.

TOTAL FITNESS AND MAXIMUM PERFORMANCE

OUR BOOK, *Total Fitness: In 30 Minutes a Week,* established a dynamic new concept of fitness. You didn't need to kill yourself trying (and usually failing) to conform to some idealized notion of the conditioned body; you needed only to condition yourself to live life fully *at your level of existence*. That is, if you weren't employed by a professional football team, you didn't need a professional football player's strength or stamina. You were totally fit, we said, if you had enough energy to fully live your working day, to enjoy your evenings and recreation and to have a reserve for ordinary emergencies.

Anyone who wants to maximize his performance must begin with a certain base of fitness. How one achieves this fitness base will be old hat to readers of *Total Fitness*. Those who have not read that book, or those who have and wish to review its principles, will find a brief summation in the next chapter.

We're starting with the assumption that you're not atrophied or weak or in poor circulorespiratory condition, that you're not overweight and don't have any joint problems. If you do have any of these problems, then you should start with a medical checkup and the *Total Fitness* program.

That program ends at a maintenance level that enables you to retain fitness for daily life activities which are not strenuous. If you are going to perform activities that require strength and endurance beyond what you've been needing in ordinary life situations, these capacities can be built in the same way that you built your strength and endurance from a subfit to a totally fit level.

Fitness relates precisely to your need for it.

Example: In golf and tennis, you need a little more strength than you would require if you weren't playing these games. But you don't need the strength of a weight lifter.

Whether you're working on your muscles or developing circulorespiratory endurance, your need determines your degree of exercise. Even three long sets of tennis or eighteen tough holes of golf don't require the endurance you'd need to run a marathon.

Running fifty miles or chinning a thousand times demonstrates your capacity to perform these stunts, but it says little about your circulorespiratory condition or your muscle strength. If you don't intend to do these things, you don't need the fitness they require. You can't use strength that isn't needed. If you're wrestling or weight lifting or playing the line in football, strength is usable to its utmost. Otherwise, if you're giving all your effort to getting stronger than you need to be, you're wasting your time.

Let's now apply this elastic concept of fitness to maximum performance.

SPECIFICITY

IF YOU WANT TO MAXIMIZE your game—whatever it is—you are increasing your fitness needs. This means that you will need to, and want to, condition to meet those needs. It means working a little longer than you would if you only wanted to keep fit to live your day fully, enjoy your recreation and have a reserve for emergencies. Above all, it means working *specifically* to develop the strengths you need for the game you want to play.

"Specificity" means the special adaptation that is made to the type of demands being imposed. It applies to work or play. Just because you are conditioned to engage in a sport doesn't mean you're conditioned to chop wood or clean a house. In *Total Fitness*, we described the woman who returned after a skiing vacation superbly conditioned—for skiing. The first day she cleaned her house, she strained her muscles.

The body responds to demands imposed on it. Form follows function. As you function habitually in a certain way, your body conforms its shape to the new demand.

Getting in shape for one event doesn't get you in shape for another. A basketball player who increases his running endurance during his season doesn't increase his swimming endurance proportionately. A competitive swimmer can't run up and down a basketball court much more effectively at the end of the swimming season than at the beginning.

Conditioning for maximum performance is a program in itself. The best single way to train for a sport is to practice the sport. But if your goal is to move into a higher class of play, there's more to it than that.

When you play a match every day, you improve up to a point, particularly if you play against better and better players. But in doing so, you're using the limit of your present strength and endurance capacities and skills in every game. You're fatigued at the end and feel that you've given your all. But you're not improving your condition as well as you could.

When you're using all you have in the latter part of the contest—the point where winning takes place— you miss the crucial shots because of the fatigue that inevitably comes before exhaustion. Psychologically, you're further handicapped. You know from experience that you're not at your best in the closing moments of a contest. So you lose your confidence.

The maximum performer does it another way. In training, he concentrates on all the elements he needs to develop a reserve of strength, endurance and whatever else the game demands. During the match, he plumbs but never empties that reserve. He finishes his match with ease; even though he's played his best, he's never exhausted.

PROFILING YOUR PERFORMANCE NEEDS

TRAINING FOR MAXIMUM PERFORMANCE is exquisitely efficient. You do what you need to do, and not an ounce more. Most amateur athletes assume that staying in shape for their sport automatically includes daily bouts of jogging. Unless their sport includes a lot of movement at jogging speed, they're mostly wasting their time. Jogging might be beneficial at the outset of pre-season training to gently condition the body tissues for unusual stresses and strains, but it gives no training value for a specific event.

Suppose you're a tennis player. About the only time you move at jogging speed on a tennis court is when you're retrieving balls during your warmup. To train for tennis excellence, you train at game speed.

Whatever the sport, conditioning for maximum performance is performed in the same posture, with the same intensity and rhythm inherent in the event. But it's not *just* the event; it's the manner in which you perform that event—or wish to. If tennis is your game, do you play singles or doubles? Your conditioning program will vary, depending on your answer. Do you play, or wish to play, an hour every day? Two hours twice a week? Do you play in tournaments? Are the tournaments decided in three- or five-set matches? Every response changes your program.

We're going to set up your program now in terms of your objectives. Because each person approaches his activity in a different way, determined by his age, physical capacity and objectives, each training program should be and is different.

It's up to you now to decide what kind of performer you want to be. Provide yourself with a good challenging goal—but be sure at the same time that you won't literally or figuratively break your heart.

Remember the human sense of maximum: to be as good as you can be in the time you're willing to commit.

We're going to devise your program with a convenient rating scale that will tell you at a glance where the emphasis needs to be in your conditioning, so that you spend your time and effort where it counts the most.

CONDITIONING PRIORITIES

LOW—Some, but minor importance. A certain degree of development necessary, but high development not needed. Usually accomplished in early conditioning.

MODERATE—Important, but not usually a limiting factor. May be called on occasionally, so needs to be developed to a fair degree.

HIGH—Of central importance, often the factor on which success or failure hinges. The primary goal of conditioning and maintenance.

ELEMENTS	PRIORITIES

Muscle mass
Muscle endurance
Muscle strength
Cardiorespiratory endurance
Mobility
Durability of joints or ligaments
Toughness of skin
Ability to relax

Now we're going to show you how you would analyze your activity in terms of the demands it makes on these elements of performance. Elements with high priorities will get the most attention. If you don't need a lot of strength for the sport, for example, there's no point in building your strength beyond your need. You're better off investing the effort and time elsewhere. Remember to consider *how* you intend to play the sport. If you're proposing to play goalie on a soccer team, your program of conditioning will differ radically from that of the forwards on the same team. You don't want to devote hours to something that isn't productive.

First let's identify the priorities.

Muscle mass is determined by the size of fibers in your tissues. You need mass in order to have something to work with; you achieve it by repeating efforts of moderately high intensity—for example, exercising with a load that you can lift only fifteen to twenty times. Developing the muscle mass you need is a prelude to developing muscle endurance and strength.

Muscle endurance enables you to contract your muscles many times without developing fatigue.

Muscle strength is the brute force you can apply in an all-out rapid single contraction of a muscle.

Circulorespiratory endurance is the ability of your heart and lungs to keep you moving for a long time.

Mobility is your body's flexibility—ability to reach, turn and bend.

Durability of joints or ligaments enables you to withstand sudden jolts and repeated shocks.

Toughness of skin relates to ability to withstand friction or tearing.

Ability to relax is the capacity to release excess tension in the body.

Now, let's rate each of the elements in terms of its importance to an event—L for low, M for moderate and H for high—and record each rating alongside the element. Suppose, for example, we were analyzing tennis for someone who played competitive singles.

Does tennis require muscle mass? A certain amount, but not an exceptional amount. So we'd place an M in the rating column.

Muscle endurance? Absolutely. A lot of running, jumping and movement of the arms. An H would be marked in the rating column.

Muscle strength? A great deal in the hand and forearm, a moderate amount in the rest of the body. We'll put our H in the rating column, but make the note "forearm" alongside as a reminder that the need for strength is localized.

Circulorespiratory endurance? Tennis is not a continuous all-out event like a mile run, but there are enough periods of prolonged rallies involving successive starts and sprints to tax anyone's stamina. So we need an H here to be sure we have this stamina when we need it.

Mobility? We'll give this one a "high." It's important, but not maximally important as it would be to a gymnast or a swimmer.

Durability of joints or ligaments? A great deal of strain, requiring much preparation. An H in the rating column.

Toughness of skin? Tennis has a terrific tendency to cause blisters. It's important to toughen the hands and feet. An H in the rating column.

Ability to relax? A fairly important element, so it rates an H.

Summing up your program if you were trying to

achieve proficiency in tennis, here's what you would do:

Concentrate more on muscle endurance than on developing muscle bulk or strength, except for the strengthening of the hand and forearm.

Develop circulorespiratory endurance by working up to game speed and a little higher for a period a little longer than the length of an extended match.

Give a healthy amount of attention to developing your mobility; total attention to exercises that build up the knee and ankle joints and ligaments; careful attention to fitting your shoes and gradually toughening the skin of your hands and feet; and a respectable amount of attention to learning to relax.

One important caution: The need for various qualities depends on the manner in which you play your game, the intensity and your expectations. The priorities assigned here are for the average player who wants to improve and is willing to work at it.

Later on, after we've learned how to condition for maximum performance, we'll help you put the process into the perspective of your own sport. All that's important to remember at this point is the principle that training should correspond to your need.

A BONUS FOR BEGINNERS

BEING OUT OF SHAPE at the outset of a training program is something of a psychological bonus. From your starting point, you're going to improve at a much more rapid rate than the trained performer.

It's the first exposure that has the greatest effect when the body is adapting to any new condition. Subsequent exposures to the new condition help to improve the body's responses, but the gains become less and less as the adaptation becomes more and more complete.

I call this training phenomenon the "effect of first exposure" and it applies whether you're exposing yourself for the first time to heat, high altitude, heavy loads or fast movement. That single exposure does more to acclimate you to the next exposure than the next exposure does to the third, and so on in ever diminishing proportion.

Nearly half of all the improvement you can expect will be achieved in the first quarter of your training program. As you progress, the gains become less and less pronounced, until, near the end, they are almost unnoticeable. The very slight gains in performance ability and capacity at the end of a training program

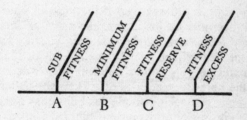

are made at great expense of time and energy. It takes a dedicated athlete or fitness fanatic to commit himself to work that much for that little gain.

The point is that you can make measurable strides in your performance without that low-yield investment. If you want to make the investment, it's entirely up to you. But by the time you're ready to make that decision, you will have advanced to a condition far beyond the condition in which you began.

Be sure that added training is going to be profitable. You'll want to develop enough strength to play the sport, but not more than you need.

Point B would be the minimum level of fitness you'd need to perform your event. At point B you're able to last out an ordinary match. It would be to your advantage to train to point C, in order to have a sufficient reserve for the occasional more-arduous-than-normal match or oppressive climatic conditions. But you'd really want to think carefully about the benefits to be gained by advancing to point D. Could you really use them? Even if they might increase your fitness to a fractional degree, would you become more proficient if you invested the time and effort on the further development of your skill?

WARMING UP AND COOLING DOWN

PERFORMANCE IS IMPROVED if the muscles have been slightly warmed up just before the activity. There are two key ideas here. *Slightly:* It does you no good to overheat or dissipate energy you'll need for the event unless you happen to be a baseball pitcher or a ballet dancer with very special needs. They are under such strain and need such extreme flexibility that a sacrifice in stamina is made to prevent injury. In other cases, if you begin to perspire heavily, you've warmed up excessively. As you become more and more overheated, your body loses more and more of its capacity to continue useful physical work. *Just before:* If you complete your warmup half an hour before your event and then sit, you've all but lost the value of the warmup, and you may even stiffen up so that you are worse off than if you hadn't warmed up at all. To be most effective, a warmup should be completed no more than a minute or so before your event.

Failure to warm up before vigorous activity can risk tearing of muscle fibers from tendons. The muscles most frequently torn in this fashion are the antagonists to the muscles that are contracting to move the body. These "cold" muscles are in opposition to the force and are at the mercy of the momentum of the action as well as the force of contracting muscles.

In our workouts, we're going to do two kinds of warmups. The first is a *general* warmup, unrelated to the performance; it prepares the body overall to function well during strenuous effort. During this warmup blood circulation increases, as does respiratory capacity. Oxygen becomes more accessible to your cells. The muscle temperature rises slightly, which facilitates a faster speed of all chemical actions, including those that transmit nerve impulses. The muscles contract and relax faster. General warmup helps to prevent muscle soreness and stiffness, and increases your capacity to move more freely.

Specific warmups relate to the actual movements of your event. They rehearse the nervous systems that control movement. You become familiar with the complex movements of a contest, especially those that use your newly developed skills. Using the implement with which you intend to play, or throwing a ball in a manner that duplicates play, is a specific warmup.

To repeat, if your specific warmup is so intensive that your body temperature is raised too high, the endurance with which you perform will be diminished. A moderate warmup is always superior to a heavy warmup except, again, for people like pitchers and ballet dancers.

Don't be like the runner who leaves his race in his sweat suit. Take yours off the moment you feel warm.

Efforts to increase your range of motion should follow, not precede, vigorous exercise. The manner will be detailed at the end of Chapter 15. Here, let's just note that if you do extensive stretchouts and *then* go into a hard workout, you're going to wind up tighter than you were when you started. Forceful stretching should be done when you're warm, not when you're cold.

If one of your warmup exercises has been to dive down and touch your toes without bending your knees, you've probably shortened your range of motion rather than increased it as you'd hoped. And you can hurt your back that way. The same result occurs if you've jerked your arms rapidly from side to side or performed high kicks. Any rapidly executed, forceful stretching motion excites nerve sensors, the muscle spindles, and Golgi tendon organs, which send signals back to the central nervous system. In this case the signal is an alarm: your joints are in danger. They're being violently used. Result: your muscles tug at the joint to limit the motion and to prevent further violence. At the same time, your ligaments, tendons and fascia, the tendinous sheaths of the body that protect it against overextension, are irritated. So the result of your violent stretching exercise may be a shortening of these tissues and a decrease in your range of motion.

Increasing the range of motion is a desirable objective of exercise. A flexible body requires less energy and can move to extreme ranges. The type of exercise you do at the end of your workout soothes those reflexes that say "that's enough." These stretching exercises break adhesions and elongate tissues. If that's the sole purpose of your workout—to increase flexibility— you should have an endurance workout of ten minutes minimum, preferably twenty minutes, allowing your body to store heat and raise your body temperature, and then proceed to your stretching exercises. If the weather is cool, this is the time to wear sweat garments. Like the pitcher or dancer, you know you're going to lose endurance by raising your body heat, but you accept this loss of capacity as a compromise, in order to increase your range of motion and diminish your risk of injury.

These are the theories involved in conditioning for maximum performance. Next, for those of you who need it, we'll review the principles laid down in *Total Fitness*. Then, in the chapter after that, we'll set up your program for maximum performance exercises.

14

The Total Fitness Program

IN ORDER TO have a fitness program, you must first determine how fit you want to be.

There are three levels of satisfactory fitness. The first is the irreducible minimum below which you're going to experience degradation of function and structure. The second is a general level of fitness that provides you with a safe margin of adaptation for change, including some emergencies, and enables you to get through the day without an undue amount of fatigue. The third level is preparation for fairly strenuous recreational or occupational activity.

The third level, as we'll see in the next chapter, requires specific conditioning. If you're going skiing you've got to do preskiing exercises or you just won't ski as well.

The second level, general fitness, requires a thirty-minutes-a-week program we will detail in this chapter.

The first level, which we call *minimum maintenance*, requires nothing more than the incorporation of a few simple habits into everyday life.

But note well: Whether you want to be a superathlete or a well-conditioned person, you must still adopt these few basic habits for everyday life. In order to reach levels two or three, in other words, you've got to sustain level one. To maintain total fitness or improve your performance, you must become, habitually, a slightly more active person, incorporating five simple requirements into your everyday life.

THE FIVE REQUIREMENTS OF
MINIMUM MAINTENANCE

1. *Allover stretch:* Turn and twist your body joints to their full range of motion. Turn your head. Reach upward and backward with your arms. Twist your trunk. Bend your waist. Use everyday situations to advantage, twisting when you're looking for something, bending or stretching when you're retrieving it. If you're alert to the opportunities, cleaning house or gardening or even shopping at the supermarket can give you your mobility exercise for the day.

2. *Standup:* Stand for at least two hours each day. If you're supersedentary, you'll need at least three hours. Standing strengthens your bones and tones your blood circulation. So take phone calls standing up; hold some standup conferences; and after you've been in your chair for a while, do some work on your feet.

3. *Overload lift:* Lift something unusually heavy for a few seconds. Think of this as your daily "overload." You can maintain your muscle tone just by lifting a hefty child once a day or carrying a heavy bag or two of groceries from the market to your car.

4. *Heart walk:* Walk briskly for at least three minutes to stimulate your cardiovascular system. If you're moving briskly enough to feel your heart beating in your chest, that's okay; but if you start to feel a throbbing in your head, it's time to slow down.

5. *Caloric burn:* Burn up 300 activity calories a day in physical activity.

The energy required to maintain life is called the basal metabolic rate. You use this up, whether you do anything else or not, just to keep the body going;

pumping the heart, breathing, digesting, maintaining body temperature.

An office worker who rides to her job, takes an elevator to her floor and sits all day uses 800 calories above her basal metabolic level for these functions. Supposing her basal metabolic rate is 1500, she's burning 2300 calories doing next to nothing. If the food she's consuming exceeds that amount of calories even slightly, she's going to get fat. If she could step up her activity enough to balance her caloric intake, she would arrest this insidious accumulation of fat.

When you've been leading an otherwise sedentary life, any physical movement that increases your pulse rate twenty beats above resting level significantly steps up your metabolic rate. Walking, lifting, carrying, climbing, sexual activity—any of these will do it. Even making ordinary motions more vigorously than you normally make them will burn activity calories.

If you want to use your 300 calories up in one hour or less, you can play tennis, dig in the garden, chop wood, and so forth. The alternative, if any of these is too arduous, is to work the burning of these calories into the day. If you stretch, stand, lift and move briskly during the day, you're almost surely burning your extra 300 calories.

Minimum maintenance is dynamic. As your condition improves you can do more and more without increasing your effort. Our subsequent programs are based on the premise that you will incorporate minimum maintenance into everyday life.

Next, Total Fitness.

HOW THIS PROGRAM DIFFERS

THE TOTAL FITNESS PROGRAM is different from any other fitness program.

All other programs measure the work you produce

—the distance you run or the speed at which you run it or the number of times you can accomplish a specific task. *This* program ignores exterior accomplishments in favor of interior results. *This* system is interested in only one thing—the effect you produce on your body. *You* regulate that effect entirely. *You* produce exactly the response to effort that you wish and require.

The problem with other exercise systems is that they assign tasks that either are too difficult at the outset or become easier and easier to perform. It's all very well to run or swim faster or farther, but if your internal system is not responding to the right degree, you're not achieving fitness.

Other systems program you into specific tasks. This system offers you your choice of any activity you find enjoyable. All that matters is that the activity churns your system to a level appropriate for *your* particular circumstances.

You monitor that activity. You set the pace in terms of what the activity is doing to your circulorespiratory system—your heart and vessels and lungs. You do this by taking your pulse which you'll shortly learn to do.

The loads you lift or numbers of repetitions are not equivalent to effort. They tell you nothing about the body's response to the exercise. They don't tell you if you're working hard enough or not hard enough. There is only one way to tell whether you're working at the right intensity, and that is by measuring the amount of effort directly.

In the laboratory this can be done in many ways. We can measure how much oxygen you consume while you're working, how much air you're ventilating, how much your blood pressure is rising and how fast your heart is beating. Of all these, heart rate is the easiest to measure; it has the further advantage of computing the relative effort expended by various systems of the body and coming up with a final score, which is a reliable indicator of the intensity of physiological effort.

Any change from day to day in your physiological status automatically becomes part of the consideration in determining how much physical work you have to do. When you're fatigued or not feeling well, your heart rate responds more swiftly to stress; the weaker you are, the less work required to get your heart rate up.

In the old way of exercising, you had to perform a certain task a certain number of times. It made no allowance for the condition of your system at the moment you performed the exercise. The new way automatically compensates for your condition by using your very own computer. On days when you're not feeling well, it takes less work to obtain the desired heart rate or level of physiological activity. So if your program is to maintain a heart rate of 130 beats per minute for five minutes, you're always giving the same effort for that exercise. If you're fatigued, then you have to put out less work to reach the same effort level. As training takes place, then you have to do more work to produce the same effort.

ALL ABOUT YOUR PULSE

THE PULSE IS A PRESSURE WAVE initiated by the heart. It travels throughout your arterial system each time your heart beats.

It indicates the change in the condition of your artery at the end of each heartbeat, at the point at which you feel the change.

In most people, the pulse can be felt wherever a large artery lies near the surface—at the temple, in the throat, at the wrist, inside the thigh, on top of the foot.

When you read a pulse, you're not reading the amount of blood flowing out of the heart into the body, nor are you reading blood pressure. The pulse is nothing more nor less than an accurate index of how many times the heart is beating against the column of blood in your circulatory vessels.

But what a wonderful index it is! It informs you of every change that is taking place in your person. It tells you if your body temperature is rising or if you're cooling down. It tells you how fast you're burning up energy and using oxygen from the air. It tells you how your body is handling the chemical wastes in your blood. It tells you how your muscles are involved and working. It even tells you about the state of your emotions and attitudes. It pulls all of these things together, weighs them and comes out with a single signal that reports your overall condition.

The pulse is so simple to measure, and yet it's the body's most important single indicator of well-being, stress or illness.

Not only is the pulse a simple and reliable index, it's easy to locate and count. After light exercise, it's impossible to miss. After moderate exercise, you don't even have to search for it. If you just sit quietly, you can feel it beating.

Your pulse rate changes throughout the day. It is lowest *after* you have been asleep about six hours. On awakening it will increase five to ten beats per minute. During the day your resting pulse rate gradually increases, and at bedtime it is probably another five to ten beats per minute higher. Any activity, such as eating, elevates the pulse rate. A bout of unusually hard work, such as a Sunday of heavy gardening, can cause the pulse rate to be elevated for the rest of the day and much of the night.

An accelerated pulse rate in itself isn't dangerous. Nor does it indicate that there's something necessarily wrong with you. All it means is that the body is working under a heavy load. The efficiency of the body can be measured by how much external work is being accomplished at a moderate heart rate of about 120. If it takes very little physical work to produce this kind of heart rate, that means you're "inefficient." Your system is probably deconditioned due to lack of exercise.

The accompanying table indicates the approximate pulse rates that are reached at various intensities of continuous exercise.

SCALE OF PERCEIVED EXERTION	PULSE RATE
1 * Very, very light	Under 90
2 * Very light	90
3 * Light	100
4 * Fairly light	110
5 * Neither light nor heavy ("moderate")	120
6 * Somewhat heavy	130
7 * Heavy	140
8 * Very heavy	150
9 * Very, very heavy	160

HOW TO COUNT YOUR PULSE RATE

FIRST, YOU'LL WANT to find the best place to feel your pulse. Be active for a minute or so in any manner you wish—take a brisk walk or climb a flight of stairs—in order to amplify your pulse. Now explore the following:

   The radial artery in your wrist, just inside your
      wristbone at the base of your thumb joint.
   A carotid artery on one side of your throat, either
      just above your collarbone or below your jaw.
      Remember, don't close off the second carotid
      artery on the other side while you're doing this;
      you may shut down the blood supply to your
      brain.
   A temporal artery at the side of your forehead
      (temple) just in front of your ear. Again, press
      on one side *only*.

I prefer the radial artery in the wrist. If that's the system you elect, use the following procedure:

Place your wristwatch on your wrist so that you can see its face when the palm of your hand is up. Next, place the wrist on which you have your watch in the palm of your other hand, so that the wrist falls into the crotch between thumb and forefinger. Let the tips of your fingers curl toward your thumb. Now your third and forth fingers will rest over your pulse. The little pads at the ends of those fingers will fit right into the groove of the wrist. The pad on your middle finger is the pulse "feeler." If you press slightly against the wrist with your fingertip feeler, you should be able to find your pulse. Don't panic if you can't find the pulse at first; it takes a few minutes of practice.

What you feel at each beat is not blood flow, but a pulse wave that moves along the arteries about twelve to eighteen feet per second.

Doctors and nurses use one of several methods in taking the pulse: counting it for a minute, counting it for thirty seconds and multiplying by two, or counting

for fifteen seconds multiplying by four. We use still another method: counting for six seconds and adding a zero. We do this for a good reason. A longer count is more accurate in general terms and is ideal for taking the pulse of someone at rest, but a long count does not tell us about your exercise response as accurately as does a six-second count taken immediately after the exercise. Then the pulse (and heart) is beating at a rate that most nearly reflects the exertion you achieved during your movements. Within fifteen seconds, the pulse has diminished from that peak, within thirty seconds still more, and within a minute still more. The variation between the pulse rate immediately after exercise and the rate one minute later can be as much as thirty beats.

You're now going to determine your pulse rate by counting the number of pulses in six seconds and adding a zero to get the per-minute rate. Catch the rhythm of pulsations for a few seconds. When your pulse coincides with an easy time interval (at one of the five-second marks), start counting. Begin with "zero" as the second hand crosses over the five-second mark. If you don't say "zero" you'll miscalculate. Then count the number of pulses in six seconds.

YOUR TRAINING PULSE RATE

THE ACCOMPANYING CHART will locate your training pulse rate (TPR) for each eight-week period if you are just starting a fitness program. If you're already training at a higher pulse rate, there is no need to fall back to a lower rate.

The training pulse rate is figured by multiplying the difference between 220 and your age by 60 percent the first period, 70 percent the second, and 80 percent the third and thereafter.

If you're 40 years old, for example, the remainder

from 220 is 180. Multiplied by .60, that's 108. We round it off to 110.

AGE	TPR-1	TPR-2	TPR-3
Under 30	120	140	150
30-44	110	130	140
45-60	100	120	130
Over 60	100	110	120

TPR   = Training pulse rate.
TPR-1 = TPR for the first 8 weeks—about 60% maximum PR (220 minus your age, × .60).
TPR-2 = TPR for the second 8 weeks—about 70% maximum PR.
TPR-3 = TPR for the third 8 weeks—about 80% maximum PR.

THREE SHORT STEPS TO FITNESS

WHAT FOLLOWS APPLIES equally to men and women. The exercises are the same because the requirements are the same. Women need good muscles every bit as much as men do. To obtain good muscles, they must first develop a certain quantity of tissue. Then they must develop two muscle qualities, endurance and strength. Their work or sport requires both. Finally, the circulorespiratory endurance of a woman is no less vital to her health and fitness than is that of a man.

The total fitness program is best performed on alternate days—ten minutes a day. Three days a week. You can do more, but you don't have to. Each session is compact; it asks you to concentrate your effort into one brief span. There's no way around that requirement, because you need to raise your heart rate to be fit, and only compact action does that. But the fitness program itself spreads out over twenty-four weeks and continues throughout your lifetime.

Each of you will start these exercises according to your readiness for them. Each of you will make the exercises a little bit more difficult according to your individual capacity to extend. The degree of difficulty doesn't matter, so long as it's a slight overload for you. Don't compare what you're doing with what anyone else is doing.

THE FIRST EIGHT WEEKS: REBUILDING TISSUE

DURING THE FIRST eight weeks your ten-minute exercise session will be divided up into three parts:

1. One minute of limbering
2. Four minutes of muscle building
3. Five minutes of any continuous activity that raises your heart rate to the desired level

LIMBERING

The object of these four limbering exercises is to increase your range of motion so that you can move more easily. There is no drill. Use whatever rhythm pleases you. Don't count; there's no need. Just spend about fifteen seconds on each exercise.

1. *Reach:* Reach up as high as you can toward the ceiling with one arm. Your hand should be directly over your head. It's a prolonged reach we're after. Feel the elongation all the way to your ankle, all the way along your side. When you feel all loosened up, drop your arm, and repeat the exercise with your other arm. Be a cat; reach to your outer limit.

2. *Twist:* Arms extended sideward, twist your trunk in either direction as far as you can turn. Then twist in the opposite direction. In the military, this exercise is performed with a snap. These are nonmilitary proceedings. No snaps, please.

3. *Bend:* Lean over, with knees slightly bent, grasp your thighs behind the knees with your hands, and pull your shoulders gently toward your knees. Don't use force. Don't use momentum. Just an easy tug. Some people will get closer to their knees than others. It's all relative to your condition. If you're in terrible shape, then even gaining proximity to your knees is a triumph, and you've done yourself a world of good. If you're already fairly supple, you should soon get fairly close.

4. *Turn:* Turn your head to the side, with your chin over the top of your right shoulder. Place your right hand against your chin, on the left side of your face. Place your left hand on your head from behind. Right and left hands now turn the head just a little farther than it can turn on its own. Gently, please. Don't try to jerk your head, or snap it. Now reverse the process, with your chin over your left shoulder, your left hand against the right side of your face, the right hand grasping the head from behind. Slowly loosen your neck muscles.

In the first few sessions, one performance of each of the movements is sufficient. Later you may wish to do them twice or even three times. But do them in a leisurely, languid manner.

Now that you are limbered you are ready to develop muscle tissue.

MUSCLE BUILDUP

During the next four minutes you're going to concentrate on developing muscle fibers by pumping motions of your muscles, against resistance. As you continue to exercise, it will be easier for you to overcome the same resistance. So you should gradually increase the resistance.

You'll do two exercises, alternating them for a full four minutes. The first will expand the muscles of your shoulders, chest and arms. The second will expand the muscles of your abdomen and back. Don't worry about your legs; they'll get all the exercise they need at the end of this session.

1. *Expansion Pushaways*

Stand a little beyond arm's reach from a wall. Put your hands against the wall at the height of your shoulders. Lean forward until your chest comes near the wall. Then push away until you're back in the starting position. If that's too hard, step in closer. Do the exercise about fifteen or twenty times, or until the exertion begins to feel heavy. This is one set.

If the exercise was a workout for you at a set of fifteen pushaways or less, keep that position the next session.

When you can do a set of twenty or more with ease, move to a position with the feet farther away from the wall.

In successive workouts you'll be able to do more repetitions. Just keep backing away from the wall until you find the position that gives a moderate effort. If you can do a set of more than twenty pushaways before the exertion begins to feel heavy, shift to a more challenging position next time.

Some people will find at the outset that the pushaway from the wall is too easy. In that event, try a kitchen counter, or a bathroom sink, or a chest of drawers—anything that lowers the height of your hands below the height of your shoulders. If you can

do only fifteen pushaways before the exertion becomes heavy, you've found your starting place. We want an exercise that begins to feel difficult after fifteen executions. At each session, you'll be adding more repetitions as your condition improves. When you can do a set of twenty with only a mild effort, increase the difficulty of the pushaway exercise.

From the counter or sink or chest of drawers, move next to a table, and repeat the same routine.

From the table, move to a chair or a bench.

From the chair or bench, move to the floor. Put your knees on the floor. When you're able to do a set of twenty pushaways, try them with your knees off the floor, pushaways in this floor position are commonly called "pushups."

For the person who is in fairly good shape to begin with, twenty pushaways in the foregoing positions may soon become too easy. He can increase the resistance by positioning his feet higher than his hands. The feet are placed first on a low bench, then on a chair, then on a table, etc., until the extreme case, when the feet are directly over the head. None of us will likely get there; none of us needs to; but it's a good illustration of the many ways in which the difficulty of our push-away exercise can be increased.

2. *Expansion Sitbacks*

This exercise will restore the muscles of your abdominal wall.

The abdominal muscles are the hardest ones to involve in beneficial exercise. They're mainly supportive muscles, not primarily designed to flex isotonically—i.e., with movement. They function isometrically, holding without moving, and that's the way they should be exercised.

Whenever you do an ordinary isotonic "situp," there's a tendency to call on two large hip flexor muscles, the psoas and the iliacus, to do most of the work, taking the load off the abdominal muscles. Some time ago I started searching for an exercise that would overcome this problem and really give the abdominals a workout. Using electromyographic studies of the muscles during various movements, I found a simple solution: to reverse the situp process. If you started with your chest at your knees and went backward, instead of rising from the floor to your knees, the ab-

dominals would act more strongly as supporting muscles while the body was being lowered.

In the traditional situp, it's almost impossible for the abdominal muscles to bring the shoulders up without strongly involving the psoas and iliacus muscles.

On the way back from a situp, the tendency is to relax the abdominal muscles and collapse. Consequently, it is the hip flexors, not the abdominal muscles that are getting the best workout.

In the *sitback*, it's almost impossible to lean backward without involving the abdominal muscles. You don't need an electromyograph to check those; you can do it yourself just by touching the abdominal muscles with your fingers. You'll feel them harden as they come into action, and soften as they relax.

The sitback has a psychological as well as physiological advantage over the situp. For the person who's out of condition, the situp can be all but impossible. There's no way to reduce the difficulty beyond a certain minimum. You've got to get off the floor. The sitback permits every degree of difficulty.

We're not interested in how far back you go. We're interested in exercising you to your own personal degree of effort. We define this degree as a slight overload. But you're the one who gauges that effort in terms of your own resources. When you've gone back to a point where the return will be moderately difficult, that's a good position for you.

In whatever position you do the expansion sitback, remember to oppose the tendency to hold your breath. Keep breathing.

Sit on the floor. Don't hook your feet under a piece of furniture unless you have to. It's easier on your back if you don't. Fully bend your knees. Work your chest up against your knees, or as close as it will come. Let your head curl forward. Place your hands on your abdomen so that you can feel the muscle action. If you're not trained to exercise, you may not be able to bring your abdominal muscles voluntarily into action. A good way to teach your muscles to respond is by a biofeedback technique. Probe the abdominal muscles with your fingers while trying to harden them, and feel the muscles contract. Even when you're trained, this probing will cause your muscle to harden even more.

Move back away from your knees until you feel your abdominal musculature coming into play to a moderate degree. To find this moderate degree, it's necessary to explore. Start out by going back just a few inches, and then hold it. If that was easy, go back a few more inches, and hold that position. Keep it up until you've found the spot where you're getting a moderate workout. Once again, the body is a good estimator of what it can do. It may be that you'll go back too far on one occasion to a point where you can't hold it long enough. If that happens, just let yourself collapse to the floor, use your arms to get yourself into a less strenuous position, and resume the exercise. Now your position for moderate exertion has been well defined.

As your condition improves, your point of moderate effort will be farther and farther backward. Eventually, your shoulder blades will nearly touch the floor.

Do only one sitback per set, starting with a degree of effort that enables you *to hold the position for fifteen to twenty seconds*. The last few seconds the belly muscles will begin to quiver. Work up to a full twenty-second sitback the next set before quivering commences, then try a deeper sitback. When your back is near the floor, and you can hold the sitback for twenty seconds or more, you can proceed to "load up" the exercise by pressing harder with your fingers and pushing your abdomen harder against them. Another way of increasing sitback intensity is by folding your arms on your chest. That little change may take you back to fifteen seconds per set; you may even need to make your sitback more shallow for a few days.

The next position is arms folded and raised away from your chest. When that has been mastered, move your hands behind your head. Finally, move your arms over your head. Caution: Don't swing your arms. They're elevated for added weight, and should not be used for momentum.

Be concerned with getting the most value for each position, rather than with advancing to more difficult ones. You're getting just as much value out of the first position you use when you're in poor condition as you are from the last position you use when you're in good condition.

Important: After each set of the two muscle buildup exercises, check your pulse to be sure it isn't over your limit for your first training-pulse-rate period: 60 percent of your maximum level. If it is, take it easier. After a few weeks your exercise pulse rate will be coming down because the other work you're doing will be strengthening your circulorespiratory system.

Repeat two muscle buildup exercises in the same order; again monitor your pulse. You may not be able to hold the sitback position for as long the second set. That's to be expected.

The double sets usually take less than four minutes. The remaining minutes of your ten-minute program are devoted to your heart-rated circulorespiratory conditioning.

CIRCULORESPIRATORY ENDURANCE "LOPE"

You can choose any steady, easy activity you want that will raise your heart rate to your proper level for five minutes during this phase.

The loping activity should be a rhythmic, continuous exercise that brings the large muscles of the legs into action.

The most obvious steady, easy endurance exercise is running in place. It's also the most boring. The second most obvious exercise is jogging. For most people it's the second most boring. Do either if you wish. Or try dancing. Dance in any way you like for five minutes. The only requirement is that your movements be energetic enough to get your pulse rate up to your

moderate level by the end of the second minute, and to maintain that level for another three minutes.

If the spirit moves you, you might want to try incorporating the "fitness hop" into your movements. Hop twice on the left foot, then twice on the right foot, then twice on both feet. Repeat. If there's a radio or record player handy, tune in and turn on. Otherwise, you can hum or whistle or just think of a tune. The rhythm of "Tea for Two" is particularly effective for the fitness hop.

Don't forget: Move around when you take your pulse. Never come to a complete standstill. The same applies to the end of your workout.

That's your program for the first eight weeks. It should take you two or three sessions to find your patterns, positions, speed and endurance. By the end of the first week, you should have a comfortable ten-minute routine.

For the following seven weeks, your only requirement is to keep intensifying your activity. Stretch farther. Put more vigor into your workout. Change the position of your pushaways and do your sitbacks with more and more vigor.

On your circulorespiratory endurance lope, the intensification is automatic. You have to do more to get your pulse up to the proper rate. That's your own internal computer at work.

A reminder: Your proper rate is calculated by subtracting your age from 220, then multiplying the remainder by 60 percent. Example: $220 - 40 = 180$; $180 \times .60 = 108$. Call it 110. That's your starting training pulse rate. But don't fall back if you've previously trained at a higher level.

THE SECOND EIGHT WEEKS: BUILDING STAMINA

Now you've got some muscles, not to look bulky—you won't—but to hold your frame erect, give you some confidence in yourself and move you where you want to go. Our next job is to give those muscles a capacity for *endurance*, so that any sudden situation requiring extra effort won't throw you off schedule for a week.

We're also going to move up a notch in our circulorespiratory conditioning. Again, the aim is endurance.

MUSCLE ENDURANCE

We no longer have to worry about expansion—the building of muscle tissue. By now, you've got all the bulk you need. Nor do we need to worry about range of motion. If you're doing enough stretching in your minimum maintenance program, that's plenty. However, you may want to do the limbering routines as a warmup before your workouts in this period.

The second eight weeks require a new series of training methods to achieve the new objectives. We'll utilize the first four minutes for muscle endurance training, the last six for circulorespiratory endurance training. Now that we have an improved heart and circulation, we're going to start pushing the new capillaries into skeletal muscles. This will induce the chemical and structural changes necessary to give the muscle cells the endurance they need for prolonged activities such as tennis, skiing, carpentry, gardening, and so on.

We're also going to take up *interval training,* which helps us get the heart rate up to higher levels without fatigue. But first, let's work on the muscles.

1. *Endurance Pushaways*

Your first exercise is to do twice as many pushaways as you were doing in the first eight weeks, and feel that the exertion is moderate at the end—not light, not heavy. In order to do that many without a heavy effort, you'll have to lighten the resistance considerably from what it was at the end of that first eight weeks, when you were exercising for muscle bulk. It may be that you had worked your way from the wall through all the stages to the floor. Nonetheless, it would be a good idea to go back to the wall the first time you try to do about forty pushaways. If that's too easy, try the next hardest level the next time you exercise.

The objective is to do twice as many *and do them fast.*

You'll adjust the intensity by moving your feet away from the wall. Start at just beyond arm's length. Once again, if that's too hard, step in closer. The important thing is to be able to do about forty pushaways. If you can easily do more than fifty, you're standing too close. Once you've found the position that enables you to just barely get forty without the exercise becoming heavy, maintain that position until you can get a moderate exertion at about fifty. Then move to the next position. As you step away from the wall, you automatically increase the load.

Pushaways from the wall can be very easy if you stand next to the wall, but if you get back far enough you'll find them an interesting challenge.

Doing forty to fifty pushaways isn't a rigid rule. It's just an order of magnitude. In order to gain endurance, you have to do relatively lighter work rapidly for a greater number of times. If you quit before twenty, you're not doing an endurance exercise. If you get thirty-five and have to stop, or if you get sixty without feeling tired, fine, that's your workout for the day. Make adjustments the next time you exercise. Stand closer or farther away; go faster or slower.

2. *Endurance Sitbacks*

Assume the same position you did for the regular sitback—on the floor, knees bent, head forward, chest near knees.

Now lean back just a little, about a third of the way to the floor. Hold that position for forty or fifty seconds if you can. If that was easy, move back a notch the next time you exercise so that you're approximately halfway between your starting position and the floor. Try again to hold for forty to fifty seconds: If that wasn't enough, next time move back to the three-quarter position, and try to hold that for forty to fifty seconds.

While you're leaning backward, probe the abdominal muscles in all areas, low and high, with your hands. This helps to keep the muscles hardened.

When the exertion starts to become heavy, your belly will begin to quiver. That's your signal to straighten up or relax backward onto the floor.

It may take you a few days to establish just how far back you should go. If you're back too far, you'll start to quiver before thirty seconds. If you're too far forward, you won't quiver until after forty seconds.

As soon as you've finished the sitback, do another bout of endurance pushaways.

When you've finished the second bout of endurance pushaways, do another endurance sitback.

Two sets of the two exercises should take you about four minutes. Don't hurry yourself, but try to develop to a point where you can do the two sets within four minutes.

Reminder: Check your heart rate every two minutes. Keep it within prescribed limits. Your upper limit during this second period is now $220 - 40 = 180$; $180 \times .70 = 126$. The nearest interval of ten is 130. You can go to 130 beats a minute, or 13 beats in 6 seconds. No higher, please—unless you've been used to exercising at a more advanced TPR.

CIRCULORESPIRATORY ENDURANCE INTERVALS

Now, interval training.

It consists of six minutes of exertion in which sallies of intensive exercise are alternated with intervals of active rest. The conventional method is to run for a number of seconds, say thirty, then slow to a walk for about thirty seconds, then run and walk alternately.

There is a cardiovascular training level for each individual below which the system is not stimulated sufficiently to produce a training effect. If you fall below that level, as you would if you sat down to rest, you've wasted a lot of effort; the time you're below isn't doing you any good, because you're not getting a training stimulus. Nor are you gaining anything from the energy you spend to get back up to the level that does you good. So the trick is to orchestrate your activity in such a way that the slow periods give you enough of a rest to be able to maintain vigorous activity in the fast periods, without being so inactive that you're penalizing yourself.

When you perform your body creates lactic acid and other metabolites that cause discomfort after prolonged effort. In interval training, you can work longer without fatigue because these brief periods of active rest allow for the reconversion of these products so that they don't limit your performance. You'll be doing more physical work and putting more of a load on your circulorespiratory system after interval training than you will after continuous distance training. You can stand a heavier load in interval training because you haven't let your metabolic waste products pollute the working mechanisms of your body.

During your endurance lope in the first eight weeks, you worked to 60 percent of maximum. Now to increase your circulorespiratory endurance we're going to speed you up so that your training pulse rate goes to 70 percent of maximum during the fast portions of the six-minute period.

Start out—running in place, jogging, fitness hopping, dancing—at your old loping rate for thirty seconds.

In the next thirty seconds, speed up your motion to an extent that raises your pulse rate to your 70 percent level. It will take a few tries to find out what effort is required to achieve that result. You know basically that if you go faster, your heart rate will increase. How much faster is something your body will teach you by the second or third session.

Now a minute has passed. In the next thirty seconds, slow your activity, giving yourself a rest, but not to such an extent that your heart rate falls below your loping pulse rate. In other words, if you were doing your loping workout at a pulse rate of 110, let your pulse lower to that rate during this active rest interval.

After thirty seconds of active rest, speed up for thirty seconds of intensive exercise. Then slow down for thirty seconds. Continue these intervals for six minutes.

Reminder: Take your pulse after two minutes. Don't exceed your training pulse rate: 70 percent of the difference between 220 and your age. At the same time, don't be alarmed if you haven't quite made it to your training pulse rate after two minutes. It may take another interval of intensive exercise to do that. After the fourth minute, take your pulse again during your active rest interval. If you're too high, don't move so fast during your next thirty-second intensive exercise burst. If you're too low, move faster.

Even if you miss your training pulse rate by ten beats per minute or so for several sessions, it's no big deal. Eventually you'll find the target. Toward the end of your second eight-week period, you'll be moving a lot faster to produce your training pulse rate than you were at the beginning. When that begins to happen, you're really getting in shape.

THE THIRD EIGHT WEEKS: ADDING STRENGTH

NOW WE'RE GOING to put more quality into your program.

We're moving up to 80 percent of all-out effort. These are energetic, fast workouts. You can't move well with your brakes on. You can't get speed unless you're relaxed. Excess tension acts as a brake on the body's ability to perform work.

MUSCLE STRENGTHENING

You've gained muscle mass during the first eight weeks. You've gained muscle endurance in the second eight weeks. The final ingredient is muscle strength.

We've already seen some increase in strength during the previous periods. Inevitably, the exercises you've done have made once dormant muscles stronger. But to bring muscle strength up to a respectable level, you've got to do exercises designed for that purpose. Remember, you can't work effectively for mass, endurance and strength at once. You can only work for one at a time.

Basically, training for strength takes less time during your workout session than building for bulk or endurance. You achieve strength by using heavier loads and fewer repetitions. These exercises take only two minutes out of our ten-minute program, leaving eight minutes to complete our circulorespiratory endurance training. Once again, you may want to do the limbering routines as a warmup before your workouts.

1. *Strength Pushaways*

The first exercise for muscle strength is the pushaway. But the exercise takes on decidedly different characteristics. For the endurance pushaway, we went to an easier position so that we could do forty pushaways. Now we want to make things so difficult that we can do no more than five. So we may have to do floor pushups with some adjustments.

You can make the pushup exercise more difficult by elevating the feet—placing them on a chair, or a stair, or a table, or even up against the wall until you are doing pushups in a handstand position.

Ideally, you would make the exercise so difficult that you could do only one pushaway or pushup. With the same degree of difficulty, you would then try to train up to five. Then you'd intensify it even further so you can do only one again.

2. *Strength Sitbacks*

Same position as for earlier sitbacks—on the floor, knees drawn up, head forward.

Now assume a position you can hold without trembling for only six to ten seconds. After ten seconds, let yourself go down to the floor, and rest.

There are two basic ways to create that much difficulty for yourself. The first is to press your hands against your abdomen and push the abdomen against your hands as hard as you can for 6 to 10 seconds. After each push, shift your fingers to a new area of your abdomen and repeat. The second way is to extend your arms over your head, hold a weight in your hands or in your arms, folded across your chest. Obviously, a deep sitback may very well be enough at first to give you a good challenge. But if it isn't, try your arms in different positions. If that isn't enough, add weight. A heavy dictionary or encyclopedia or a heavy utensil will do.

When you've finished your strength sitback, do another bout of strength pushaways. Then another sitback, another pushaway, another sitback. Three times for each exercise, alternating.

You're going to be falling all over the place at the outset. Don't worry about it. It's only for two minutes. It may seem arduous, but it's also amusing. What's remarkable is that by the third week you'll be doing harder things than those you were unable to do in the first week.

You'll feel it when you've given a sufficient effort: it's at the onset of trembling of your abdominal muscles. No need to go beyond that. The effort of the first week will be insufficient for the third week to give you a strength workout, because you're getting stronger. Once again, you'll feel it and make the necessary adjustments.

Reminder: Don't exceed your training pulse rate. It's now 80 percent of 220 minus your age. That's high enough.

CIRCULORESPIRATORY SPRINT INTERVALS

In the next eight minutes we'll use a more energetic form of interval training.

At 80 percent of maximum, a 50- to 60-year-old person by this point can exercise at a training pulse rate of 130. A 40-year old person can go to 140.

To achieve these levels, you're going to shorten your sprinting interval to fifteen seconds.

Alternate slow lopes and fast sprints each fifteen seconds for eight minutes.

Again, it will take two to three minutes to work your heart rate up to your goal. Take your pulse after two minutes, four minutes and six minutes, and make the appropriate adjustments so that you are exercising at 80 percent of maximum pulse rate.

YOUR TOTAL FITNESS DIVIDEND

YOU'RE FIT NOW. You can start thinking about what you're going to do with all the qualities you've gained. Up until this point, the exercise has been done solely for the purpose of getting the foundations built. Now that they're built—and they are—you can direct the effort in specific ways; for example, toward increasing your abilities in whatever sports or other recreational activities give you pleasure. You're ready to move full bore into your specialty.

FITNESS AT A GLANCE

DAILY MINIMUM MAINTENANCE ACTIVITIES

Allover stretching
Standing two to three hours during the day
Overload lift
Heart walk to elevate your pulse rate for three or
    more continuous minutes
Caloric burn: at least 300 activity calories

TOTAL FITNESS: 24 WEEKS

First Eight Weeks: Rebuilding Tissue

Limbering
  Reach
  Twist
  Bend
  Turn
Muscle building pushaways: two sets of 15-20
Muscle building sitbacks: two sets, one sitback
  per set, held 15-20 seconds
Endurance pulse-rated exercise at 60% effort

Second Eight Weeks: Building Stamina

Limbering
  Reach
  Twist
  Bend
  Turn
Muscular endurance pushaways, two sets of 40-
  50
Muscular endurance sitbacks, two sets, one sit-
  back per set, held 40-50 seconds
Endurance pulse-rated exercise at 70% effort

Third Eight Weeks: Adding Strength

Limbering
  Reach
  Twist
  Bend
  Turn
Strength pushaways, two sets of 1-5
Strength sitbacks, two sets, one sitback per set,
  held 6-10 seconds
Endurance pulse-rated exercise at 80% effort

15

Early Conditioning for Maximum Performance

EARLY CONDITIONING IS the process of preparing yourself for more strenuous activities than those for which your total fitness program prepared you. It has two central objectives: first, to develop increased circulorespiratory endurance so that you can handle more strenuous exertion and, second, to build general body musculature as well as tendons and ligaments so that they can better withstand the stresses and strains of heavier-than-usual loads.

Your total fitness program got you in shape for ordinary daily life activities, for recreational games and for the occasional emergency. It also prepared you for maximum performance conditioning. Because your needs for strength and endurance are increasing, your first task is the same as it was when you began your total fitness program—to build a bigger "engine."

As in the fitness training program, all endurance performance training is monitored by the effect it produces on your heart. That effect, in turn, is determined by taking your pulse. Each person has a different target pulse rate in fitness training, determined by his age and condition when he starts.

The out-of-condition person starts at 60 percent of

220 minus his age, moves to 70 percent after eight weeks, and to 80 percent after another eight weeks.

In training for maximal performance, it's assumed that you've worked up to 80 percent of 220 minus your age. That's the level at which you begin your new training program. Example: A 50-year-old man would subtract his age from 220, giving 170, then multiply by .80. Result: 136. He would work out on the 130-140 range.

CIRCUIT TRAINING

CHAMPIONS TRAIN in "circuits." Training in a circuit —a series of stations—enables you to do far more than if you trained constantly at one exercise, just as interspersing the cleanup chores at home enables you to work more efficiently than if you made all the beds or polished all the floors or moved all the furniture in one continuous bout of work.

At each "station" on a circuit, you do a different exercise. Each exercise emphasizes the activation of a different system or body part than the previous exercise or the next one. Cardiorespiratory conditioning is alternated with muscular conditioning. You let one body system take it easy while you exercise a different one.

The following circuit training program pretty well matches the program of a champion. The champion would be exercising at a higher intensity at each station, repeating each exercise a greater number of times, and performing the exercises at a more rapid rate. Those who are in the early states of conditioning for maximum performance will use the same exercises but will do less work.

In the course of your conditioning, you'll use two or more training circuits. The first will be for "early conditioning," to get you into the overall shape necessary for heightened activity. The next training circuits will be for "specific conditioning" for the sport of your choice. In all cases, the circuit training schedule will consist of five phases.

CIRCUIT TRAINING SCHEDULE

1. Limbering circuit
2. Warmup circuit
3. Training circuit
4. Calmdown circuit
5. Flexibility circuit

The *limbering circuit* gets you loose, puts you in the mood for exercise, and prepares the body for activity.

The *warmup circuit* eases you into the exercises you'll do for overload conditioning. You move slowly, accustoming yourself to the movements, doing few repetitions, not straining in the least, simply getting your body prepared for the vigorous bout of exercises to come.

The *training circuit* is the one during which you are exercising to bring about the body changes that give you greater endurance and make you stronger. You move fast and nonstop from station to station, not straining to the point of injury, but giving yourself a very brisk workout at 80 percent or more of your maximum capacity.

The *calmdown circuit* repeats the intensity of the warmup circuit, with the same slow movements and few repetitions, but this time with the reverse purpose. Coming off a vigorous bout of exercise, you never want to stop abruptly; you should continue activity at an easy pace to maintain circulation and remove metabolic wastes.

The *flexibility circuit*—which should follow any vigorous bout of activity, whether it's a workout or a competition—is the period when you stretch out the tissues that are limiting your range of motion. After these flexibility exercises you keep moving until you are breathing easily, your heart rate is near the resting level, and most of your excess heat has been dissipated. This is the way you prevent stiffness.

LIMBERING CIRCUIT

WHILE WALKING for about two minutes, gradually increasing the pace from moderate to brisk, do the following exercises, approximately thirty seconds each:

1. *Rotating stretch:* While walking slowly, reach your arms out to each side, and rotate them in a horizontal plane, twisting from side to side and stretching your shoulders and back.

2. *Overhead stretch:* Reach one arm at a time overhead and lean from side to side, stretching your waist as you do. Increase walking tempo slightly.

3. *Propeller stretch:* Make large circles with your arms, moving them like dual propellers. After fifteen seconds, reverse direction of arms. Walk at a fairly brisk rate.

4. *Swinging stretch:* Greatly exaggerate your normal arm swing, and lengthen your stride so as to stretch your torso and hips while walking very briskly. The exaggerated body motion resembles that of a cross-country skier.

TRAINING CIRCUIT FOR EARLY
CONDITIONING

DURING THE WARMUP circuit, you progress nonstop from station to station, until you've completed all six exercises. Remember, this is a warmup, so take it easy.

During the training circuit, progress once again nonstop from station to station at 80 percent or more of your maximum capacity.

During the calmdown circuit, do all six exercises nonstop a third time, but just going through the motions of each exercise.

Station	Exercise
1	Rope skipping
2	Sitbacks
3	Reverse pushaway
4	Prone lift
5	Bench stepping
6	Pushaways

STATION 1: ROPE SKIPPING

The emphasis here is on developing both the muscles of the legs and lightness in the feet. During the training circuit, skip rope for a full minute, fast enough to increase your pulse rate to 80 percent of your maximum. After you've developed some proficiency, try skipping on one foot ten times in a row, then shifting to the other foot. Another variation is to jump from one side of a line to the other—particularly good for skiers.

STATION 2: SITBACKS

This exercise is a slight variation from the one used in the total fitness program. It's done from a chair.

Sit near the front edge of the chair, so that your back won't touch the backrest. Put your hand on your breastbone, and feel it rise as you lift your chest. This movement puts a stretch on the abdominal muscles. Now lean back, until you feel a slight strain. Next, put your two hands on the upper abdominal wall, one hand below the other, fingers in opposite directions, and push out with your abdomen as you press in with your hands. Breathe normally as you thrust your belly against your hands with a firm pressure—not a maximal effort. Hold this position for fifteen to twenty seconds. Now move your hands down to the lower part of the abdomen, the "potbelly" area. Again, feel every muscle in that area pushing against your pressing hands for fifteen to twenty seconds, still breathing normally. Finally, put your hands at the sides of your abdomen, making sure your chest is still elevated, and push your abdominal muscles against your hands, while pressing your hands against your belly. Continue for fifteen to twenty seconds.

During the training circuit, lean back a little farther and push a little harder with your hands. Your abdominal muscles will adjust to the resistance.

One tip for starting in the right position. After you've leaned back, imagine someone's going to hit you in the belly, or tickle you there with a feather. You'll automatically constrict. It's from that point that hand pressure is applied.

STATION 3: REVERSE PUSHAWAY

Stand with your back to the wall, feet about a foot from the wall. Lean back, touch the wall, and slide down, until your thighs are parallel with the floor, or as close to parallel as is comfortable. You may need to adjust your feet. Now, place your hands against the wall behind you, fingers down, at the level of your hips. Push gently away from the wall and hold it for fifteen to twenty seconds. Return to starting position. Repeat for another fifteen to twenty seconds. In the training circuit, use near-maximal tension.

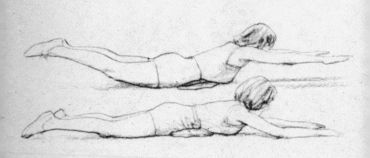

STATION 4: PRONE LIFT

Lie face down, arms extended, with a seat cushion, pillow or folded blanket under your midsection. Raise your hands and arms approximately four inches from the floor; raise your legs at the same time and hold them off the floor for fifteen to twenty seconds. Rest a moment and repeat. While you're holding the lift position during the training circuit, tighten your back muscles strongly.

STATION 5: BENCH STEPPING

This is one of the finest exercises you can do to build your leg muscles and improve your circulorespiratory endurance. Face a bench or a sturdy box a foot or more in height. Step onto the bench with the left foot, then up with the right foot, then down to the floor with the left foot, then down with the right foot. Repeat ten times, then step up with the right foot, then the left foot, step down with the right foot, then the left foot. Continue alternating the takeoff foot in this manner for at least one minute. During the training circuit, speed up to raise your pulse rate to 80 percent of your maximum.

STATION 6: PUSHAWAYS

Even if you're in pretty good shape, don't be ashamed to start this exercise with your hands against a wall, a dresser, a table or a countertop. The point is to be able to do the exercise fifteen or twenty times easily during the warmup and calmdown circuits, and change to a more strenuous position during the training circuit. With your feet at arm's length or more from the object on which you rest your hands, push away from the object until your arms are straight, then return to starting position. As your condition improves, move your starting position closer to the floor, finally to the floor itself. If floor pushups can be continued easily for the time allotted, elevate the feet, placing them on a step, chair or up against a wall in a handstand pushup position.

FLEXIBILITY CIRCUIT

THE TIME TO INCREASE your range of motion is while you are warm *after* your other exercise, when the muscles and ligaments are nicely stretched from the workout you've given them. The flexibility circuit consists of ten brief exercises; properly and faithfully executed, it will diminish the possibility of injuries to the hamstrings and other vulnerable muscles.

1. *Autotransfusion:* Walk slowly for a minute, reaching your arms overhead and clenching your hands repeatedly. During exercise, the blood has been collecting in the extremities, causing them to swell. This exercise removes the excess blood from the arms and hands, as the following exercise does from the feet.

2. *Inverted pedaling:* Lie on your back with your legs in the air and your hips elevated with the support of your hands. Pedal slowly for a minute or sixty revolutions.

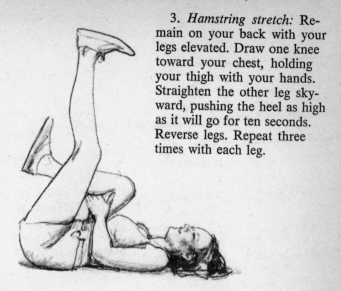

3. *Hamstring stretch:* Remain on your back with your legs elevated. Draw one knee toward your chest, holding your thigh with your hands. Straighten the other leg skyward, pushing the heel as high as it will go for ten seconds. Reverse legs. Repeat three times with each leg.

4. *Knee hug:* Stay on your back, and use your hands on your thighs to draw both knees toward your chest to slowly stretch the lower back region. Hold for ten seconds. Rest five seconds and repeat.

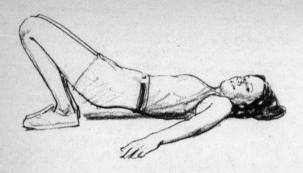

5. *Hip raise:* While lying, place the soles of both feet on the floor next to your buttocks. Slowly raise your hips and hold them off the floor, stretching the low back by slowly lowering the vertebrae from the neck downward to the floor for ten seconds. Rest five seconds and repeat.

6. *Adductor stretch:* Remain lying with your knees flexed. Place the soles of your feet together and let your knees fall outward. Press your hands on the *outside* of each knee for ten seconds, and gradually resist an attempt to move your knees wider apart. Remove your hands and relax the legs so the knees fall sideward as far as they will go. Now keep the legs relaxed and place your hands on the *inside* of your knees, and gently but firmly press the knees farther

outward, stretching the leg adductor muscles for about ten seconds. Relax five seconds and repeat the entire sequence.

7. *Neck rotation:* Sit, and turn your head to the left as far as it will go. Place your left hand on your left cheek and resist an attempt to turn your head farther. Then release the pressure of your hand, relax your neck, let your head turn completely to the left, and then assist the turn with your left hand by pressing it gently but firmly against your right cheek. Now turn your head to the right, resisting with your right hand on your right cheek. Release the pressure, relax, and turn completely, assisting the turn with your right hand pressed gently but firmly against your left cheek. Repeat. *Resist* each turn five seconds; *assist* each turn ten seconds.

8. *Hip flexor stretch:* Squat with hands on the floor, arms outside of your knees. Extend your left leg backward. Keeping your back and left leg straight, press your right knee toward the floor until you feel a slight stretch in the left groin area. Hold ten seconds. Now do the exercise with right leg extended. Repeat.

9. *Heel cord stretch:* Stand at arm's length from a wall with your heels flat on the floor, the balls of your feet on a small board an inch thick. Lock your knees and lean forward as far as you can without lifting your heels, supporting yourself with your hands against the wall. Hold for ten seconds. Relax five seconds and repeat. As flexibility increases, move feet farther and farther from the wall.

10. *All-body stretch:* Mark a real or imaginary X on the floor, two feet from a wall. Mark another real or imaginary X at shoulder height on the wall, above and on line with the floor X.

a. Stand upright facing away from the wall X, with your feet astride the floor X.

b. Touch the floor X with both hands, with your heels flat on the floor and your knees slightly flexed.

c. Return to standing position.

d. Twist left and reach out toward wall X with your right *hand*. Don't move your feet.

e. Twist right and reach out toward wall X with your left hand.

f. Return to front and touch floor X.

g. Return to stand.

h. Twist left and touch wall X with your left *elbow*.

i. Twist right and touch wall X with your right elbow. Repeat entire series four times.

16

Evaluating Your Progress

THIS CHECK ON your progress is begun after you've spent the first two weeks on the training circuit for early conditioning. Repeat this check every week or two. When your scores on repeated tests show no further appreciable gains, you're ready to move on to a training circuit specified for your sport. If you're not satisfied with your performance, remain with the early conditioning program awhile longer. Once you've moved into a specific conditioning phase, use this check every few months to be sure you're maintaining your strength, endurance and flexibility.

STRENGTH

Pushups—Start with your hands by your shoulders and your chest touching the floor. Push your body up from the floor until your elbows are fully extended, keeping your back straight. Return and touch your chest to the floor and repeat, as rapidly as possible. Record the number of complete pushups you can do in one minute.

Vertical jump—Dip your fingers in a cup of water. Bend at the waist with your side to the wall and jump, touching as high as you can with your wet fingers. Measure the height of the finger mark.

Standing broad jump—Stand on a line and jump from it as far as you can without falling back. Measure the distance you jumped.

ENDURANCE

Step test—Step up and down on a bench or box thirty times a minute for five minutes if you can make it. See how many minutes and seconds you can continue, and also check your pulse immediately after stopping.

FLEXIBILITY

Shoulder—Touch your fingers behind your back by reaching the shoulder with one hand and over the shoulder with the other. Measure the gap or the overlap. To measure, hold the ruler at the zero end with one hand and slide the other hand toward the zero as far as possible. Remove the ruler with the sliding hand and read the measure.

Back—Sit on the floor with your legs straight, and reach toward or past your toes without bending your knees. Measure how far you reached.

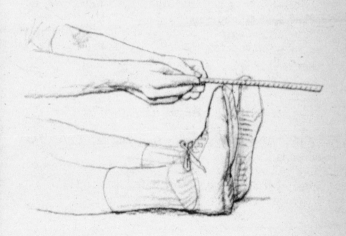

Trunk—Sit in a straight-back chair with your feet locked against the insides of the front legs of the chair. Without twisting in the seat, turn your shoulders and see how far you can reach with your hand along the back of the chair. Try both sides.

RESULTS

Test	Date	Date	Date	Date	Date
Pushups					
Vertical jump					
Standing broad jump					
Step test: Time					
Pulse					
Flexibility					
Shoulder					
Back					
Trunk: Left					
Right					

17

Specific Conditioning for Maximum Performance

ONCE YOU'VE COMPLETED your early conditioning, you're ready to move into training that's specific for your sport. There are two choices, one for locomotor sports, the other for brachiating sports.

Locomotor sports are those that make great use of the legs. They include tennis, track, backpacking, cycling, swimming, basketball, skiing, rock climbing, scuba diving, soccer, football.

Brachiating sports are those that make great use of the upper part of the body, particularly the arms. They include tennis, golf, baseball, handball, squash, swimming, racquets, gymnastics, wrestling, fencing, rowing and bowling.

Some sports, like tennis, have elements of both locomotion and brachiation. The upper body is used in stroking the ball, the lower body in getting into position to stroke it. Because the whole body loses quickness when the legs tire, anyone conditioning for maximum performance in tennis must give particular attention to his legs, building a reserve of strength as well as endurance. Except for the serve, tennis is a crouching game. In tournament play, it's the legs that fatigue and cause a slowing of the footwork and eventually the strokes.

Specific circuit workouts should be done every other day, three days a week. If you're a tennis player, or you play some other sport that involves both brachiation and locomotion to intense degrees, ideally you would work out six times a week, alternating the workouts. If you don't want to exercise that much, work out three times a week, alternating the schedules thus:

Monday–Locomotion

Wednesday–Brachiation

Friday–Locomotion

Monday–Brachiation

Wednesday–Locomotion

Friday–Brachiation

Obviously, six days a week on alternating schedules is better. But you'll still improve on the three-days-a-week schedule. The degree of improvement depends on the investment you're willing to make.

Inasmuch as the abdominal area is not used strongly in sports, exercises for the abdomen are not in either specific circuit. Nonetheless, you'll want to maintain the abdominal strength you've developed. To do so, add the sitback exercise you did in training for early conditioning to your limbering phase of the specific conditioning circuit schedules. The order of the limbering circuit will thus become:

1. Sitbacks
2. Rotating stretch
3. Overhead stretch
4. Propeller stretch
5. Swinging stretch

SPECIFIC CONDITIONING FOR
LOCOMOTOR SPORTS

SINCE LOCOMOTOR SPORTS are almost invariably endurance activities, the exercises are performed to build muscular endurance rather than muscle strength.

Always begin your workout with the limbering circuit and finish off with the flexibility circuit.

As in your schedule for early conditioning, do your warmup circuit gently, your training circuit with vigor, and just breeze through your calmdown circuit.

Station	Exercise
1	Side-to-side jumping
2	Quad setting
3	Kangaroo hop
4	Heel and toe raises
5	Bench stepping
6	Half-squats

STATION 1: SIDE-TO-SIDE JUMPING

Knees slightly flexed, jump to right over a narrow stripe on the floor, then quickly back to the starting position, then repeat to left—a specific preseason exercise for skiers, but applicable to any locomotor sport. Continue for at least one minute and during the training circuit increase your pulse rate to 90 percent of maximum if your sport requires extraordinary endurance; otherwise continue at 80 percent.

STATION 2: QUAD SETTING

Sit at the end of your chair seat and lean backward. Now extend one leg fully and tighten the quadriceps —the anterior thigh muscles—so that you pull your kneecap back. Push on the kneecap to make sure it's locked in place. Hold the position forty to fifty seconds, probing the thigh muscle with your fingers to be sure it is contracting strongly. Repeat the exercise with the other leg. During the warmup and calmdown circuits, use less than all-out contractions. During the training circuit, contract the muscles as hard as you can.

STATION 3: KANGAROO HOP

Stand with your feet apart, crouch forward and jump upward, bringing your knees up toward your chest. Continue hopping for one minute. During the training circuit, try to get a little more height each leap, and elevate your pulse rate to 90 percent of your maximum if you are training for an event that requires extraordinary endurance; otherwise continue at 80 percent.

STATION 4: HEEL AND TOE RAISES

Stand and slowly rise on your toes and return to the floor. Repeat, changing the position of the feet so that the feet point outward, straight ahead and inward at various times. Second half of exercise at each position: rock back on your heels slowly and raise your toes. Repeat, changing positions of feet and alternating toe and heel raises. During the training circuit, intensify the effort by rising higher.

STATION 5: BENCH STEPPING

This is the same exercise as at station 5 in the early conditioning program.

Face the bench. Step up with the left foot, then up with the right foot, then down with the left foot, then down with the right foot. Continue for one minute. Then step up with the right foot, then the left foot, step down with the right foot, then the left foot for another minute. If endurance is your goal, raise your exercise pulse rate to 90 percent of your maximum; otherwise continue at 80 percent.

STATION 6: HALF-SQUATS

Start in a standing position in front of a straight chair, legs and feet spread about a foot apart. When shoes without heels are worn, put a small board about an inch thick under your heels. Bend at the knees, and lower your buttocks to touch the seat of the chair, lifting your arms in front of you for balance. Return to starting position. Repeat forty to fifty times. Increase the speed and load as your condition improves. Squat can be done with a barbell, book bag or other weight held on the shoulders, behind the neck, leaning forward slightly to maintain balance.

SPECIFIC CONDITIONING CIRCUIT FOR BRACHIATING SPORTS

BRACHIATING SPORTS can be either endurance or strength events, or combinations of the two. The exercises that follow should be tailored to the endurance or strength needs of the sport—using moderate loads and high repetitions for muscular endurance, and heavy loads with few repetitions for strength.

Once again, always begin your workout with the limbering circuit and finish off with the flexibility circuit. Walk through your warmup circuit, do your training circuit energeticially and finish off with an easy calmdown circuit.

Station	Exercise
1	Eight-count pushup
2	Arm curls
3	Arm stepping
4	Pushbacks
5	Arm isometrics
6	Half-lever

STATION 1: EIGHT-COUNT PUSHUP

This is a whole-body exercise with both strength and endurance benefits.

Start in a standing position. At the count of one, bend at your knees into a crouch, keeping your back straight, and place your hands on the floor in front of you. At the count of two, throw your legs backward until they are straight. At the count of three, bend at the elbows and graze the floor with your chest. At the count of four, push away from the floor until your elbows are straight again. At the count of five, graze floor with your chest again. At the count of six, push away again. At the count of seven, return to the same crouching position as count one. At the count of eight, return to the starting position. During the training circuit, repeat the exercise rapidly for at least a minute.

STATION 2: ARM CURLS

If you have a barbell or a dumbbell, use it. Otherwise, fill a small bag with books—not too many at first. If the handle is big enough for both hands, do the exercise using both arms simultaneously. Otherwise, do one arm at a time. Start with the palms forward, arms extended toward the floor, weight in the hand or hands. Curl the weight toward your chest, then return to the starting position. Repeat. If it's endurance you're after, use moderate loads and repeat forty to fifty times during the training cirucit. If strength is your goal, increase the load so that you can complete only five curls or less.

STATION 3: ARM STEPPING

This exercise adds power to your arm and shoulder muscles.

Place your hands on the second step of a stairway and stretch your body out as though you were going to do a pushaway. Your shoulders should be directly over your hands. Now move your right hand to the *third* step, then your left hand to the third step, then your right hand back to the second step, then your left hand back to the second step. Repeat ten times, then start with your left hand, then your right hand, return with your left hand, then your right hand. During the training circuit, repeat the exercise rapidly for a minute or so.

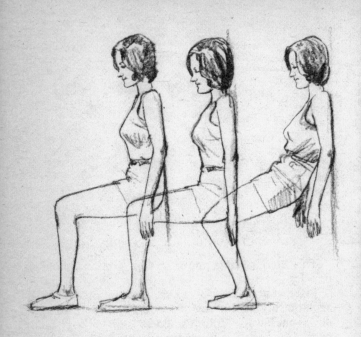

STATION 4: PUSHBACKS

Assume a sitting position with your back against a
wall, as if you were seated in a phantom chair. Press
your palms against the wall just below your buttocks.
Hold the pressure for ten seconds. Then relax your
arms and press against the wall with your back by
pushing against the wall with your feet. Hold this pressure for ten seconds. Alternate palm pressure and foot
pressure for a minute. During the training circuit,
press with all you've got.

STATION 5: ARM ISOMETRICS

Hook your fingers in front of your chest, with your elbows out at shoulder level. Attempt to pull your hands apart, pulling for ten seconds. Move your hands behind your head and pull for another ten seconds. Return to the front and press the palms together. Push the hands together, trying to push one hand or the other off center for ten seconds. Repeat the series. During the training circuit, pull and push to your utmost.

STATION 6: HALF-LEVER

Crouch between two straight chairs with your hands on the seats of the chairs. Extend your legs in front of you. Raise your body by straightening your elbows. Lower your body very slowly. Repeat for a minute. During the training circuit, let your body descend as far as possible.

In the next chapter, we'll fit the exercises we've just learned into your overall program.

18

Your Maximum
Performance Program

WHATEVER DEGREE OF change you have in mind,
the program in which you'll accomplish your objective
will consist of four stages.

1. DEVELOPMENT

Correction of health defects
Reduction of excess fat
Reduction of excess tension
Early conditioning circuit training
Building mobility
Skill analysis; changes in form or style

2. REFINEMENT

Specific conditioning
Dynamic relaxation
Non-injurious drills to incorporate new skills into game
elements

3. REHEARSAL

Game practice
Acclimatization

4. COMPETITION

Tapering of Training
Peaking of effort

The time you'll devote to each stage will depend on
the amount of change you're after. The more time
spent overall, the more changes you'll achieve. Be sure
to spend some time at each stage. Remember, the
greatest gains come in the early part of each stage. As
you prolong each stage, your gains each week will be
diminished, but for maximum performance you are
seeking the extra talents you will be needing at crucial points in the game, and the extra stamina you will
be needing during the closing moments.

NUMBER OF WEEKS AT EACH STAGE

	Degree of Commitment*		
	Low	*Medium*	*High*
Development	4	8	12
Refinement	4	8	16
Rehearsal	4	8	12
Competition	Varies	Varies	Varies

* Degree of commitment:

Low: Willing to go halfway to my ultimate capacity. I'm prepared to invest 12 weeks of training
prior to competition in order to improve my performance.

Medium: I want to reach 80 percent of my capacity, and am willing to invest 24 weeks of training to
that end prior to competition.

High: I want to be the best I can possibly be, and
am willing to go all out for a full year—for example,
40 weeks of training prior to a 12-week period of competition.

Underlying every program—no matter how long its duration—is the same philosophy: that the route to maximum performance is not through performance alone.

You don't get to be the best possible performer by practicing only the event itself. If that's all you do, you won't ever do your best.

This is a tough notion to sell to tournament players, some of whom win all the time by playing all the time, and the rest of whom see that that's all those winners do to win. As a consequence, each day they play. They set up a performance goal without regard to whether it's just enough, too little or too much to stimulate development. They play just hard enough to win. Whoever trains in that manner forgets that it's his body that's performing, not the stopwatch or tape measures or scorecards that quantify the result. He may also be risking injury. And he's surely not performing to his potential—even if he's winning.

Assuming you've decided that you want to develop to the maximum of your ability in a specific period of time, you're not going to get there if you start right off in competition. At the end of the season, you're only going to be partway to where you might have been had you taken things in their proper order, using the fundamentals of training.

The natural question is, "How long must the overall program be?" It's also the most difficult to answer, beyond saying that the more you train the better. But here is a way of looking at training that might help you to find your own answer.

In training, you're always building up to a peak. After a short recovery period, you're starting again and building toward the next peak. If your peak is as glamorous as the Olympic Games, that's a four-year cycle; and if, let us say, you've won your silver medal, you take a short rest and then start over again in order to win your gold. In football, a bowl game is your ultimate goal. That means a fifty-two-week cycle. After the bowl game, you get a little rest and start over again. Swimmers have a winter and summer season, with a championship at the end of each season. So for swimmers, it's a six-month recycling program—which, at the championship level, is about as small as a cycle can be. There's so much to be done between each peak that if you try to peak more frequently than twice a year you will probably not perform as well.

Recreational play is a different matter. The recreational player has obviously not got the Olympic Games or a bowl game in his sights. His sport may or may not be seasonal. But he ought to reflect a bit on this concept of peaking.

Assuming you're this recreational player, why not look on the program you're about to undertake as one that will lift you to a new peak—from which, if you wish, you can then organize yourself for an assault on an even higher peak? You might very well be content to remain at the first new peak, without going farther. The option is yours. The beauty of this program is that it permits you to establish a realistic goal for yourself —one that you can achieve in the time that you can give it—without foreclosing your prospects.

That gets us down to the minimum time period for any improvement. Bearing the foregoing qualification in mind—that improvement is relative to the amount of time you give it—a slight, but measurable improvement may be seen in a week of concentrated training, and marked improvement may be expected if the program is extended to a luxuriant fifty-two weeks. A period somewhere in between those extremes—let's say twenty-four weeks—gives us a manageable and tolerable time to make possible the accomplishment of most all of the essential benefits of training. Give yourself a minimum of twenty-four weeks, if you can, but give whatever time you can, in any case.

PRACTICE TIMES

EACH PRACTICE IS DIVIDED between fitness and skill workouts. How long should each of these be?

If your event is one of pure strength or endurance, your fitness workout will occupy most of your workout session.

If your event is a highly skilled one, not requiring much strength or endurance, you can give most of your time to the development of skill.

Here again, it's up to you. The more time and effort you invest, the more you'll profit.

FITNESS

1. Thirty minutes for your fitness workout.

2. An additional period for further circulorespiratory training, using any leg movement—running, hoping, dancing—that gets your heart rate up to your prescribed level. This period can vary anywhere from ten minutes to slightly longer than the period of the event for which you're training. If your fitness level is below par, however, it would be a good idea to start with long slow distance (LSD) training: long brisk walks, some slow running, or uphill walking, for at least half an hour of continuous vigorous effort.

If your circulorespiratory conditioning is done on a different day from your training circuit, remember to precede it with the limbering warmup and follow it with the flexibility circuit.

If you do your training circuit and circulorespiratory conditioning on the same day, you can hold off your flexibility circuit until the end of your session.

SKILL

Skill training is one case in which more isn't better. Overlong practices that cause fatigue or boredom are undesirable. The less fit you are, the shorter the practice period should be.

For the development of most motor skills, you'll make a lot more progress by breaking the weekly practice time into brief segments, rather than doing one continuous drill. It's far better to have four one-hour practice periods in four consecutive days than to practice all afternoon on a single day. Even better would be eight half-hour practice periods dispersed through the week.

Remember to set a level at which you wish to perform that is one you can realistically achieve. If you've got a full-time job, you're not a naturally gifted athlete, and you've made Jack Nicklaus your model, you've set an unrealistic goal.

At the outset of your development program, you'll be concentrating mostly on the development of sufficient fitness to support the new demands for body strength and endurance. On days when both fitness and skill practices are scheduled, however, the skill workout should *precede* the fitness workout. This order becomes increasingly important as the emphasis on skill practice increases.

Keeping these goals and protocols in mind, let's now set out the four stages of your program.

1. DEVELOPMENT

HEALTH

The beginning of the development stage is a great time to have that annual checkup and to correct all the defects and weaknesses that may exist in your body. If you've had a low-grade infection, now is the time to fight it and get rid of it. If you have spurs or torn ligaments, now is the time to remove or repair them. This is also the time to determine whether you have any vitamin or mineral deficiencies. This is not a shotgun approach, in which you grab a bunch of bottles in a health food store and begin ingesting the contents. Supplementary vitamins and minerals ought to be taken as specifically and carefully as you take medicines. The reason this is a good time to clean up infections, incidentally, is that all medicines have side effects. In this first stage you'll be operating at such a low level of performance that the side effects won't bother you, whereas they might in more intensive phases.

If you're overweight, this is the time to begin a fat reduction program. There is no handicap more destructive to maximum performance than unneeded fat. To get rid of it, the method we recommend is the pound-a-week weight loss on a wide variety diet detailed in *Total Fitness*. Eat everything you want to, just eat a little less—200 calories a day less. Increase your caloric burnoff through extra activity by 300 calories a day. As you get into the next stages, your caloric burnoff will be stepped up to 500 calories or higher, so you'll be reducing fat just by holding the line on food intake. A 500-calorie adjustment each day totals 3500 calories in a week, or a one pound of fat loss accomplished without discomfort as your tissues improve.

Whatever's troubling you, get it corrected. If you have a foot problem, try to find other shoes or have your present ones modified. Start intensive therapy for any chronic aches and pains. If necessary, undertake the therapy yourself. The best therapeutic device you can have in your home is a hydrocolator, a pad soaked in boiling water that is then wrapped in Turkish towels and applied to your sore spots. The next best thing is an electric heating pad, which is a lot easier to use but not as effective. Either the hydrocolator or the electric pad should be applied twice a day for an hour each time to help heal muscular trauma. Remember, heat should not be used until at least twenty-four hours after injury, after swelling has subsided. Cold is what you should use immediately after an injury—as it inhibits bleeding, suppresses swelling, and numbs pain.

If you're just coming off an intensive season, and you've literally risked your neck in order to win, you need a rest period to repair the microtrauma, those small tears in muscle and connective tissue. You may have upset your endocrine system because of the stress to which you've put yourself. If you've been traveling during a competitive season, you may have picked up some minor infestation that will be bugging you for months if you don't do something about it. Now's the time to get a complete clinical examination, which includes blood and fecal analysis in addition to the standard urine and x-ray evaluations. Now's the time to get your immunization and vaccination treatment.

FITNESS

Begin the training circuit for early conditioning, explained in Chapter 15, exercising at a training pulse rate of 80 percent of your maximum. For a 40-year-old person, this means a training pulse rate of 144. The formula is $220 - age \times .80$. Rounding off, the 40-year-old person would train at a 140–150 pulse rate.

If you are an athlete who has just completed a season of competition, this is a period of active rest. Your training pulse rate should not exceed 80 percent during this phase, even if yours is an endurance event.

For convenience, we'll reproduce the early conditioning schedule described in Chapter 15.

TRAINING CIRCUIT FOR EARLY CONDITIONING

Station	Exercise
1	Rope skipping
2	Sitbacks
3	Reverse pushaway

4	Prone lift
5	Bench stepping
6	Pushaways

Phase one is the limbering circuit.

Phase two is your warmup circuit. You take it easy, doing six listed exercises, one after the other.

Phase three is your training circuit. You exercise at 80 percent of your capacity.

Phase four is your calmdown circuit. You take it easy, again.

Phase five is the flexibility circuit.

Keep the load well within your capacity so that you can achieve success. If necessary, make the exercise easier and easier until you find a level at which you can succeed with a mild effort. Then gradually work your way up from there. If you feel stiff or sore after a workout, it's a sign that you've worked out too hard. Your body doesn't need this kind of demand, and the tissue damaged must be allowed to repair before you proceed. Overwork means time lost. Your objective is to build up any muscles that have been neglected, and to pay attention to the connective tissue, building up and hardening the bones, thickening the ligaments and tendons that hold the joints together.

Give considerable attention to the exercises in the flexibility circuit to increase your range of motion. Use relaxation procedures to relax excess tension.

Avoid dehydration in these heat training sessions by drinking some water before you start exercising, and replace the fluids as you lose them by frequent drinks of water. If you prefer sweetened beverages, it's best to drink some water along with them, as their usually heavy concentration draws fluid from the body to dilute them in your intestines before they can be absorbed. On days when you are going to sweat a lot, take extra salt with your meals and choose salty snacks. If you use salt tablets, chew them first, then wash them down with lots of water. The irritating action of salt in your mouth will be the same or worse on the lining of your stomach and intestines if you swallow the tablets whole—so don't do it.

Circulorespiratory training: This training is in addition to your circuit training. It can be performed at any time of the day, three or four days a week. Move at a rate fast enough to elevate your heart to 80 percent of your maximum for six to ten minutes. This continuous type of effort is accomplished by running, swimming or rowing long distances at a fairly slow rate. In running, this is called long slow distance, or LSD.

SKILL

Now is the time to ditch the parts of your game that aren't working well for you. Paralysis by analysis won't hurt you here. You're returning to fundamentals, in order to build them anew.

In the development stage you don't compete. You pick your game apart and rebuild the elements. Each element becomes a plaything. What you're most concerned with is analysis. It would pay you to stop everything else for a while—stop fooling around, stop doing things wrong—and have an expert look you over. If you have access to a video-tape machine, so much the better; your movements can be analyzed by your instructor, and he can coach you into an improved style.

This is the one phase in the training cycle when you can learn to do things a new way. After this, it's too late, because your attention should no longer be on technique. You know that your competitive edge is going to deteriorate while you're rebuilding your game, so you can start out by sacrificing your present game for a future, better one.

Your instructor will translate his analysis of your improved form into useful cues. He will keep the new skill acquisition simple and the load within your capacity, so that you know nothing but success. Remember, you should always succeed in conditioning for maximum performance. If, by chance, you don't succeed, you know that you've tried too much too soon and that you should revert to more secure ground.

2. REFINEMENT

HEALTH

Continue any treatment or fat-reduction regimen established during the development stage. Treat muscle soreness at once and avoid overwork like the plague. Pay strict attention to blisters that may develop on hands or feet. For protection against blistering, use petroleum jelly to reduce friction. On tender areas apply tincture of benzoin and let it dry, to toughen the skin before applying the jelly. Wear gloves or an extra pair of socks to protect against friction. Protect blisters with gauze and tape bandages.

FITNESS

In the development step, you added muscle bulk. Now in the refinement stage, your objective is to give the quality to that muscle that you'll need for your event. If it's muscular endurance you need, you'll do the exercises with loads so moderate that you can complete forty to fifty repetitions. If it's explosive strength you're after, you'll exercise against a resistance so heavy that you can't possibly do more than five repetitions. All work will be performed at 80 percent of your capacity unless your event requires great endurance, in which case you will advance to 90 percent.

Now is the time you'll want to make your choice of options for specific conditioning.

If yours is a "locomotor" sport that makes heavy demands on the legs, you should follow the schedule explained in Chapter 17 and repeated here for convenience.

SPECIFIC CONDITIONING CIRCUIT FOR LOCOMOTOR SPORTS

Station	Exercise
1	Side-to-side jumping
2	Quad setting
3	Kangaroo hop
4	Heel and toe raises
5	Bench stepping
6	Half-squats

If yours is a "brachiating" sport that emphasizes and engages the upper body a great deal, then you should follow the schedule explained in Chapter 17 and repeated here for convenience.

SPECIFIC CONDITIONING CIRCUIT FOR BRACHIATING SPORTS

Station	Exercise
1	Eight-count pushup
2	Arm curls
3	Arm stepping
4	Pushbacks
5	Half-lever
6	Arm isometrics

If the sport has features of both, alternate the schedules.

Cardiovascular training: We're moving now from long slow distance to interval training. This more intensive training makes demands on your oxygen systems and calls on your heart and lungs.

Work: Move for five minutes at 80 percent heart rate.

Recover: Slow down for a while, until your heart rate drops to 60 percent, and then speed up again.
Work.
Recover.
Work.
Recover.
Remember to add the limbering, warmup and flexibility cool-down phases to your workout sessions.

SKILL

We're moving into the arena now, still not at game level, but beginning to simulate game conditions. We're becoming "one with the arena," getting to know the terrain, the environment, the shape and size. In football, we're scrimmaging. In tennis, we may play without keeping score. In golf, we're still hitting practice balls, but we're much more deliberate in our work, setting up theoretical playing conditions, working from practice traps. Golf is a peculiar sport, in that if you actually play a round, you're only hitting the ball some forty to sixty times (not counting putts). That's not really enough practice—unless you've established to your own and your coach's satisfaction that your new stroke is grooved to the point that it will stand up under pressure.

In the development stage, we analyzed the mechanics. Now in the refinement stage, we're putting the parts together and practicing the entire routine. Our objectives are to quicken the response, improve coordination, reduce extra motion and tension, and get comfortable with our new style.

That last is so important it's worth all the time you can give it. We enter maximum performance from a relaxed state. The whole basis of skilled movement, speed, accuracy and efficiency is to perform without excess tension. You can always build up from a relaxed state; it's more difficult to begin in a state of agitation and then calm down. This is the time to incorporate Dynamic Relaxation into your event.

If you feel halfway through the refinement stage that you want to enter into an informal game, be sure that it's at a low level. Ideally, this would be a combination drill-play experience with partners or your pro or members of your squad; and you and your friend would have the option of stopping play at any time to work on what you want to. If you do play a regular game, tell your partner that your objective is to use your new mode of play, and that in no case will you revert to your old style in order to win a point.

3. REHEARSAL

HEALTH

Great care should be taken to prevent injury. All of your previous injuries should have been repaired by this point, and you should be completely rehabilitated physically.

FITNESS

Continue your quality training program, but increase the intenstiy to 90 percent effort. For the 40-year-old person, this would mean circulorespiratory conditioning at a pulse rate of about 160.

Whereas in training for fitness for ordinary life activities, you never need to go above 80 percent of 220 minus your age, in training for maximum performance you eventually work to 90 percent of 220 minus your age. A 160 heart rate is plenty high for anyone 40 years or older; there is no point in trying to get it higher than that, unless the pulse is going to rise above 160 in a maximal endurance event such as distance running. Heart rates over 160 represent strenuous exertion for people over 40 years of age. Those at younger ages can more easily tolerate higher heart rates and can train above the 90 percent level if the event requires that extreme degree of effort.

If what you'll eventually be doing will be performed in a climate radically different from the one you're used to, now is the time to begin to condition for that. As an example, if the peak of your training is to be in a tennis tournament in New Orleans in the summer, you face the problem of heat exhaustion and dehydration. So part of your training during the month beforehand should be to build up a tolerance to heat by wearing a sweat suit every other day when you train. Don't wear a sweat suit every day, because body heat storage cuts back on the intensity of your muscular workout—and your level of training.

Cardiovascular conditioning: You'll do sprint intervals—one to two minutes of activity at 90 percent effort, followed by a minute of active rest, again without letting your heart rate go below 60 percent of 220 minus your age. Maintain this for 10 to 20 minutes.

SKILL

The rehearsal stage is when fitness and skill come together in a mode specific to the arena. All training is done in the conformation of the event. That is, all your training will attempt to anticipate the very conditions that exist in the event itself. Whatever physical load you're asked to bear during the event, you'll bear in practice. You'll play to the duration of the event, at the speed of the event, in the posture of the event.

It's imperative that you train specifically. At this point, further nonspecific training won't help you much, if at all.

Now you can compete, but preferably with non-threatening opponents. If you're on a team, this means playing with opponents from out of your league. The games can be against superior, inferior or equivalent teams, as long as it's a winning-doesn't-count situation.

If it's an individual sport you're playing, the same applies. Play anyone you want to, but not under circumstances that pressure you to win at all costs.

Your skills are all being used at game rhythm now, and you're consciously working on that rhythm. Even variations of a motion, such as the serve in tennis, should be done in your game rhythm. Try what many top athletes do, which is to verbalize the rhythm or set it to a tune. Hum the tune or feel the rhythm as you make your movement.

Work on reflexive action. Try to shorten your response time to signals, by responding to cues rather than to complex details.

Keep working on relaxation. Make an inventory of muscle areas from time to time, particularly little areas of residual tension in the neck, shoulders and thighs. Quickness and power develop from a relaxed body, not a tense one. Practice the Dynamic Relaxation Run described in Chapter 4.

4. COMPETITION

HEALTH

Gauge your opponents, and apportion your effort. Be cautious. Do what's necessary to win without injuring yourself. Don't invite staleness or overfatigue by playing all out in every encounter. Orchestrate your effort so that it peaks when you get to the championships. If you go all out at all times prior to the championships, you're inviting microtrauma, small injuries that will keep you from your goal.

FITNESS

Continue your training program at 90 percent effort, or gradually move up to 100 percent if it's an all-out strength or endurance event.

Maintenance of specific acclimatization is important now if you plan to compete at altitudes or temperatures different from those in which you've trained. To whatever extent you can, duplicate the conditions of the new environment every other day.

Any circulorespiratory training should correspond exactly to the requirements of your event. Train at the speed of the event, for the duration of the event, with the same active rest intervals that you get in the actual event. This adjustment of the training load to match peak competition efforts with no further overloading is called *tapering*.

SKILL

You've got it now—at least all you can or should try to get before your important competition.

This is not the time to make changes. Avoid all analysis. Anything that needs changing will be done after the season. To change now would be to risk your chances of winning.

19

Focusing on Your Sport

Now THAT YOU understand the characteristic of training for maximum performance, let's put those principles into specific terms, so that you can be certain you're making maximum use of your training time.

Of the more than 300 sports, we've selected 30 that are either popular or serve as good examples of many other sports. What follows are brief guidelines that show what to concentrate on in preparing yourself physically for the activity of your choice. Now's the time for you to rate each of the required elements with a low, medium or high priority, as we did for tennis in Chapter 13. To assist you, we've rated each sport in terms of the needs of the average player. Our ratings are not exact for every condition: you should change them up or down, depending on your manner of play and your expectations.

Each of the sections also includes guidelines on what general principles of learning and skill we've previously discussed will help you improve your game.

ARCHERY

A BRACHIATING SPORT. You'll need arm, shoulder and back strength, meaning that you'll want to concentrate on the exercises found on pages 252-62. Isometric arm exercises, shown on page 261, are especially applicable to preparation for archery performance.

But archery requires skill more than it does strength, so you'll want to give 75 percent of your time to the perfection of the art (Chapter 10). Skill in archery is enhanced by establishing a Zen-like interrelationship between the archer, bow, arrow, course and target (see pages 113-15).

Conditioning Priority

Muscle mass	M
Muscle endurance	M
Muscle strength	H
Circulorespiratory endurance	L
Mobility	M
Durability of joints and ligaments	M
Toughness of skin	L
Ability to relax	M

BACKPACKING AND MOUNTAIN CLIMBING

CLIMBING—AN all-but-inevitable component of backpacking—requires agility, muscular endurance and strength and cardiorespiratory endurance. Endurance training will be particularly helpful when you get to high altitudes.

Preparation for backpacking and mountain climbing should give 80 percent to locomotor conditioning (pages 249-55), with heavy emphasis on circulorespiratory endurance exercises (page 272), and 20 percent to brachiation conditioning (pages 252-62), with arm presses as the principal exercise.

Conditioning Priority

Muscle mass	M
Muscle endurance	H
Muscle strength	H
Circulorespiratory endurance	H
Mobility	M
Durability of joints and ligaments	M
Toughness of skin	H
Ability to relax	M

BADMINTON

BADMINTON CAN BE played with satisfaction at the beginning and expert levels, and everywhere in between; it's that kind of game. As skill improves and game intensity increases, the play requires quick changes of direction. Maximum performance in badminton requires muscular and circulorespiratory endurance, particularly in singles competition.

Early training (Chapter 15) involves both locomotor conditioning (pages 249-55) and brachiating conditioning (pages 252-62). Quickness and agility are perfected through skill practice (Chapter 10). In the first stages of development, give 70 percent of your time to physical conditioning and 30 percent to skill and strategy. As the competitive season approaches and your condition improves, reverse the priorities.

Throughout your training, work hard on flexibility (pages 233-41) to enhance the speed and angle of motion required in badminton.

Endurance training should conform to the event. Simulate the movement, speed and duration of the game. (See pages 178-84.)

Conditioning Priority

Muscle mass	L
Muscle endurance	H
Muscle strength	M
Circulorespiratory endurance	H
Mobility	H
Durability of joints and ligaments	H
Toughness of skin	M
Ability to relax	M

BASEBALL

BASEBALL PLAYERS have a special problem. Except for pitchers, catchers and first basemen, they are not as active during a contest as players in most other team sports. Their special problem, as a consequence, is a tendency to accumulate excess body fat.

The conditioning program for baseball and softball players, therefore, should combine brachiation circuit training (pages 252-62) with long slow distance (LSD) running to burn calories. Five miles a day at any speed usually shifts the balance of food intake and caloric burnoff so that fat is reduced without starvation dieting. Running in rubberized suits may show substantial weight loss on the scales, but this is mostly water loss, not fat loss; as soon as the water is replaced —as it must be—the weight will return. The prime objective during the baseball season is to refrain from increasing body fat and thereby reducing your playing effectiveness.

Baseball is essentially a contest between the pitcher and the batter, with the batter winning usually no more than 30 percent of the time. Batting requires a firm grip, which can be developed by using the isometric exercises on page 261; batting also requires body stability, which is developed best by the eight-count pushup exercise found on page 257.

At the outset of training, pitchers should devote 90 percent of their time to brachiation training (pages 256-62) to protect against arm strains, and the other 10 percent to locomotor training (pages 249-55). Once the arm is fit and skill training begins, the priorities are 90 percent on skill development. (Chapter 10) and 10 percent on fitness training. This priority holds during the competitive season. The flexibility circuit (pages 233-41) should be practiced almost daily unless the pitcher's joints are already lax.

During the season, other players should divide 30 percent of their training time between locomotor and brachiation training, and give 70 percent of their time to skill training. All players, regardless of their position, should concentrate on arm strength exercises (pages 258, 259).

Skill in pitching comes from mastery of the summation of forces described on pages 140-45 and the windup on pages 144-45. Batting skill employs the same two principles. Players should learn to stay low (page 150) and to sink slightly before moving to increase takeoff speed (pages 151-52).

Not much running is done in baseball. In the course of a two to three hour game, most players would run no more than a mile—half of that to and from their positions. But because running during play must be performed at maximum, some locomotor training (pages 249-55) is advised. This training will also add to power at the plate, as the legs are very much a component of the swing. See especially the first principle in Chapter 11 on Super Ks (page 140).

Conditioning Priority

	Pitchers only	All others
Muscle mass	M	L
Muscle endurance	H	L
Muscle strength	H	L
Circulorespiratory endurance	L	L
Mobility	H	L

Durability of joints and ligaments	H	M
Toughness of skin	M	L
Ability to relax	H	L

BASKETBALL

THE REQUIREMENTS for strength, endurance and durability of ligaments and joints are such in this vigorous sport that they demand long-term conditioning before basketball pratice begins. At the outset, you would devote 90 percent of your time to conditioning, and only 10 percent to skill development. Both locomotor training (pages 249-55) and brachiation training (pages 256-62) are essential in the early stages.

During the periods of rehearsal and competition (Chapter 18), training priorities shift radically. Now you'll spend 20 percent of your time on the maintenance of condition (pages 277-79), using the kangaroo hop exercise (page 252) in particular, and 80 percent of your time on the perfection of skill (Chapter 10) and strategy (pages 345-46).

The basketball player wants to establish a friendly harmony with the ball (pages 115-17) and develop a delicate finger touch (pages 142-50) for shooting accuracy.

To get height, the player first sinks low (page 150) to gather for the upward spring.

As anyone who has ever played it knows, basketball requires rapid and constant action. Endurance will keep you going in the crucial fourth quarter. Start with long slow distance training (pages 267, 272), but move as soon as possible to training at the speed of the event; for the length of the event, at least, and slightly longer to develop a reserve for the occasional overtime; and in the mode of the event. (See page 280.)

Conditioning Priority

Muscle mass	M
Muscle endurance	H
Muscle strength	H
Circulorespiratory endurance	H
Mobility	H
Durability of joints and ligaments	H
Toughness of skin	H
Ability to relax	M

BOWLING

BOWLING IS A MILD ACTIVITY requiring little strength or endurance. The weight of the ball can be adjusted to the bowler's strength and hand size. Although the accuracy needed to compete with experts demands extensive training, skill in bowling is easily acquired. The secret is to practice each component—address, walk and delivery—separately until all are ready to be put together (pages 114-15).

All bowling practice is at game speed (pages 128-30). The biggest problem is that first results tend to provide poor feedback (pages 120-22). As skill improves and the ball is delivered properly over the guide spots, it avoids the gutter and knocks down the pins —changing the bowler's image (pages 123-26).

Inasmuch as skill is almost everything and conditioning little or nothing, practice time should be devoted almost exclusively to skill (Chapter 10). Brachiating exercises (pages 256-62) will strengthen the arms, back and shoulders, and the flexibility circuit (pages 233-41) will improve your mobility.

As in archery, skill in bowling is established by an interrelationship between the bowler, ball, alley and pins (pages 113-15).

Conditioning Priority

Muscle mass	L
Muscle endurance	L
Muscle strength	M
Circulorespiratory endurance	L
Mobility	M
Durability of joints and ligaments	M
Toughness of skin	M
Ability to relax	M

BOXING

THE PURPOSE OF boxing is to produce a concussion in the brain of the opponent, rendering him harmless. Any unconsciousness signals brain damage; the extent of damage is roughly in proportion to the number of minutes of unconsciousness accumulated over the term of the boxer's career.

To avoid knockout, watch the opponent's waistline, which moves before the hand and signals the punch (page 142). If your opponent becomes furious, you have a strategic advantage (page 22).

Boxing is both a brachiating and locomotor sport. Conditioning should alternate between these programs. (See Chapter 17.)

Conditioning Priority

Muscle mass	M
Muscle endurance	H
Muscle strength	H
Circulorespiratory endurance	H
Mobility	H
Durability of joints and ligaments	H
Toughness of skin	H
Ability to relax	H

CYCLING

LEGS, LEGS, LEGS. Get them in condition with loco-motor training (pages 249-55).

Go for muscle endurance rather than strength (pages 210-15) and for circulorespiratory endurance, first by long slow distance training (pages 267, 272) and then by interval training (pages 213-15, 274-78). Gradually elevate your heart rate to at least 80 percent of maximum, and 90 to 100 percent if you'll need that kind of exertion in a race (pages 276-78).

Learn to pace yourself rather than using undue effort at the outset that will leave you without gas near the finish (page 69).

And learn to relax, using Dynamic Relaxation (Chapter 4) and the Dynamic Relaxation Run (pages 37-38).

Conditioning Priority

Muscle mass	H
Muscle endurance	H
Muscle strength	M
Circulorespiratory endurance	H
Mobility	L
Durability of joints and ligaments	H
Toughness of skin	H
Ability to relax	H

DIVING, SPRINGBOARD

THE TWO MOST important needs for diving are muscular strength and flexibility. Get in condition with the locomotor circuit (pages 249-55) and the flexibility circuit (pages 233-41).

Skill emphasizes balance and agility. Remember

that the head leads the body (pages 145-46). And train away from the pool by using mental practice (pages 134-36).

Conditioning Priority

Muscle mass	M
Muscle endurance	M
Muscle strength	H
Circulorespiratory endurance	L
Mobility	H
Durability of joints and ligaments	M
Toughness of skin	L
Ability to relax	M

FENCING

CONDITIONING FOR FENCING should emphasize brachiation exercises (pages 256-62), with some locomotor conditioning as well (pages 249-55). The need is for muscular endurance, so do the exercises with that objective in mind, using light loads and many repetitions; for a discussion of this principle, see pages 210-15.

Mobility is another high priority. Condition for it with the flexibility circuit (pages 233-41).

Skill effectiveness develops with your increasing ability to make lightning decisions. The process becomes automatic after sufficient effective practice. (See Chapters 9 and 10, also pages 151-52.)

Conditioning Priority

Muscle mass	M
Muscle endurance	H
Muscle strength	M
Circulorespiratory endurance	M
Mobility	H

Durability of joints and ligaments	M
Toughness of skin	M
Ability to relax	H

FIELD HOCKEY

A HARD RUNNING game played with a stick and a hard ball. Running and stopping to turn sharply on grass strain the knees and ankles in particular, which means that you'll want to give a lot of time to locomotor exercises that condition the joints and ligaments of your legs (pages 249-55). Do the exercises to develop endurance, primarily, using light loads and high repetitions.

Skill requires agility and fast response. See, especially, Chapters 10 and 11.

You'll perform better and last longer if you're without excess tension. Practice Dynamic Relaxation (Chapter 4).

Conditioning Priority

Muscle mass	M
Muscle endurance	H
Muscle strength	H
Circulorespiratory endurance	H
Mobility	H
Durability of joints and ligaments	H
Toughness of skin	H
Ability to relax	M

FOOTBALL

CONDITIONING FOR FOOTBALL is a year-round commitment. It's no good to try to get in shape just before the season; you can't do enough in that amount of time to achieve the condition required for maximum performance. There is a brief period, following the season, that's dedicated to recovery. During this period, the players should tend to any ailments developed during play, and begin therapy to correct defects, speed recovery and strengthen weak areas of the body. At the same time, players should avoid deterioration by performing minimum maintenance activities (pages 189-91) in addition to their therapeutic exercises.

After the first month, the players should start a new conditioning cycle, commencing with the replacement of fat with muscle using the tissue rebuilding exercises on pages 199-210. During this period, the intensity of circulorespiratory exercise need not exceed 60 percent. Building stamina comes next (pages 210-15). Finally, strength (pages 215-18).

Fitness evaluation tests (Chapter 16), taken both before and after spring practice, can inform each player of his further needs for conditioning exercises.

Daily practice should start with the limbering circuit (pages 223-26). *After* skill and strategy sessions have been held, the practice can conclude with early conditioning circuits (Chapter 15) conducted at about 80 percent of capacity, and finally the flexibility circuit (pages 233-41). Players already sufficiently lax can be excused from the flexibility circuit.

Conditioning for maximum performance in the fall season begins immediately after the end of spring training. Since football requires both leg and arm action, both locomotor (pages 249-55) and brachiation (pages 252-62) circuits are employed. Linemen can exercise at 80 percent of capacity, but backs and ends need to boost their cardiorespiratory conditioning to 90 percent of maximum during early preseason, and gradually close to 100 percent as competition nears.

Every practice starts with the limbering circuit (pages 223-26) and concludes with the flexibility circuit (233-41), with the exceptions made for those with lax joints, as noted above. Joints that are too lax are highly susceptible to injury, thus the exclusion.

Football players need muscle mass but not added

weight in the form of excess fat. Excessive body fat is a hindrance, impairing speed, agility and endurance. Players with excess fat should convert it to vital tissue (pages 268-70). Body fat control is better assessed by waistline girth changes than by scale weight, due to changes in muscle weight caused by training regimens. (For a comprehensive discussion of weight control, see Chapter V of *Total Fitness*.) Weigh-ins before and after practice are fluid-loss indicators, useful guides for water and salt replacement.

The training table diet for football players is, or should be, a normal balanced one that includes a wide variety of foods. A slight shift toward carbohydrate foods a day or two before games and the addition of salty foods in hot weather are the only modifications needed.

Conditioning Priority

Muscle mass	H
Muscle endurance	H
Muscle strength	H
Circulorespiratory endurance	M
Mobility	M
Durability of joints and ligaments	H
Toughness of skin	H
Ability to relax	H

GOLF

GOLFERS, ESPECIALLY those who can't break 100, seem to be avid analysts. They study golf magazines, books and syndicated newspaper columns with a view toward adding every nuance to their game—all this during extended periods of play. Many try to pick up pointers from fellow players and caddies between shots during a game—even during tournament play. The idea of taking a month or more away from game play for stroke analysis and game rebuilding under professional guidance is unthinkable for most players, yet this is just what they need to bring their scores down. It is during the period of development (pages 268-70) that such analysis and game rebuilding best occur. Then the player can go back to the driving range or the course and start a period of refinement (pages 273-76). His greatest effort at this point should be to resist all challenges and wagers; if he succumbs, he'll be enormously tempted to revert to his old stroke just to win a hole. Even during the rehearsal stage (pages 276-78), competition should be confined to a friendly, sociable match. Only in the competition stage (pages 278-79) does the remade golfer put his new game to the test.

Golf is a game of skill, not strength or endurance. Obviously, you want to be fit enough to swing a club with vigor. For this, brachiating conditioning (pages 256-62) at 80 percent of maximum effort will be more than sufficient. All practice and play should be preceded by a limbering circuit (pages 223-26) and followed by a flexibility circuit (pages 233-41) to avoid stiffness and increase mobility.

To learn why a novice should begin the game on the putting green, see pages 57 and 113-15. To learn how to get extra distance, see sections on the virtue of a tight grip (pages 146-47 and 166-69), on getting your back into the ball, and on summating your force (pages 140-46). Developing just the right amount of tension is discussed in Chapter 3, how to practice is in Chapter 10; how to "target" your shot is on pages 136-37, and how a holistic approach applies to the art of golf is on pages 113-15.

Conditioning Priorities

Muscle mass	L
Muscle endurance	L
Muscle strength	L
Circulorespiratory endurance	L
Mobility	M

Durability of joints and ligaments	M
Toughness of skin	M
Ability to relax	H

GYMNASTICS

TUMBLING IS THE first skill learned in gymnastics. It teaches you how to fall without injury. Before tumbling, however, comes the long conditioning needed to build muscle tissue (Chapter 15), to become flexible (pages 233-41) and to prepare for locomotor and brachiating movements (pages 251-62).

Most gymnastic apparatus events are brachiating movements. Floor exercises and vaulting combine brachiation with locomotion. High degress of muscular strength and endurance are needed to execute the required movements. Bear in mind that these two qualities are come by separately; loads and numbers of repetitions of exercise vary with your objectives— heavy loads and few repetitions for strength, light loads and many repetitions for endurance. (See pages 210-17 for a fuller discussion.)

The musculature of the arms and shoulder girdle, not used strongly in most other sports, is dominantly used in gymnastics. Body mobility is vital; all workouts should end with the flexibility circuit (pages 233-41).

Conditioning Priorities

Muscle mass	H
Muscle endurance	H
Muscle strength	H
Circulorespiratory endurance	M
Mobility	H
Durability of joints and ligaments	H
Toughness of skin	H
Ability to relax	H

HANDBALL

HANDBALL, WHETHER IT'S PLAYED using one, two, three or four walls, puts great demands on circulorespiratory endurance, agility, speed of movement, flexibility and muscular endurance. Played with both hands, handball contributes to symmetrical development. The continuous running and sudden changes in direction during the game make handball a locomotor as well as a brachiating sport.

Fitness for handball, then, should emphasize muscular endurance in both the upper and lower body. Locomotor and brachiation training should be alternated (Chapter 17). To build up circulorespiratory endurance, interval training (pages 211-15) should follow long slow distance training (pages 267-70 and 272-78). The flexibility circuit (pages 233-41) should conclude your workout.

Dynamic Relaxation (Chapter 4) will put you at just the right level of tension to maximize your movements.

In preparing for handball, give 30 percent of your time to fitness and 70 percent to skill. Many of the Super Ks in Chapter 11 apply to handball, particularly the technique of using all your body in your shot, whipping not batting the ball (pages 140-46), playing low and getting into position fast (pages 147-52).

Conditioning Priorities

Muscle mass	M
Muscle endurance	H
Muscle strength	H
Circulorespiratory endurance	H
Mobility	H
Durability of joints and ligaments	H
Toughness of skin	H
Ability to relax	M

ICE HOCKEY

A HARD, slippery surface, large, hard hockey stick, hard, fast-moving puck, sharp skate edges and points and hard fence and goal cage make hockey an extemely hazardous sport. Anyone playing hockey owes it to himself to be in the best possible condition. Fitness requirements are across the board; you need muscle bulk, muscle endurance and muscle strength in both the upper and lower body. Locomotor training (pages 249-55) should be alternated with brachiation training (pages 252-62), and the exercises should be performed in varying ways to achieve the three objectives of bulk, strength and endurance: first, moderate loads and fifteen to twenty repetitions for bulk; later on, after you've acquired sufficient bulk, high repetitions using light loads to obtain endurance; finally, maximum loads and one to five repetitions for strength. (See pages 199-210.)

For circulorespiratory endurance, interval training (pages 212-15) should follow long slow distance training (pages 272-73).

Workouts should be divided evenly between fitness and skill training. Dynamic Relaxation (Chapter 4) not only will put your tension level where you want it, but will help you to keep your cool during the close combat that characterizes hockey.

Conditioning Priorities

Muscle mass	H
Muscle endurance	H
Muscle strength	H
Circulorespiratory endurance	H
Mobility	H
Durability of joints and ligaments	H
Toughness of skin	H
Ability to relax	H

JOGGING AND DISTANCE RUNNING

MUSCULAR STRENGTH IS not a prime requirement in these events; the name of the game is endurance. To that end, you'll be doing yourself an enormous favor by losing excess fat in preparation for your event. You'll want to be sure that all the tissue you're going to be propelling over those long distances is healthy tissue, working in your behalf.

As a first step, then, you might want to review the pound-a-week weight loss program found on page 269.

If you're in poor condition as you begin your development program, it would be wise to start by walking until you can complete two miles without fatigue. Next, walk the same distance more briskly, or walk up hills, working yourself up to a training pulse rate of 70 percent of your age-adjusted maximum, using the formula found on pages 197-98. Then, start jogging the two miles, making sure that your pulse remains between 70 and 80 percent of maximum.

Once your running has become vigorous—above 70 percent of maximum—precede your workout with a limbering circuit (pages 223-26) and follow it with a flexibility circuit (pages 233-41).

Finally, train with the locomotor circuit (pages 251-55) to increase your running power and endurance.

Endurance for running is developed in two stages. At the outset, you'll want to train at 70 to 80 percent of your maximum heart rate with long slow distance (LSD) running. Once your running at that speed has improved—you'll know it has by the relative ease with which you can run distances that were difficult for you at the outset—it's time to increase to the intensity of the event. You do this by increasing the speed with which you run, until your heart rate is in the 90–100 percent of maximum range during the latter portion of your run.

Fatigue in long runs is due mainly to an exhaustion of stored energy, i.e., a depletion of carbohydrates. As carbohydrates deplete, the body uses fats.

In the early part of a distance run, the runner is operating at about 80 percent of capacity. Later on, toward the end of a long run, the runner may need to use energy to his maximum capacity in order to maintain his initial speed. If the runner attempts to go all out too early in the race, the waste products of his energy utilization (metabolism) will accumulate to such an extent that he will feel intolerable pain. Learning to orchestrate your race to your heart rate, therefore, plays an important part in your performance. To be certain you understand the principles of heart-rated training, review pages 191-98.

Remember that running in heat makes extra demands on your circulation, which reduces performance. Dehydration, due to inadequate replacement of fluids, and overheating can cause collapse and even death. If you intend to run in hot climates, you should acclimate yourself gradually to those conditions. The same for running at altitudes above 5000 feet.

Whatever the conditions, two training sessions a week will improve your performance somewhat; five or six sessions a week will produce maximal improvement.

Conditioning Priorities

Muscle mass	H
Muscle endurance	H
Muscle strength	H
Circulorespiratory endurance	H
Mobility	L
Durability of joints and ligaments	H
Toughness of skin (feet only)	H
Ability to relax	H

JUMPING, HIGH AND LONG

A PURELY LOCOMOTOR SPORT. Conditioning should emphasize the lower body (pages 251-55). Both muscular endurance and strength are needed; the exercises must be performed separately and differently to achieve each of these objectives (pages 210-18)— low loads and high repetitions for endurance, maximum loads and few repetitions for strength. Body mobility is imperative. All workouts should conclude with the flexibility circuit (pages 233-41). Finally, circulorespiratory endurance should be developed, using interval training (pages 213-15) after first spending several weeks on long slow distance conditioning (pages 267-70 and 272-78).

Learning to rehearse your jump in your mind will greatly improve your performance (see pages 134-36).

Conditioning Priorities

Muscle mass	M
Muscle endurance	M
Muscle strength	H
Circulorespiratory endurance	M
Mobility	H
Durability of joints and ligaments	H
Toughness of skin	M
Ability to relax	H

ROWING

A BRACHIATING SPORT, requiring more fitness than skill, but a sublimely satisfying one to those who practice it. In training for rowing, give 80 percent of your time to the development of fitness, emphasizing muscular endurance, particularly in the upper body. Do the brachiation circuit exercises many times with light loads (pages 252-62).

Rowing at a fast pace puts a strain on the circulorespiratory system, which, of course, helps condition the system. Further conditioning can be accomplished through interval training (pages 213-15) after an initial several weeks of long slow distance training (pages 267-70 and 272-78).

Rowing skill improves as rhythm improves. The right state of tension—just enough, not too much—can enhance rhythm. So utilize Dynamic Relaxation (Chapter 4).

Conditioning Priorities

Muscle mass	H
Muscle endurance	H
Muscle strength	H
Circulorespiratory endurance	H
Mobility	L
Durability of joints and ligaments	H
Toughness of skin	H
Ability to relax	H

SKATING, ICE AND ROLLER

CONDITION YOUR LEGS for muscular endurance, using the locomotor exercises on pages 249-55—low loads, high repetitions.

Mobility is important in skating. The flexibility circuit should conclude every workout (see pages 233-41).

Optimal tension greatly enhances performance. To skate fast, you must learn to relax your muscles. Practice Dynamic Relaxation (Chapter 4).

Conditioning Priorities

Muscle mass	M
Muscle endurance	H
Muscle strength	M
Circulorespiratory endurance	H
Mobility	H
Disability of joints and ligaments	H
Toughness of skin	M
Ability to relax	H

SKIING

SKIING DOWN A MOUNTAIN SLOPE produces feelings of exaltation and enervation in equal quantity. There are few sports where improved condition so improves one's ability to perform the sport as he would like to. The emphasis in conditioning should be on the lower body, but the upper body shouldn't be neglected. Train for muscular endurance with the locomotor exercises (pages 249-55), using light loads and many repetitions. Give some time to brachiating exercises (pages 256-62).

Circulorespiratory endurance training is a must, if you're to ski at all well. Spend several weeks, at least, on long slow distance training at the outset of your conditioning program (pages 267-72). Then move to interval training (pages 213-15). The recreational skier can exercise at 80 percent of his maximum heart rate (pages 197-98 and 273-78), but the racer should move to 90 percent and approach 100 percent as competition nears.

Undue tension is a frequent problem and major handicap in skiing well. Practice Dynamic Relaxation (Chapter 4) in your workouts, particularly when you're skiing poorly.

Conditioning Priorities

Muscle mass	M
Muscle endurance	H
Muscle strength	H
Circulorespiratory endurance	H
Mobility	H
Durability of joints and ligaments	H
Toughness of skin	H
Ability to relax	H

SOCCER

SOCCER IS THE ONLY major game requiring chiefly co-ordination of eyes and feet. To play it well, you need timing, balance and speed. And you must be in super shape. Soccer involves long periods of continuous play; substitutions are seldom made and, in certain instances, not permitted. Locomotor conditioning (pages 249-55) for muscular endurance is essential if you expect to play well.

Circulorespiratory endurance is another imperative. Start with long slow distance training (pages 268-72) and move after several weeks to interval training (pages 213-15), matching your movements to those you make in a game. Finish your workouts with a flexibility circuit (pages 233-41).

And practice Dynamic Relaxation (Chapter 4) to put yourself into an otpimal state of tension. Excess tension while following the ball and anticipating a pass is fatiguing; overanxiety can destroy your coordination. Dynamic Relaxation should be practiced during the rehearsal stage of your program (pages 276-78) so that your relaxed technique can be incorporated into your play.

A number of Super Ks in Chapter 11 are applicable to soccer, particularly those dealing with skill in kicking, rapid starting and balance.

Conditioning Priorities

Muscle mass	M
Muscle endurance	H
Muscle strength	M
Circulorespiratory endurance	H
Mobility	H
Durability of joints and ligaments	H
Toughness of skin	H
Ability to relax	M

SPRINTING

RUNNING A SHORT DISTANCE at top speed—whether it's a dash in track, or running bases, or open-field running in football—involves the same ingredients: a fast reaction time; an ability to accelerate from a dead stop to maximum speed; and an ability to maintain that speed for as long as required.

Fast reaction time and the ability to sustain maximum speed are probably more affected by heredity than training, which means that sprinters are more likely born than made. High knee lift, long stride and forceful push off the rear leg tend to characterize champion runners, but styles vary widely among individuals to no apparent disadvantage, and attempts to change minor variations may be a waste of time.

Much can be done, however, to maximize performance in sprinting. Reaction time represents only about 1 percent of a race; explosive power in leaving the blocks, about 5 percent; power to accelerate, 64 percent; speed (which is a combination of stride rate and length) about 18 percent; and the ability to maintain speed about 12 percent. If the power to accelerate is the major factor in sprinting performance, it follows that the major objectives of fitness training should be the development of muscular endurance, muscular strength, flexibility, and the reduction of excess fat.

As we've learned, muscular endurance and muscular strength are developed in different ways (see pages 177-78). Your program should incorporate both procedures. For flexibility, concentrate on the flexibility circuit (pages 233-41) at the end of each workout.

Warming up, raising muscle temperature a degree or two, probably reduces the possibility of muscle pulls, and may, in some runners, contribute a trifle to speed, especially if the sprint is executed after a minute's recovery from the warmup, Be sure you understand the function of the limbering circuit (pages 223-26), which should precede all training for maximum performance, as well as the warmup circuit (page 222). For a runner, a warmup circuit would consist of a slow rehearsal of the motions he'll perform at top speed. Remember not to overdo it; if you start to perspire, you're using energy that would be better spent when it counts.

Other than to maintain general fitness, a sprinter has no need for brachiation conditioning. He should concentrate, instead, on locomotor conditioning (pages 249-55).

Conditioning Priorities

Muscle mass	H
Muscle endurance	H
Muscle strength	H
Circulorespiratory endurance	M
Mobility	H
Durability of joints and ligaments	H
Toughness of skin	M
Ability to relax	H

SQUASH, RACQUETS, PADDLEBALL AND PLATFORM TENNIS

THESE ARE GAMES in which the need for fitness is in proportion to the degree of skill with which they're played. Among novice players, the duration of each rally might be short. As skill improves, so does the ability to sustain a rally. At the top, it's a zestful game of brilliant rallies, requiring much muscular and circulorespiratory endurance—not so much for the player who dominates the middle as for the opponent he's manipulating.

These games combine locomotion and brachiation. The two training circuits should be alternated, and done in a manner to enhance endurance (Chapter 17). As the games put a premium on agility, body mobility is important. Flexibility circuits should conclude each workout (pages 233-41).

For circulorespiratory endurance, interval training (pages 213-15 and 274-76) at 80 percent of maximum heart rate is adequate for recreational players. Tournament players would want to move up to 90 percent and even 100 percent just before competition begins.

Conditioning Priorities

Muscle mass	M
Muscle endurance	H
Muscle strength	M
Circulorespiratory endurance	H
Mobility	H
Durability of joints and ligaments	H
Toughness of skin	M
Ability to relax	M

SWIMMING

GETTING FIT FOR SWIMMING depends to some extent on your objectives. If you're a marathon swimmer, a certain amount of body fat might actually be an advantage, since body fat increases buoyancy and insulates against chilling in cold-water swims. For any kind of speed swimming, however, fat is a drag; it should be reduced.

Competitive swimming calls for efficient stroke mechanisms, muscular endurance and a great capacity for energy expenditure. Sprint swimming requires an inordinately higher rate of energy expenditure than distance swimming because of increased body lift and because of wave and eddy resistance at high velocity.

Muscular strength is not improved during a season of competitive swimming unless the swimmer employs weight training or other strengthening procedures. This indicates that swimming does not involve a high degree of strength, probably because the peak resistance of water against arms and legs is too low to overload muscle strength, even in sprint swimming.

So it's muscular endurance that's needed, mostly in the upper body. Brachiating exercises (pages 256-62) should be emphasized, but some time should be given to locomotor exercises (pages 249-55), as well—in each case, low loads and high repetitions to maximize endurance.

Warming up is not a vital factor in swimming performance. It should be kept to a minimum, so that energy can be invested in the performance itself.

Mobility *is* a vital factor, however, which means that flexibility circuit training should conclude all workouts (pages 233-41).

Experienced swimmers have learned to relax in the water, but often become tense before races due to overanxiety. Training to relax such excess tension will enhance competitive performances. Practice Dynamic Relaxation (Chapter 4).

Skill: Most of the propulsion in swimming is derived from the arms. It's important to pull the arms through the water nearly to the finish of the entire arc. Near the end of the stroke, the forearm and hand are pushing the water directly rearward. That last effort is what distinguishes the excellent swimmer. (See pages 147-49.)

Beyond that, skill is a matter of idiosyncratic style (see pages 17-19). There is no perfect way to do something. There's a way that's right for you, which you and your coach should seek to develop (see Chapter 12). You should work to achieve the idea of swimming (pages 123-28) to see how it's going to feel. Only with that idea in mind can you make real progress.

Conditioning Priorities

Muscle mass	H
Muscle endurance	H
Muscle strength	H
Circulorespiratory endurance	H
Mobility	H
Durability of joints and ligaments	L
Toughness of skin	L
Ability to relax	H

TENNIS

A PROPERLY ORCHESTRATED program can lead to enormous improvement in tennis for even the average player. Most players try to improve their game by taking a lesson or two to correct a flaw. As we've seen (pages 120-23), that's not the route to maximum performance in any sport, tennis least of all.

Conditioning specifically designed to strengthen the stress areas in tennis will do wonders for your game. Tennis, with its violent and sudden movements, puts great strains on your arms and legs. At least a year of very gradual conditioning is needed to build the body's defenses. But it's not just a matter of guarding against injuries; you'll play like a different person when you're properly conditioned.

Tennis is both a locomotor and a brachiating sport. The manner of alternating exercises for the upper and lower body is elaborated in Chapter 17. You need a certain amount of muscle bulk, but not a great amount. Once you've developed muscle bulk, your objective should focus on overall muscle endurance by exercising with low loads and many repetitions. Your wrist, arm and shoulder muscles need strength as well as endurance, which means maximum loads and few repetitions when the exercises are performed for strength. Remember, you can only work for one objective at a time (Chapter 14); if muscle tissue, endurance and strength are all essential, they should be developed one at a time, in that order.

Long-term progressive conditioning that thickens and strengthens the wrist, arm and shoulder muscles will prepare them for the great stresses experienced when a ball is smashed with a firm grip, and thereby diminish the risk of "tennis elbow."

Legs need endurance, particularly if you're playing competitive singles. When the legs go in the latter stages of a match, your game usually goes with them. Locomotor exercises (pages 251-55), particularly the bench-stepping exercise (page 254), should be performed with endurance in mind.

Exercising for circulorespiratory endurance will add endurance to the leg muscles at the same time, if the exercises are done correctly. Begin with long slow distance training at 80 percent of maximum heart rate, but move to interval training within several weeks. The jogging you do in LSD training will get you fit for jogging, but not for tennis; you don't jog in tennis, you run in bursts, and so to train specifically for tennis, you must run in bursts. The bursts should approximate the length of time you rally when you play, and should be followed by an interval of active rest—walking briskly—approximately equal to the time you would take to start a new point. Recreational players can continue at 80 percent; tournament players should train eventually at 90 to 100 percent.

One marvelous way to develop both circulorespiratory endurance and muscle endurance for tennis is to simulate the very movements you would make on the court. Racket in hand, pretend to begin a point. "Serve" the ball, then hit ground strokes, move in to the "net" for some rapid volleys, then move back to return a lob, and put it away with an overhead. "Play" like this for a minute, walk rapidly for ten to fifteen seconds as though you were retrieving a ball, then resume "play." The more "points" you play, the better your condition for that arduous third set in the tournament.

To develop mobility, always finish your workouts with the flexibility circuit (pages 233-41).

Too much tension often impedes good play. Learn to develop an optimal state of tension by practicing Dynamic Relaxation, particularly during warmup and rallies before play (Chapter 4).

If your next tournament is in a warm and/or humid place, wear warmup clothing during practice to acclimate yourself to play in the heat. Drink water before and during sessions.

Skill: Efficient stroke mechanics will help to protect your arm, in addition to winning points. To make a quantum jump in ability, you should set aside a special time of several weeks and even months to rebuild your game (pages 120-23 and Chapter 18). During this period, all competition should be avoided.

The relationship of a tight grip to power tennis should be understood, and the proper grip developed (see pages 146-47 and 167).

Many of the Super Ks in Chapter 11 apply to tennis, particularly those dealing with the use of the entire body rather than just the arm, to gain power; the "summation of forces" principle; the windup; finishing the stroke; aspects that quicken movement and relaxation. The aspiring tennis player should study the entire chapter with care.

Your ability to keep the ball in play is an important indicator of your increasing skill. After stroke mechanics have been mastered, maximal performance comes from focusing on the action of the ball (pages 109-11 and 149, not on the antics of your opponent or your own mistakes. Learning to sight and frame (pages 131-34) will help focus your game.

If your fitness is low on the evaluation scale, tennis

practice sessions should be short, not exceeding half an hour. Practicing while fatigued leads to careless stroke habits as well as injuries (pages 130-31). As fitness improves, the duration of practices can be gradually increased.

Conditioning for tennis should always follow skill practices; it should never precede play. If your practices are intensive, they should be scheduled on alternate days; brachiation and/or locomotor routines can be done on days between skill practice.

Spend 40 percent of your available time on developing fitness, 60 percent on developing skill.

Conditioning Priorities

Muscle mass	M
Muscle endurance	H
Muscle strength	H (wrist and forearm), M (rest of body)
Circulorespiratory endurance	H
Mobility	H
Durability of joints and ligaments	H
Toughness of skin (hands only)	H
Ability to relax	M

VOLLEYBALL

THIS INCREASINGLY POPULAR sport requires quick movement and fine coordination if it's to be played well.

Conditioning involves both locomotor (pages 249-55) and brachiation (pages 256-62) exercises. The emphasis is on strength, so after you've built muscle bulk (pages 198-203), use maximum loads and few repetitions. The kangaroo hop exercise (page 252) is particularly good for volleyball.

Circulorespiratory endurance training should begin with long slow distance running at 80 percent of maximum heart rate. After several weeks, take up interval training (pages 213-15 and 268-72). Recreational players can remain at 80 percent; competitors should move into the 90 to 100 percent range as competition nears.

The kangaroo hop, incidentally, can give you a terrific circulorespiratory workout if you continue it long enough.

The Super Ks on movement in Chapter 11 are applicable to volleyball; other Super Ks can add authority to your spike. Special attention must be given to learning how to fall and recover fast.

In terms of reaction, sighting and framing (pages 131-34) can help focus your attention so that you're not diverted unproductively.

Conditioning Priorities

Muscle mass	H
Muscle endurance	H
Muscle strength	H
Circulorespiratory endurance	M
Mobility	H
Durability of joints and ligaments	H
Toughness of skin	H
Ability to relax	M

WATER SKIING

THIS SPORT TAXES both the upper and lower body. After you've developed sufficient muscle tissue, use light loads and many repetitions for endurance. Train with the brachiation and locomotor circuits (Chapter 17) to develop muscular endurance.

Dynamic Relaxation (Chapter 4) will put you in an optimal state of tension to smooth your performance.

Give conditioning 40 percent of your time, skill development 60 percent. Skill is basically a matter of balance. See the Super Ks chapter, particularly page 149.

Conditioning Priorities

Muscle mass	M
Muscle endurance	H
Muscle strength	H
Cardiorespiratory endurance	L
Mobility	L
Durability of joints and ligaments	H
Toughness of skin	L
Ability to relax	M

WEIGHT LIFTING

WEIGHT LIFTING IS PRIMARILY a brachiating sport with support required from strong legs and back muscles. You need both muscle strength and endurance, as well as sufficient bulk to develop these qualities. Be sure you understand that the manner in which you exercise varies with your objectives (page 214 and Chapter 18): moderate loads and fifteen to twenty repetitions for developing bulk; light loads and high repetitions for developing endurance; and maximum loads and few repetitions for developing strength. You can't develop all three at once; they must be developed in sequence.

Your performance in weight lifting is mostly a matter of your fitness to perform. Give a minimum of 70 percent of your available time to conditioning, the remainder to developing skill. Learn to use momentum (pages 148-49) and to use your legs, not your back, when you lift.

Conditioning Priorities

Muscle mass	H
Muscle endurance	H
Muscle strength	H
Circulorespiratory endurance	M
Mobility	M
Durability of joints and ligaments	H
Toughness of skin (hands only)	H
Ability to relax	M

WRESTLING

THE SPECTATOR OFTEN assumes that the wrestler with the bigger chest and greater arm strength will win the match. Experienced wrestlers know better. Wrestling skill is the dominant performance factor.

This is not to suggest that fitness isn't important; to the contrary, because the sport is so exhausting, 60 percent of available time should be given to the development of muscular endurance and strength, circulorespiratory endurance and flexibility. Conditioning should concentrate on brachiation (pages 256-62), but leg strength should not be neglected (pages 249-55). For endurance, use light loads and many repetitions; for strength, maximum loads and few repetitions. Circulorespiratory endurance begins with long slow distance training (pages 268-72), then moves to interval training (pages 213-15). Always finish your workouts wtih a flexibility circuit, to develop increased mobility.

In the 40 percent of available time given to skill, work on speed, mechanics and agility. Many of the Super Ks in Chapter 11 are pertinent to wrestling.

Conditioning Priorities

Muscle mass	H
Muscle endurance	H
Muscle strength	H
Circulorespiratory endurance	H
Mobility	H
Durability of joints and ligaments	H
Toughness of skin	H
Ability to relax	M

20

Constant Performance:
Avoiding Injury and Illness

ONE OF THE ultimate achievements of maximum performance is learning to stay in one piece.

Remember the campus hero, the one with all the bandages, who'd given his all for Alma Mater? His contribution would have been much greater had he used restraint. Because he'd been hurt, he couldn't play.

I've heard coaches say, "Show me a player who isn't injuring himself and I'll show you a player who isn't putting out." This is nonsense. What good is a player whose performance is hobbled by injury?

When you give your all in an uncontrolled reckless attempt, you're not giving your best. More than likely, you're on a course that will eventually deprive your teammates of your services. In the words of the sailors on square-rigger ships, one hand for the rigging and one hand for yourself.

Anyone who's attempting to achieve maximum performance runs on the ridge of injury. Maximum performance, by definition, means to explore undeveloped areas of use. Any unknown contains risk. Only if you take the risk can you extend your maximum. The trick is to stay on the safe side of the ridge.

To court injury and play out the drama of the wounded hero is absurd. The reasonable position to take is, "I don't want to be injured, but I'm ready to be injured if it should happen. That's the chance I take. On the other hand, I realize that injury is going to be painful, and I realize that it will set back my performance. So I'm going to do everything sensible that I can to avoid it."

Good sense, alas, is not always demonstrated by athletes in do-or-die competition. Their "win at all costs" spirit leads them to sacrifice their future chances for distinguished performances.

Just as the winner must pace himself to win a distant race, so one must extend himself very gradually to achieve a worthy lifetime goal. Too many potentially great athletes wear themselves out in high school.

Among athletes, there are extremes of caution and recklessness. I first encountered the overcautious types years ago, when I was head trainer at Springfield College. They liked to bear visible signs of injury, swathing themselves in yards of tape until they looked like survivors of a major disaster. They enjoyed the sympathy, but it wasn't only sympathy they were after; it was an excuse for not playing as well as they might or as was expected of them. Some may have played better because the wraps served as a security blanket and made them less anxious.

At the other extreme is the athlete who wants admiration so badly that he'll do foolish things to get it, such as deliberately diving headlong into the path of a kicker's foot. He actually takes satisfaction from being a bloody mess—proof to his teammates that he's "risked his life" in their behalf.

Equally imprudent is the performer who's so eager for self-improvement that he becomes impatient in his training. He competes for blood the first day out, trying to lift the heaviest weight, and he turns his circulo-respiratory conditioning into all-out races. That's where most mistakes are made and most injuries occur.

There should be no reason to risk injury in a practice session. Yet that's where the majority of injuries occur.

If you're given a weight to lift, unless you're told to stop, your tendency is to lift it until you can't lift it anymore. First, you want to challenge your own limits. Then, too, you're probably persuaded that it's the last, most difficult repetition that gives you the greatest benefit. For the minuscule gain you may get from that one last lift, you're putting the whole gain from previous conditioning on the line. Stop now before you hurt yourself and let the gradual improvement over time lead you to increased performance.

Obviously, any repetition you do that injures you gives you no benefit whatever.

Improved skill in an event should reduce the chance of injury because the performance is better controlled. But with improved skill often comes the temptation to take more chances, a process somewhat analogous to tailgating. When you first learn to drive, you are cautious and keep well behind the car in front of you. As you become more and more experienced, you increasingly diminish that distance. It's not a good idea, but it happens. If you get too close, it's just a matter of time before someone in front of you has to make a sudden stop and he and you get hurt.

There are certain signals in training and performing that tell you you're tailgating your muscular actions. They appear in the form of microtraumas, those little points of soreness that result from a particularly heavy practice or an intensive competition. Learning to recognize and respect these signals is as important as anything else you do to maximize performance.

TRAUMA AND THE CASUAL ATHLETE

THE CASUAL ATHLETE usually has the full-blown athletic spirit but lacks the preparation of the body that will withstand the stresses and strains of all-out competition.

The roots of this circumstance are grounded in the historic British sport ethic, which held that the true amateur met his opponent at the same level, without advantage of training. Anyone who practiced—or, worse, worked out under the eyes of a coach—well, that was simply not "cricket." You're a good sport only if you show up every Sunday morning in the appropriate attire, ready to join fully in the game with whatever body you have. You are expected to give it everything you've got, and more. If you don't exhaust yourself, that's not "cricket" either.

The essence of this traditional amateur sportsmanship, therefore, is an invitation to traumatic injuries and submaximal performance. Players who haven't been taught to move properly and avoid injuries are expected to give their utmost during a game.

Trauma is injury or damage to tissue due to the application of a force. When trauma occurs, the treatment consists of two basic steps: (1) ice and pressure to prevent swelling the first day and (2) heat to promote healing after twenty-four hours and thereafter.

But *anticipation* of injury is by far the best course. Injuries needn't occur if you're prudent—and the essence of prudence is to set a pace that's within your capacity.

A corollary myth to the one that the last repetition gives you the most benefit is that training to complete exhaustion increases your endurance. Training to exhaustion trains you to give up. You should never exhaust during performance. You couldn't finish if you did. The only part exhaustion plays in a training program is learning how to avoid it. When you're fatigued to the point that your performance is affected, that's all the pain you need to endure. You're not gaining anything beyond that point, and you're losing coordination and diminishing your desire to train.

The sign of a mature athlete is his willingness to take time out when he feels overheated or fatigued. Most of us will keep a game going rather than acknowledge to the other person that we're more tired than he is. But the game has become a dull contest of physical stamina instead of the more exciting and pleasurable expression of one's idea in terms of skill and strategy. Now we are playing the man instead of the ball, and the essence of the game is lost.

"Quit" is too heavy a word for most of us. It implies that we're inferiors, failures, weaklings. "When the going gets tough, the tough get going" is physiological nonsense. When the going gets tough for you, you should stop, rest and start in again when you're fresh.

The most fulfilling contest is a battle of skill and strategy, not fatigue.

Today, competition at high levels makes much more physiological sense than it did when the British cricket ethic prevailed. Our swimmers, runners and other endurance performers finish relatively fresh. The contribution of science to modern conditioning has been to reduce the element of exhaustion as a differentiating factor. Theoretically, the well-conditioned athlete has developed to the point that he has a reserve beyond what he'll need for his event.

If you have just enough energy to finish your race in a state of exhaustion, it means that in the last few moments of the race you've been poorly coordinated— running with the bears grabbing you. Once again, that's why training for an event by practicing the event will never get you to your maximum. You'll never develop the reserve that permits you to finish strongly.

Exhaustion, in itself, is not a hazard to a healthy person. When I was at Harvard, my well-trained colleagues and I performed an experiment to perceive the effects of daily exhaustion on the body. Every day we ran uphill on a treadmill as fast as we could until we literally dropped. Fellow subjects caught one another so they wouldn't be thrown to the floor. Aside from some shin splints and blisters, there was no damage to the body. All systems, particularly the cardiovascular system, received an advanced training effect from the work.

The hazard, then, is not exhaustion itself but how

you misuse your body when you are near exhaustion. You begin to move awkwardly, calling on muscles that shouldn't be employed. You try to run at full speed when your muscles can no longer elongate fast enough. It's then that the classical hamstring injury occurs.

The skier who takes one last run when he's tired risks more on that run than he's risked all day. The tennis player who plays one more set after the onset of fatigue is more likely to develop tennis elbow or other trauma from that set than from all the rest of his play. It's in the closing moments of an event that injuries are most likely to occur. Fatigue invites carelessness and poor body mechanics.

SOME GUIDELINES
FOR AVOIDING INJURY

IF YOU'RE GOING TO PLAY to your maximum within your present condition, and the game requires a partner, select someone whose attitude corresponds to yours. Neither of you is going to strive to win at all costs. And if either of you gets a little tired, you're not embarrassed to suggest a break. You're playing against your opponent's skill, not his endurance. That's where the real game is.

Accept your present level of capacity, and play within that capacity. Keep your expectations at a modest setting. If you're unwilling to experience pain in the pursuit of sport, if you don't want to work too hard, if it's not your nature to drive yourself, you can nonetheless have a fulfilling competitive experience at this level.

If, however, your objective is to pit yourself against all comers, then a new set of cautions prevail. You accept a slightly higher risk of injury, and you've got to condition yourself to last throughout the event, so that you finish well short of exhaustion. Saying that in an outstanding performance one gave 150 percent of his capacity reveals a complete misunderstanding of maximum performance. A true compliment would be to say that the great performer gave 90 percent of his capacity.

After a season of competition and an interval of rest, start your redevelopment program at 80 percent of your capacity—no matter what level you were performing at when the last season ended.

When you're out of shape, it's not too important what exercise you do or the mode in which you exercise so long as you put tension on your muscles and stimulate your heart and lungs. When you're in shape, if the activity you have in mind requires great strength, put in at least six weeks on high-resistance, low-repetition work before you try the strength event. If cross-country running is your game, start by brisk walking and gradually increase the distance to two miles; then gradually step up the speed over a six-week period. Otherwise when you run uphill, you're going to tear your calf muscles loose, when you run downhill you're going to tear your knees apart, and when you run on the flat you're going to tear your hamstrings.

Keep your priorities in mind. Remember the hurdler who doesn't set up his hurdles until he's trained for speed and power. If you can manage to reorder your priorities so that you're willing to peak six months from now or, even better, a year from now, you'll not only achieve a higher level of performance but greatly diminish the risk of injury.

Schedule frequent rest periods during the early periods of any conditioning program.

Employ the circuit training principle. Put a stress on one body part through one activity, leave it and work on a different part. Get all your work done by distributing the work.

Always follow the principle of progressive overload. Remember that even though you've been playing for years in a certain style, when you change that style you're putting a new strain on your muscles, joints and ligaments. They have to be redeveloped progressively in the new mode. Redevelopment comes gradually; any change in style requires about two months of a progressive overload to rebuild you to your old strength.

If you feel punk, skip your quantity work. Be content with a few brief bouts of quality work with plenty of rest in between. If you're in training, you have a bank of physical capital. On days that you're overfatigued and need rest, you can draw on this bank. It's reducing your capital slightly, but not so much that it's serious. Where you get into trouble is when you continue to train when you're overfatigued. You may be trying just as hard day by day but you're actually doing less and less work, which causes you to decondition. It's better to take it easy for a day, or two days if needed, to recover from the overfatigue.

Learn to distinguish staleness from overfatigue. Staleness is boredom, nothing more. It comes from a depression when hard training no longer results in marked improvements and when trying your best no longer results in winning.

During this period of ennui, you withdraw psychologically from the arena in both competition and practice. The best remedy is to break completely from the arena for a while so that you can return with a fresh view. While away, however, you should find some recreational activity that will keep you in shape, because the total amount of work you're doing can't be reduced without a loss of performance. Staleness is very much like what happens to you when you perform at high altitudes or in the tropics. All three phenomena depress physical activity and thereby your state of training. It's not the altitude or the heat or the staleness that are doing it, it's that you're not working hard enough,

LEARNING TO DEAL WITH PAIN

IDEALLY, ONE SHOULD be able to start from poor condition and become a highly capable achiever after a year of progressive overload training without having had one day of stiffness, soreness or severe distress. The reality is that competition creates all kinds of uncontrolled circumstances that cause injury.

The end point of any strength effort is pain, but as you become familiar with it you actually welcome it because you recognize it as a sign that you're performing near your maximum.

From early years, we associate pain with injury and even the propsect of death. In training, we modify the significance of pain. We learn that it's not necessarily associated with injury, and we learn not to fear its onset.

We've said that we almost never perform to our physiological capacity. Learning to perform better means learning to narrow the gap between our psychological and physiological limits. The psychological limit is governed by our awareness of pain more than by any other factor. To change our *concept* of pain, therefore, is basic to extending our performance potential.

Pain is a variable sensation. You can probably recall when you had an ache of some kind and something happened to make you forget all about your pain. I remember my father returning to Danbury one day from a trip—he traveled a great deal and was always anxious to get home—to find my mother suffering from an upset stomach and me with a headache. That just wasn't the way he wanted it to be. So he packed us into the car, and off we went to Bridgeport and sat in a vaudeville theater and laughed at the comedians until the tears streamed down our faces. Afterward, we went to a restaurant and ate a nice dinner, as healthy and as happy as Dad wanted us to be. Pain is like fatigue in this regard; you may feel very tired but then you get involved in something interesting and suddenly you don't feel tired anymore.

Almost any distraction can diminish your sense of pain or eliminate it altogether. I recall one visit to a hospital in which I was asked to swallow a tube and keep it in my stomach so that measurements could be made of my gastric acidity. The effort provoked severe reflex responses. I choked, gagged, started to throw up. Then a nurse handed me a girlie magazine, I began to look at the pictures and moved from a sense of life-threatening distress to one of relative calm as the tube went down my throat.

Most pain associated with unusual exertion is caused by a sudden lack of circulation through the muscle. When you have angina, it's caused by insufficient blood supply to the heart muscle. The same thing can happen in your neck muscle. If you can get that muscle relaxed and the blood circulating again, the pain will go away.

The first approach to this type of pain, then, is to deliberately reduce it by relaxing the muscle and improving circulation. You achieve this through movement, massage and reduction of tension via relaxation techniques.

The pain from an athletic performance is another matter. It's usually due to a pulled muscle or a swollen one. If the pain disappears after a day or so, it was probably due to the swelling of the muscle. We perceive this kind of pain as *stiffness*. It's not sore to the touch and it doesn't hurt when we move. We just don't move very well.

Soreness is more serious. It's probably due to a slight rupture of tissue, it's very sensitive to touch, and it persists for several days. You can work stiffness out and you don't have to rest, but soreness requires healing and care to avoid further damage. So the prescription for soreness is rest.

SOME SIMPLE PRECAUTIONS

A BURRO WON'T CHANGE the speed at which he moves even if you beat him or throw rocks at him. Put him with another burro or in a pack of burros and they will collectively establish a pace of their own which is near that of the slowest burro and collectively refuse to go any faster. You will probably never see an exhausted burro.

We know for sure that we don't have such a mechanism to control our effort. Accordingly, we have to watch for certain signals: hard breathing, a pounding pulse, excessive perspiration. Any one is a signal that if we don't slow down, the end of our effort is imminent.

Excessively hard breathing—often referred to as hyperventilation—is a somewhat ambiguous signal when it occurs at high altitudes. Positively, it's a means of gaining more oxygen at levels where oxygen is thin. But most novices tend to hyperventilate too much, which can cause sickness—dizziness and spots before the eyes. Wherever the symptoms occur, the remedy is the same: slow down, and slow your breathing for a while until the unwelcome sensations disappear. Then you can take your mind off your breathing.

Skill development is a protective means. A person who is well skilled in his event tends to be injured less because he uses the proper mechanics. Poor mechanics result in self-inflicted injuries—locking your elbow in the follow-through of a throw, for example, or wrenching your back in the middle of an awkward swing. The force doesn't have to be great. According to a law of trauma, it's not the force of the blow that produces damage, it's the position of the joint when the blow is struck. The body tissues have great resistance to force. But the human anatomy is strung out. We have long arms and legs, which makes us quite susceptible to injury if a blow is applied while these extremities are extended.

If you fall on an extended arm, you're almost sure to damage it or your shoulder. But if you've accustomed yourself to falling—as anyone should who plays a sport in which falling is likely or even possible—you automatically curl up or go into a rolling motion to dissipate the forces. Practice that motion early in your training. It's not hard, and it doesn't hurt. If you learned to do somersaults as a child, you can learn to curl and roll now.

The problem in most children's sports is the lack of understanding of kinesiological principles on the part of volunteer coaches, as well as the propensity on the part of both the young players and the coaches to emulate the toughness and skills of the professionals. That's not a good idea. A Little Leaguer, for example, shouldn't try to throw a curve ball, because there's a tendency to hyperextend the elbow in the follow-through. The momentum causes the ends of the bones at the elbow to snap against each other. Unless the child can learn to follow through without hyperextending the elbow, he should be discouraged from throwing curves. Growing children are susceptible to joint injury, particularly to repeated stress. Every shock produces a slight injury which may go unnoticed or appear as a negligible soreness. This should not be neglected, however, as these multiple small injuries or microtraumas often don't heal properly because of the repeated insults. Trying to "work them out" is the worst possible remedy. Until after the age of fourteen the epiphysis, or covering of the bone end, is not fully developed, the tissue is sensitive to irritation, and the bone ends can be permanently damaged. This not only would put the young player out of action, but would keep him from top performance for the rest of his life.

Equipment—the best equipment—is mandatory. In a contact sport, it's a matter of self-defense. I wish that weren't true. When I'm in a contact sport, my equipment should also protect *you*. My helmet should be soft, my shoulder pads rounded. Nothing on my person should be a weapon against you. We have the materials, particularly slow-recovery plastics used now in test-pilot helmets with great success, that would protect the opponent as well as the wearer. But somehow this concept of the function of equipment doesn't sit well with our subconscious cultural notion that football, like bullfighting, is an affirmation of manliness. Consequently, the only way to protect yourself now is to wear something heavier, sharper and more abusive than your opponent is wearing. The result: we both get hurt. How primitive!

If you jog or run, wear shock-absorbing shoes. With the exception of sprints, the heel receives the first impact of foot strike. This impact force as the heel receives the body's weight is greatly magnified by the momentum of the body's downward fall. For a person weighing 150 pounds, this could be tenfold or 1500 pounds while jogging with a jolting gait, wearing shoes with only a thin sole beneath the heels, and jogging on hard surfaces.

Almost anyone who jogs gets shin splints, tears of the bone covering called periosteal tissue. This tearing is thought to be caused by the tugging of the muscle that's fastened into this tissue each time your heel strikes, as well as the pull of that muscle in preventing the ball of the foot from slapping the ground as an aftereffect of the heel strike.

Just as you spread the force of a fall by rolling, so you can spread the jolt of your heel strike with a cushioned rocker heel.

But there's a more certain way to avoid jogging injuries, and that is to change the way you jog.

CRUISING: A BETTER WAY TO JOG

VERY FEW THINGS distress me so much as the sight of unskilled runners jogging on a hard surface, pavement in particular. You can almost see the shock waves pass from their heels to their heads with every single stride. They have no idea that they're traumatizing their bones and joints and increasing the prospect of arthritis and degenerative disease of those bones and joints in later years. Running on a relatively soft surface like turf helps considerably, but even that can be damaging if it isn't done correctly.

Jogging is splendid cardiovascular exercise when it's performed at a tempo consistent with one's training pulse rate, but orthopedically it's dangerous. Thousands of erstwhile joggers have had to give it up because of injuries to their back, knees and feet. Unskilled jogging is just what the word implies: it "jogs" the ankles, heels, knees and spine at every step. Each one of these jolts causes microtrauma. A jog of only a mile sends more than two thousand jolts through the body.

There's a simple way to take the jolts out of jogging, while simultaneously preserving the cardiovascular benefits. We call this method *cruising*.

The objective of running is to move in a horizontal plane. Unnecessary vertical movement is costly. The efficient runner, then, would be one who eliminates all unnecessary up-and-down motion of his torso and glides along the surface. If you were watching him from the other side of a shoulder-height hedge, his head would seem to move smoothly across the top of the hedge, as though he were riding a bicycle.

This cruising motion can be achieved with the slightest change in running mechanics. You simply lower your center of gravity ever so slightly, until your knees feel slightly bent.

Learning to cruise is easy. First, walk with an exaggerated up-and-down motion, simply to make yourself aware of the vertical component in forward movement. Next, keeping the same stride, bend the knees ever so slightly and consciously try to eliminate all up-and-down motion. A simple way to check yourself is to try the movement mirrored by a large picture window or the display windows of a store.

Once you can walk in a cruising mode, practice speeding up until you can break into a slow run with your head nearly level. You'll find that you're moving faster than before, principally because your stride length has increased. Cruising makes you want to move fast; you feel as if you're suddenly running downhill. It's efficient and comfortable because it eliminates the jolts by using the hips, knees and ankles as shock absorbers.

Cruising is good for speed and distance running and for running sports like soccer, basketball and tennis. Keeping your center of gravity a little low not only gives you more agility but protects you against wear and tear. Cruise, don't jog, on hard surfaces in particular. One caution: If you lower more than an inch, you'll feel an extra load in your quadriceps and even weakness in the knees. This means you're too low, so just elevate slightly. Eventually, cruising will strengthen your quadriceps and knees. Until you've finished your special conditioning for locomotor activities, it's best to avoid downhill running. It's too hard on the knees.

INJURY PREVENTION AND EARLY CARE

ANY FREQUENT or persisting disability may indicate an abnormality or other problem that should be examined by a physician. But many common injuries can be prevented or minimized if you're well informed and use good sense. It's impossible to avoid sudden stops and starts, great force and stretch and still play well; nor can you cover yourself completely with protective padding and expect to perform at your best. What you can do to prevent injury is to take sensible precautions and play as well as you can within the limits imposed by your present level of conditioning, skill and real need to go to extremes. Remember, the prolonged rest required to recover from many injuries means a loss of fitness and a long period of reconditioning. Ask yourself, "Is this sacrifice really necessary?"

GENERAL MUSCLE PULLS, STRAINS, SORENESS AND BRUISES

Prevention:
1. Well-fitting protective equipment and padding.
2. Long-term conditioning for specific stresses.
3. Thorough warmup before violent exertion.
4. Avoidance of excess effort, sudden stops and starts, bouncing exercises and jerky muscle contractions.
5. Cooldown stretching after workouts.

Early Care:
1. Immerse the injured part in ice water immediately and hold it there for thirty minutes.
2. Dry thoroughly and wrap the injured part with an elastic bandage to compress the area and prevent swelling. Do not restrict circulation.
3. Apply ice packs over the compression bandage and elevate the injured part to avoid further swelling.
4. While waiting to see your physician, leave the bandage compression on and apply ice packs during the next twenty-four hours. Do not move the injured part.
5. Rest the next day, and use crutches if necessary to avoid weightbearing.
6. After swelling subsides, remove the compression bandage and, as discoloration and discomfort disappear, very gradually return to action.

BLISTERS

Prevention:
1. Apply a thin layer of lubricating jelly over friction areas to prevent heat buildup. Eliminate the cause of any reddening of the skin.
2. Wear a pair of thin cotton socks under an outer pair of thick woolen socks.
3. Test fit of shoes by standing with full weight on toes. Check to see that there is a little room beyond the big toe and across the top of the shoe, that the ball of the foot fits into the widest part of the shoe, and that there is no slipping at the heel.

Early Care:
1. Avoid further friction, forceful motion or blows.
2. If the blister breaks, wash the area with soap and water, trim the top away and apply 70 percent alcohol or tincture of benzoin. Shield the area with zinc oxide or similar ointment and bandage to avoid infection.
3. If the blister is unbroken, swab the area with tincture of benzoin, then bandage to prevent the blister from breaking.

FOOT STRAINS

Prevention:
1. Wear shoes with a high counter (above the heel), a firm shank to prevent pronation and support the arch, a heel height close to an inch, and a fairly thick, flexible sole for shock absorption.
2. Run barefoot on resilient surfaces. Start slowly for short distances, gradually increasing speed and distance over long term.
3. Run with the foot in balance, taking most of the weight on the outside borders of the foot.

Early Care:

1. General care described for muscle pulls. Ice packs are excellent for most injuries because cold slows bleeding, numbs pain, and, with compression, prevents swelling.
2. Use pad in heel of shoe to elevate heel.
3. Use corrective support if needed.

SPRAINED ANKLE

Prevention:

1. Have training and competition shoes fitted for width as well as length to provide sufficient room for the foot. Place the shoe on a table and be sure that the back of the shoe is perpendicular to the surface; use a running shoe with a wide flare at the heel to give stability on soft surfaces. For hard surfaces, a cushioned heel is advised.
2. Gradual strengthening of foot and leg tissues by long-term locomotor circuit training.
3. Limbering circuit to warm up before running.

Early Care:

1. General care with ice described before, with this exception: Immerse the foot, *shoe and all,* in a tub of ice water for thirty minutes after injury.
2. Have physician check for fracture.
3. Keep foot elevated.

SHIN SPLINTS (Dull Ache in Lower Shin Area)

Prevention:

1. Avoid running and jumping on hard surfaces such as dry clay or cement. Select soft grass or other resilient surfaces and run easily.
2. Insert sponge rubber pads beneath the heel and beneath the forefoot in your shoes. Insert a small pad in the toe of your shoe to involve your toes more strongly in the foot action. Make sure that

your shoes are large enough so that these inserts
don't make the fit too tight.
3. Avoid sudden stops.

Early Care:
1. General care with ice described before.
2. Apply compression bandage to both foreleg and
ankle.

ACHILLES TENDON PULLS

Prevention:
1. Long-term endurance conditioning of leg muscles
using locomotor circuit training.
2. Always finish workouts with the flexibility circuit.
3. Avoid fast starts until muscles are strong.
4. Avoid excessive forcible use or stretch.

Early Care:
1. General care with ice described before.
2. Medical examination if pain is severe or function
impaired.

HAMSTRING PULLS

Prevention:
1. Always execute limbering circuit and warmup circuit before intensive exercise.
2. Slow down or take rest pauses at onset of fatigue.

Early Care:
1. General care with ice described before.
2. If there is little or no pain and no tenderness,
gently and gradually stretch the muscle to reduce
spasm.

KNEE SPRAIN (Runner's Knee)

Prevention:
1. Avoid knee-separation exercises such as full squats,

duck walks and sitting with pressure against fully flexed knees. Use quad-setting exercise to strengthen knee joint (see pages 249-51).
2. Do not use heel cleats.
3. Run on even terrain or change sides every half mile or so when running on crowded roads. Reverse direction on track or beach every half mile or so.
4. Avoid running downhill: run up, walk down.
5. Wear knee pads during basketball, volleyball and other floor games.

Early Care:
1. General care with ice described before.
2. Immobilize knee joint by splinting or making a soft cast with wide elastic straps.

TENNIS ELBOW

Prevention:
1. Hold racket with moderate tension until arm muscles are strengthened.
2. Avoid tightly strung racket during early conditioning.
3. Wear long-sleeved warmup jacket until arm tissues are warmed.
4. During pregame rally, start with gentle, rhythmic strokes to release excess muscle tension.
5. Don't toss the ball too high during service. Lower toss eliminates excessive stretching of the shoulder to reach the ball.

Early Care:
1. General care with ice described before.
2. Sling to rest elbow. Hold it at a right angle.

MUSCLE CRAMP

Prevention:
1. Use extra salt with meals if sweating is excessive.

2. Relax excess tension and rest at onset of fatigue.
3. Loosen clothing if it is obstructing circulation.
4. Use padding to protect against blows in contact sports.

Early Care:
1. Rest.
2. Firm pressure with thumbs at center of cramped muscle.
3. Slowly stretch cramped muscle within normal range of motion, hold it in an extended position for a few seconds, then relax.
4. Use gentle kneading massage to reduce spasm.
5. Apply moist heat to relax the muscle and restore circulation, then contract and relax the muscle in light, rhythmic motions.

LOW BACK SPASM

(Note: If you cannot bend sideward or forward with your legs straight without pain, let your physician examine your back.)

Prevention:
1. Sit and sleep on firm surfaces.
2. Keep knee and hip angles equal.
3. Move frequently.
4. Develop abdominal strength with the sitback exercise.
5. Stretch low back muscle using knee hug and pelvic lift exercises in flexibility circuit (pages 233-41).
6. Keep back straight when lifting and carrying.
7. Avoid back bends, arching the back and standing with hands behind the back.

Early Care:
1. Rest.
2. Apply moist heat to induce relaxation.

3. Support the low back while sitting by using a small cushion or "bustle" against your pelvis (see page 83).
4. Insert a three-quarter-inch-thick plywood board between your mattress and box springs. Sleep on your side with one knee flexed.

RECUPERATION

THE BETTER SHAPE you're in at the time of your injury, the more quickly you'll recover.

The athlete with the broken bone has some advantages over the nonathlete with the same injury. His well-conditioned muscle and bone tissues will not deteriorate as much as those of the nonathlete. Improved circulation in the tissue will probably speed the healing process. And his habit of physical activity will stand him in good stead during his period of rehabilitation. If his leg is broken, he'll take this opportunity to develop and maintain the upper body musculature, and do what he can, as well, to retain the condition of his uninjured leg. Within days after the break he'll even start exercising the undamaged portion of his injured leg to the greatest extent possible, so as to prevent atrophy and loss of strength. He'll get an assist in this instance from the surgeon who has specialized in sports medicine and uses types of casts that permit movement of uninjured parts.

The athlete's leanness is also advantageous. Fat accumulation hampers surgery and slows recovery.

But the difference between an athlete and nonathlete isn't so great that the treatment can't be similar. Who except the malingerer wants to be incapacitated, prevented from enjoying daily life and maintaining his earning power? The best rule during recuperation is to be as active as you can be, consistent with your injury.

PERFORMANCE AND HEALTH

IF INJURY REDUCES performance potential, so does illness. Staying healthy is as much a part of maximizing performance as is avoiding injury.

There's a bit of the sybarite in all of us. Rather than flagellate myself for my sybaritic tendencies, I try to make sure I stay in good health so I can enjoy my indulgences. But I try not to become a deteriorated sybarite. I guard against the conditions in a highly industrialized society that promote deteriorative change: overstimulation, overfeeding, overmedication, and underexercise.

Some people are genetic gems. They seem to have the ability to abuse their bodies—smoking, eating, drinking and carousing to their heart's content—and get away with it. Most of us aren't like that.

A positive attitude toward health makes for good health. If you insist on being a healthy person and refuse to accept less than perfect function, you can maintain a much higher quality organism—physically, mentally and spiritually—than if you neglect yourself and wait until you get sick before you do something about it.

Because we're cerebrating animals, it's easy for us to develop unnecessary concern for body processes that, left alone, do quite well.

Respiration is an outstanding example. If you don't think about your breathing, the rate and depth of your respiration are adjusted very well to the body's need for oxygen, as well as its need to expel carbon dioxide. Yet it wasn't all that long ago that we were all taught to open the window wide each morning, stand in front of it and take several deep breaths. Breathing exercises to expand the chest and strengthen the diaphragm were a part of every gymnasium routine. Today we know that such exercises perform no useful function because the healthy human system is endowed with ample lung capacity to begin with. Even in the most severe exertion, the lung probably never approaches its full capacity to exchange air.

Elimination is another body process about which needless concern is expressed. Our acculturation conditions us to be proud of substantial bowel movements, to fear constipation and extol regularity. We arrange our diets, consume laxatives and make certain that we eat a huge serving of bran each day because we are told that tribes with extremely high-fiber diets seem to have less problems with cancer of the bowel. It could well be that life expectancy in such tribes is so short that most of the members die before the cancer years.

Digestion and elimination do proceed apace if the diet contains some roughage, such as fresh fruits and raw vegetables. Roughage is part of a normal, natural diet. If your diet is so lacking in roughage that it needs to be supplemented, then it just makes good sense to add some. But to ply yourself with roughage in order to guarantee frequent large bowel movements makes little sense.

We know now that due to variations in water intake, climate and activity, bowel movements normally vary from day to day, and that there is nothing unhealthy about a day without a bowel movement. One cause of constipation is the anxiety developed in worrying about it. Worry can contract your sphincters, making emptying of the bowel impossible.

I know many people who are so overconcerned with nutrition that they make themselves sick. Each week they read about a new mineral or chemical that ought to be added to their diets. One week they're zinc eaters. The next week they're chromium eaters. They are engaged in a futile attempt to work out a diet with all the elements in proper amount to achieve perfect nutrition. We do not have the knowledge to program a computer that might digest all the information available on vitamins, amino acids, fatty acids and carbohydrates, and the way you use each of them, and come up with as good a guide as is provided by your own innate intelligence, manifested by your hunger, appetite and thirst.

If you were simply to eat and drink widely from the abundance of nutritious foods and beverages available to you, according to your hunger, appetite and thirst, avoiding nothing but excessive amounts, you would guarantee yourself the best possible nutrition.

DIET AND PERFORMANCE

IT SOMETIMES SEEMS that there isn't anything a person won't eat, or avoid eating, if there is a hope that performance will be enhanced. The reason this quest is never-ending is that even the most senseless change in one's dietary habits often does affect performance—if the performer has faith that it will. A substance labeled "super food" will motivate some to super performances. The most sophisticated will be attracted to an impressive label of ingredients even if a gallon of the potion contains only one teaspoon of sea water and another of sugar. The hooker is the logic. "Muscles are protein. Therefore, it is logical that by eating extra protein you build extra muscle—and thereby gain extra strength." Not true.

If you're weak from starvation, some food—any food —will make you stronger. But if you're well fed, no food of any kind will make you stronger. In this condition, added strength comes only from added exercise.

The greatest aphrodisiac is the power of suggestion. Convince me that vitamin E is going to increase my libido and it certainly will.

Under laboratory conditions, some carefully controlled changes in nutrition can affect performance. Carbohydrate loading is one example. Due to the body's tendency to overcompensate, if you deplete glycogen stored in muscles by avoiding carbohydrates and exercising to exhaustion for two or three days, and then for the next three days eat only carbohydrates and do only light work, your muscles will gain more than the normal amounts of glycogen and you'll be able to run longer. The trouble is, the extra water your body absorbs with the extra sugar frequently makes you so logy or ill that your performance suffers.

It's best to stay with a diet that gives you a wide variety of foods in amounts that maintain a fairly low ratio of body fat to lean tissue.

DRUGS AND PERFORMANCE

THE USE OF DRUGS to regulate our functions and our moods often diminishes rather than enhances our performances, and they are generally dangerous. World-class champions have innocently killed themselves by taking overdoses of potent drugs in the hope of achieving superhuman performances. Primitive man drank the blood of the lion for courage, and this search for performance-enhancing potions continues at the greatest extremes. Women use male hormones and anabolic steroids to acquire the superior strength of men, accepting beard growth and other male sex characteristics as well.

The human drive for maximum performance is so strong that society has established regulations and procedures to protect athletes from themselves by administering precompetition tests for doping nearly as stringent as those applied to racing horses and dogs.

As with "super" diets, the taking of drugs often activates the power of suggestion so strongly as to increase tolerance to fatigue and pain. If you block out these protective signals, you're inviting injury.

DON'T BE AN EXERCISE ADDICT

THE SAME UNNECESSARY CONCERN that exists about body processes is evident in concern about exercise.

I've given my life to the study of exercise. Yet I'm not an exercise addict. If I miss a day of exercise I don't feel as though I'm falling to pieces. I'm not guilty of anything if I haven't run a mile in years. I don't do exercises by rote or put them into a formula, even though I'm tempted to do so because it's in keeping with the science of experimentation. I know when I haven't had enough exercise, and I don't need to be an exercise physiologist to know that. Anyone can understand and observe the difference in feeling between the weakness and lack of endurance experienced after being in bed several days and the physical exuberance at the end of an active vacation.

Your body possesses beautifully orchestrated mechanisms to announce its needs. To put these reflex, involuntary functions under cerebral control is to short-circuit your system. Even if you were a genius, with all science at your disposal, you still couldn't command the control over your body mechanisms as well as your body could do it when left to itself.

The more I study the body, the more I'm impressed by the miracle of its function. Many things humans do to improve that function do more harm than good. The Mormons have a saying: "Beware of man's intelligence." What that means to me is, let things happen naturally, because you're not smarter than the processes controlled by internal mechanisms infinitely superior to any invented by man.

Overcerebration—which is to say, overconcern—makes functions complicated that, left to themselves, would work to perfection. Any regimen can be a detriment rather than an advantage if you become its slave.

21

Winning

THE EXPECTATION OF SUCCESS is critical to its achievement, not simply from a psychological but from a physiological point of view. Psychologically, you need confidence to play boldly. This comes from an acceptance of yourself as a winner. Physiologically, your body organizes itself differently for a winning effort than for a losing one. The appropriate muscle fibers elect to participate; then they join forces harmoniously with other fibers to produce the winning effort. When you're losing, tension builds to excess, and coordination is degraded by the abandonment of familiar action patterns.

Conditioning for winning is mainly a process of positive reinforcement, in which a coach or parent never punishes, scolds or even calls attention to anything negative. Every day, in every way, you succeed, succeed, succeed, until you're conditioned to expect success.

There is only one way to guarantee this pattern: to progress from a base so simple and in increments so small that failure is out of the question. This is not just the golden road to maximum performance, it's the only road.

You don't travel this road in a state of exhaustion. Nor do you jump into a task that's too difficult or complex. Just as muscles build best by progressive overload, so the mastery of a task is accomplished best by progressive advancement from simple to complex.

Belief in your body as an ally rather than an antagonist is equally critical to success. You have the knowledge now to understand what happens when you're organizing for an effort. The most intricate, delicate and responsive system imaginable is responding to your every wish. Treat it with understanding and confidence and it will lead you to experiences you've never savored before.

Now, let's put it all together. We'll do it with the help of my niece, Tina Goldsmith, a competitive gymnast. Some years ago, Tina watched Cathy Rigby perform in the Olympic Games. Tina had never done any gymnastics, but Cathy became her ideal. She dreamed about her, cut out all the photographs she found in newspapers and magazines. It so happened that Cathy Rigby was a friend of Pat McCormick, whom I had known for years and helped train as a diver. Pat not only arranged a meeting but had us come to her home where she had some gym equipment. There, Tina's heroine showed her the elements of gymnastics. Tina has worked from that day since. She has her own collection of blue ribbons now, as well as her notebook of skill and conditioning pointers that she had asked me to give her as her training progressed. Recently, I asked her to list the most important points. Even though they were written with gymnastics in mind, they apply to any performance.

TINA'S PRINCIPLES OF
CHAMPIONSHIP PERFORMANCE

1. Don't try to push yourself beyond what your capability allows.
2. Fluidness is perhaps the most important aspect of a routine. Keep the routine rhythmic.

3. Be glad that you're excited. This excitement gives you energy and pep.
4. If you fall or stumble, at least do it gracefully.
5. Wearing a serene expression on your face can make a difference in your score. This gives the impression that you're performing with great ease and actually helps you to move more gracefully.
6. Smile at the judges before you perform and afterward. It always helps to have the judges on your side.
7. If you're scored unfairly, forget about going into a tizzy. There's nothing you can do about it.
8. Stretch every movement as far as comfortable. Go for AMPLITUDE.
9. Practicing a routine in your mind while you are away from the gym helps your actual performance.
10. Always have a definite small goal to achieve for every workout. Working small tricks to perfection makes a champion.
11. Never work to exhaustion. As soon as fatigue enters, stop and rest.
12. Always practice at performance speed.
13. Try to combine boldness with ease.
14. As you go through a routine, hum the rhythm to yourself.
15. Register your mistakes, but don't react to them.
16. Besides doing the required movements in your exercise, try to distinguish your routine by expressing your individuality.
17. During warmup, study your surroundings and go through your routine in your mind, adapting yourself to the unusual conditions.
18. After each meet, write down the thing that you want to remember about that place.
19. Study each performance that impresses you, and note in writing what made that routine special.
20. Project yourself so that the judges feel you're honestly trying to impress them. They are expecting you to give your best, so let them have it.

THE WINNING GAME PLAYER

TINA'S LIST SHOWS her extraordinary awareness of the effect on her of the arena in which she performs. The importance of this awareness is even more greatly magnified in game sports.

John Smith, the record-setting quarter-miler, is my performing guru. He has the finest sense of competitive dynamics of any athlete with whom I've ever worked. Recently, he decided to take up tennis. He'd never played before. Within a very short period, he became an excellent player. Before he ever picked up a racket, however, he studied the game. The bulk of his study consisted of watching two champions, Jimmy Connors and Arthur Ashe—both of them, like John, former UCLA students.

John likes to play chess. He believes that the strategies of chess are applicable to sports competitions. Every move must be made with future moves in mind. You can even sustain a temporary loss if it's taken in order to achieve an ultimate gain. To John's discerning eye, this understanding was missing in the game Jimmy Connors was playing that day. Connors was steady and aggressive, extremely quick and well skilled. But John felt that he was not employing the give and take of the mature strategist. Jimmy didn't set his opponent up by giving him a shot calculated to put him in a position for a kill.

Ashe, by contrast, was playing the ball with a strategy behind it. He was not running by himself or playing his own game. He was highly aware of the importance of controlling his opponent in the arena, mixing hard with subtle shots and always trying to get his opponent into a certain rhythm and position so that he could take advantage of him. And, of course, he was equally aware that his opponent might try to do the same thing to him. John Smith made Arthur Ashe his particular model in learning to play tennis.

Moving the sport from a mere race against yourself into three- and four-dimensional play is what makes the champion game player. Control of the opponent *and* the ball is a very complex skill and represents the ultimate in performance.

One has to learn first that the ball cannot be neglected. When my nephew, Derek Jones, age five, plays basketball with his two friends of similar age, the three of them are all over each other. They are obviously more interested in jumping on each other than they are in attacking the ball. When one does go directly after the ball, he has no trouble in getting it. And if he shoots quickly, he can do so before his two friends are on his back. Experience may teach them eventually to "play the ball, not the man," but I see plenty of mature adults who are reacting to the opponent and missing the ball. They are easily "faked" by a move of the head or a change in timing. I taught Derek the principle of playing the ball, and he immediately gave his secret away to his friends. Now their game is at a higher level and resembles basketball more than wrestling.

Someday, if they are the chess player John Smith is, they will be moving the ball around so as to shift their opponents into weak positions and have them at their mercy. That's complete gamesmanship.

THE YIPS

WE'RE STILL SEARCHING for ways to convert a poor competitor into a good one. Some people always come through when they need to; others always seem to fail at such moments. The characteristic is most poignantly evident in certain football place-kickers and basketball free-throw shooters. Often the only ones they miss are the ones that are critical. It seems to be a complex behavioral problem best addressed to the psychologist rather than the coach.

We don't know a great deal about the off day that each of us experiences from time to time, other than recalling what it's like. We call the phenomenon the "yips." You lose your confidence and build failure into your game. Your relationship to your environment changes. In golf, the hole looks like a thimble, whereas when you have your confidence it looks like a bucket. With confidence, you visualize the ball going into the hole; when you have the yips, you visualize missing. We know from our earlier discussion of visualization how greatly it influences the result; to imagine that you're going to miss is to all but guarantee it.

The worst thing to do when you have the yips is to begin to play to failure. As success reinforces success, failure reinforces failure. Perhaps the best thing to do on such occasions is to remember that your body organizes its systems in terms of the signals it's getting. Just telling yourself that you're going to sink that putt increases your prospects enormously; and even if you miss it, it doesn't mean you'll miss the next one.

But if we don't know much about why we have an occasional off day, we do know something about the attitudes that contribute to or detract from consistent winning.

THE COMFORT OF LIMITED SUCCESS

ONE REASON MANY of us don't perform to our maximum is that we don't want the responsibility of success. We don't want to be separated from the group by being labeled a winner. We perform well enough so that we don't get singled out as failures, and yet we don't perform so well that we're singled out as winners.

It takes guts to be a winner. You have to be bold.

You have to be ready to accept the responsibilities and sometimes the accusations that accompany victory. Anyone who's ever suddenly hit a hot streak in golf knows the muttering he arouses from opponents who question his handicap. At that point, he may subconsciously hit a ball into a trap or miss a putt just to get rid of the pressure.

Most of us are more comfortable being a close second. It's a big responsibility to be number one. Everyone seems to be after you. If something goes wrong, you're going to be criticized. Such unconscious considerations are very much part of any performance, whatever the arena. It's a lot easier to blame your inability to advance to the top in business on the excuse that you're not the salesman type. The people who get the big appointments and the best jobs and contracts—who are maximum performers at their jobs—have learned how to be aggressive without being obnoxious. They aren't afraid to close the deal , and do so in comfort. They have a somewhat inflated view of themselves that enables them to stretch themselves and do a little more than others may have thought possible. They've managed to cope successfully with the risk, explicit or implicit, that success will brand them as showoffs others won't like because they're winning the contracts and making everyone else look bad.

IF YOU WANT TO WIN
FORGET ABOUT WINNING

I KNOW THE ADVICE in this heading sounds paradoxical, but it makes great kinesiological sense.

Striving—the attempt to exceed one's capacity—always results in a diminished performance. The coach who asked for 150 percent from his players is revealing a poor understanding of body mechanisms. When a team plays "over its head," it is playing more nearly to its capacity than normal, not *beyond* its capacity.

The greatest impediment to maximum performance is that it's taken so seriously. Maximum performance isn't a laughing matter, but neither is it glum. We set achievement and success as the be-all and end-all of our culture, and even worse, we mandate that this success should come from hard work, not play. We could not construct a better formula for diminished performance. It sets our brakes against our accelerators. It produces the very anxiety that fragments thought and hampers muscles.

If you want to win, you almost have to forget about winning. You never want to think of the score, or your past mistakes, or the next quarter. To be a winner, you must commit yourself to the precise moment and movement in which you're engaged. Relax. Enjoy it. Savor it. *Focus on it.* Feel the pleasure of it, the harmony that exists between you, your opponent and the arena in which you play. The game will be over almost before you know it. You'll have had an intense and pleasurable experience. You'll have played as well as you could have consistent with your condition and training.

To focus your thoughts on winning is to diminish your prospects of winning. Your goal is to perform to your maximum; to do that, you have to have confidence in your ability in order to be able to organize your body systems, as we've seen. But to believe in your prospects for good performance and to worry about winning are antagonistic ideas. The first is constructive, the second destructive.

The recognition and reduction of overanxiety constitute an important duty of coaches and trainers. In this effort, they could profit from the example of the mother of a high school football player. On the day of an important game, she sends him off to school with a reminder to bring home a loaf of bread after the game. With one remark, she has put the game in the perspective of life.

Most of us, unfortunately, are left to our own resources in dealing with pregame anxiety. There's plenty we can do about it.

GETTING READY FOR THE GAME

To PLAY THE BEST GAME you have in you tomorrow, have a restful day today.

Don't load the day with important conferences or big decisions; try to arrange your schedule so that such matters either have been disposed of or can be taken up after your match.

Get a good night's sleep.

Have sex if your partner and you feel the urge. The excitement of an impending clash may be a sexual turn-on. There's no reason you shouldn't enjoy it, and there may be a good reason to have it, because it is relaxing and soothing. It's certainly not going to diminish your strength, as the proverbial Delilah did when she cut Samson's hair. Perhaps that was the start of the myth about the loss of physical potency after ejaculation. Only if sexual intercourse is pursued as an athletic event performed in strenuous postures and with violent movements might it fatigue the player and diminish the athletic performance that follows.

In the final moments before your match, if you're upset, stay in a quiet place, avoiding the stimulus produced by the presence of competitors or audience. Some players like to find a corner in a locker room where they can sit with a blanket over their head just to get calm.

If you feel you are underaroused, or not up to an optimal level of readiness for an upcoming match, your problem is more complicated because it has to do with motivation. The first thing you can do if you are not greatly concerned about whether you are going to win or lose is to realize that this is a good state of mind to be in. You don't have to worry about over-anxiety.

The next thing is to recognize that there is some time before the game starts in which you can do several things to change your mental attitude.

Recall the satisfaction of playing well and the pleasure of picturing yourself as a successful performer. That leads to a stimulating sense of anticipation.

Remember the investment you have made in developing your game. You don't want to waste all those hours of practice just when they are bearing fruit.

Recognize that you are not alone. You have a responsibility toward your teammates and your opponents to help them get the most satisfaction out of the game. If you play well, everyone benefits.

Thoughts like these generate readiness for action and help bring you toward the optimal level of alertness. Then, the ritual of getting ready, the dressing up in the game costume, the meeting with your teammates and opponents in the arena, the presence of spectators, and the warming up activities all contribute to the fine mental and physical tuning.

If all these fail to excite you, you'll do best by continuing to relax and let the performance itself bring out the best that is in you. You may be surprised to discover that you didn't need to be all that fired up.

When you go into the arena, get the feel of it as well as the implements you're going to use. Register the lights, shapes, textures, noises, resilient properties—in short, open your senses to everything around you, let it permeate your being, get comfortable with it.

During your warmup, practice Dynamic Relaxation to be certain that you're at an optimal degree of tension for your performance.

But there is something that underlies all such efforts to perform in a winning frame of mind. It involves, paradoxically, an examination of our traditional notions about winning.

WHEN IT'S WIN OR ELSE

AMERICA IS UNDERGOING today a long-overdue reappraisal of its competitive ethic. The fundamental charge is that because there can be so few winners, we wind up as a society with a multitude of losers, psychologically crippled by the experience of failing in a life game that deals only in simplistics.

Those who deplore the emphasis on winning in our culture are reacting understandably against the excesses committed in its name. The most vivid memory Leonard Gross's son, Jeff, has of his return to the United States after five years in Europe was a lecture by his junior high school football coach, who wrote on the blackboard, "It's not whether you win or lose, it's how you play the game"—and then wrote across it: "B.S." A child who grows up with that lesson in mind may see nothing wrong with Watergate.

The consequences are devastating in ways we least suspect. In a personal defense against the abhorrence of losing we take a safe position in the spectators' gallery, set up mental models of excellence in our favorite athletes and vicariously join the arena with them. They are so beyond our own capacity that, knowing we can't be like them, we prefer to let them function as our surrogates. The consequence is that we don't train or perform or compete, which leads to physical and emotional deterioration. Our self-image cheapens. Our life diminishes. We lose the capacity to perform not simply in the events we forsake, but in everything else we do. We can't even swizzle a dry martini with the same finesse and éclat as we could if we were fit.

I've never had much patience for the dying-civilization perception of America, but one parallel to Rome does give me pause. Not only are we not performing ourselves, we are importing performers to create spectacles for us. Kenyans and Jamaicans outnumber the Americans on several major U.S. track teams. A Brazilian is the leading player on one of the country's best basketball teams. Our fledgling soccer teams have more foreigners than Americans, with new stars from abroad being signed up monthly. And professional ice hockey, of course, is played almost exclusively by Canadians. These gladiators only further widen the distance between the spectacle of the elite performer and our own ability to perform, and further discourage us from performing ourselves. We don't even fantasize any longer about our own accomplishments. Fantasy stimulates us to perform well, by helping us visualize a wish. But before anything, we need the desire—and desire diminishes as the distance increases between reality and wish. To the extent that we let others win in our behalf, we're widening the gap.

How did winning become so paramount?

The ultimate in performance, as we suggested earlier, is a life and death matter. People will pay a good deal of money to see a man developed to a high degree of perfection who risks destruction in order to win. Bullfighting, prizefighting, daredevil cycling, automobile racing and professional football are a few obvious examples. Fencing and wrestling are more symbolic but no less valid.

Death is the theme of most sport. Symbolically, a score is a kill. Play is nature's way of preparing us for survival; that's why animals, including humans, play at killing.

Television didn't manufacture the overpowering interest in professional football; it took advantage of an interest already there. Nor did the American competitive ethic produce this fascination with symbolic combat; societies with ethics totally different from ours are at least as enthusiastic about soccer as American fans are about football.

Man appears to have a need to win and a need to test his capacity. These two needs sometimes conflict, but they can work together.

MEASURING THE CHALLENGE:
IS IT FUN? IS IT SCARY?

WHEN I WAS A YOUNG MAN, I spent one summer as a swimming instructor and conducted a swim meet every Saturday. My most vivid memory is of the mother who wouldn't enter her son in a race unless she knew for sure that he could win. If she saw the name of a child on the signup sheet who might be able to beat her child, she pulled her child from the race. Her child had a reputation to protect: he had never lost a race. Nor, of course, had he ever tested his capacity.

The person who has never made a mistake or lost a race has never discovered his limits and has never really joined the human race. Man is not designed to live an error-free existence. Every one of his internal functions—breathing, body temperature, heartbeat—is maintained by a constant search between too-high and too-low limits. In all our behavior, we hover between too-much and not-enough, too-far and too-near, too-fast and too-slow. At every moment, we are bumping against our physiological limit settings, locating what's right by finding what's wrong.

Why, then, should we feel bad if we make a mistake, or even make the same mistake twice? That's the way we learn the nature of the world. What makes sense is to touch these error limits lightly, not bump against them so hard that we get hurt. "Well, I overdid it a little," is the recognition of an informative error that serves as a good guide for the next try. Being content to win a few and lose a few is a very human posture.

We are all searching for the best ways to spend our life. Like everyone else, I have an almost infinite choice of opportunities. I make my commitments on the basis of two rules. First: Is it fun? Second: Is it scary? I know that if these two elements are present,

I'll stick to what I've started. Without them, I'll never get around to doing the necessary work.

The first ingredient is self-evident. But why should something be scary? Because it turns on that marvelous shower of impulses from the reticular activating mechanism of the brain. This shower of impulses modifies your state of awareness, just as a strong water shower makes you feel more lively. Your nerves prick your muscles into action. You stand taller, assume an on-your-toes stance, poised for attack.

We do our young people a disservice today when we insulate their lives from risk. I find myself doing it all the time. If my children need help, I help them. If someone attacks them, I defend them. It would be unnatural not to, but the degree to which we do it deprives them of the adventure they need for development.

A sheltered, effete life is not as ideal as it may seem. There have been many anthropometric studies to see if the skeletal structure of blacks is enough different from whites to explain their superiority in so many athletic events. Although some differences have been established, they aren't sufficient to explain the predominance of blacks in sports in numbers totally disproportionate to their population. Nor are their reflexes that much different from the population of whites. The best answer we can give to the apparent superiority of the black athlete is that he comes from a culture where he had to excel to be recognized. Sports gave him the opportunity he was denied elsewhere.

Affluent whites have little need to seek their social position in the athletic arena. Accordingly, most of them don't—and as a consequence most of them will experience life without the remotest notion of where their performance limits lie.

THE NEED FOR COMPETITION

I DON'T WANT TO PLAY with anyone who isn't trying to beat me. The worst put-down I can imagine is for someone to let me win.

The elements of winning and losing energize and enhance performance and productivity. Look at industries in which there's no competition. Without standards of comparison, there is no clear way to determine how well they're doing and how they might do better.

The very notion that you have someone to compete against motivates performance, because you know you will have a periodic evaluation, the outcome of which is either satisfaction or determination to improve. Losing in this construct can be highly motivating, too.

Man is a game-playing animal. One day recently I went to the beach with a party that included four boys, ages eight to eleven. One of them found an abandoned ball. Immediately, they began to wrestle one another for it. When they tired of that, they played dodge ball. Next came a passing game in which they made up their own rules; if you drop the ball you lose a point, but it only counts against you if the ball is thrown within your reach. Whoever makes a bad throw also loses a point. Pretty soon they had a well-organized and regulated game going which was more fun than just fooling aimlessly around. The point is that there's no fun unless there's a structure that offers an opportunity to show a degree of skill and/or to get credit for one's performance. Even recreational skiing, the most solitary of sports, measures performance in terms of one's ability to navigate increasingly more difficult runs.

Left alone, man will usually organize a competition. Even those persons who enjoy doing things by themselves set goals that they try to meet and perhaps surpass. So long as the standards are reasonable and don't produce too much tension, they effectively organize response.

You need a worthy opponent. If you don't have an opponent to try your skills against, you haven't expressed yourself fully.

The recent spate of criticism of our society for its winning-is-the-only-thing syndrome is well taken. But the proposed corrective—winless competition—goes too far. We don't need to eliminate winning. We simply need to put it in a more rational perspective.

What you're basically doing in competition is seeking your position in the social order. When you compete you can expect to be inferior to some and superior to others. It is not necessary to always be at the very top in everything to enjoy a comfortable position in society.

The real point to competition is not so much to conquer another person as it is to defeat your lesser self.

Accept the fact of your present level of attainment. Enjoy your performance at that level. Relish the satisfaction that comes from even tiny improvements in your performance and your position. In this game, you're a constant winner.

It bears saying once more: The world-class performer always practices in an atmosphere of success. He knows exactly what he's doing at all times. He takes it in tiny increments. Each day he succeeds at what he sets out to accomplish. By the time he approaches his meet, it's with the serene belief that he can win.

But winning in competition is only one of his rewards. He is constantly being rewarded throughout his training. Winning, to him, is much broader than the conquest of someone else. What most enriches him is the conquest of himself.

If you are to approach your own potential, the same should be true of you.

A NEW WAY TO KEEP SCORE

WINNING, IN YOUR MIND, ought to be enlarged and re-defined to include the knowledge that you've explored your own uncharted potential, and gained mastery over the inhibitors in your body that keep you from being the best possible performer you are capable of being. What is a score compared with that?

As a bonus, this more expansive view of winning enhances your competitive prospects.

The performer who does nothing but compete is taking time that would be better used toward the development of long-term gains in his style of play and a body better suited to his event. He competes so persistently because he needs continuous affirmation of his position in the social order. But there is just as much satisfaction inherent in self-improvement as there is in winning. The pleasure of competition can be readily postponed in favor of different, but no less enjoyable satisfaction. All it takes is the courage to make an independent choice.

So many of us struggle a good part of our lives to get to the top of some ladder only to discover that we hadn't wanted to climb that particular ladder in the first place. We did it simply because it seemed to be the thing to do.

We tend to react to our environment with a feeling of resignation, without recognizing that if the environment makes us uncomfortable, we can either change it or remove ourselves from it.

So many people I know have poor opinions of themselves because they have failed by others' standards. They have been put into competition against others who were out of their league and so they suffered by unfair comparison. What has been overlooked is the benefit of one's own competition with himself in a more appropriate arena.

Competition, in this context, provides us with a convenient measure of how we're doing—not against one another so much as in our quest to be ourselves.

You're not static. You're changeable, trainable, modifiable. You're not today what you're going to be forever—or even tomorrow.

The business of winning need not be exclusively a matter of combat between individuals. It is expressed best by each person's attempt to become the best possible person he or she can be.

Movement for the sheer joy of movement is a personal reward. To do it better today than you could yesterday is an added reward. To emphasize that kind of private pleasure not only is rewarding but leads to a better performance.

Victory in competition can be an enjoyable consequence of maximum performance. The real gold, however, is that endless series of tiny successes that transform you into the person you always dreamed you could be.

Index

About the Authors

Laurence E. Morehouse, Ph.D., was the founding director of the Human Performance Laboratory at the University of California at Los Angeles and founding president of the Human Factors Society of America. He has taught at Harvard, the University of Iowa, the University of Southern California and, since 1954, UCLA. In the course of his studies, he has worked with world-class athletes, astronauts, aquanauts, corporate executives and industrial designers, and been consulted by federal agencies, the military services, manufacturers, labor unions and foreign governments —all of them seeking ways to make better use of human endowments. He is the author of twelve textbooks; a contributor to the Encyclopaedia Britannica, *the* Encyclopedia Americana, *the* Encyclopedia of Sports Medicine *and the* Encyclopedia of Physical Education; *and co-author, with Leonard Gross, of the best-seller* Total Fitness: In Thirty Minutes a Week, *which has been published in thirteen languages.*

Leonard Gross, a newspaper and magazine journalist for more than twenty years, has been writing books full time since the demise of Look *in 1971; he had previously served that magazine as senior editor, South American correspondent, European Editor and finally West Coast Editor. He currently writes a monthly drama column for Westways. His ninth book, a novel, will be published soon.*